ANTHROPOLOGICAL PAPERS

MUSEUM OF ANTHROPOLOGY, UNIVERSITY OF MICHIGAN

NO. 51

LOCAL EXCHANGE AND EARLY STATE DEVELOPMENT IN SOUTHWESTERN IRAN

BY

GREGORY ALAN JOHNSON

ANN ARBOR, MICHIGAN

1973

© 1973 by the Regents of the University of Michigan
The Museum of Anthropology
All rights reserved

ISBN (print): 978-1-949098-07-5
ISBN (ebook): 978-1-949098-69-3

Browse all of our books at
sites.lsa.umich.edu/archaeology-books.

Order our books from the University of Michigan
Press at www.press.umich.edu.

For permissions, questions, or manuscript queries,
contact Museum publications by email at umma-
pubs@umich.edu or visit the Museum website at
lsa.umich.edu/ummaa.

PREFACE

MY wife and I sailed from Norfolk, Virginia on the 16th of May 1970, bound for Iran by a convoluted route. We were scheduled to participate in the Southwest Iran Project of The University of Michigan Museum of Anthropology. The project was directed by Henry T. Wright and supported by National Science Foundation Grant GS-3147. I would participate as Assistant Field Director for Survey and attempt to collect enough settlement and ceramic data for a report on the development of the state on the Susiana plain, Khuzistan.

In the more than two years that have passed since leaving for Iran, many people have contributed to the work of the survey, analysis and interpretation of the survey data, and preparation of this report. I would like to acknowledge their efforts and aid here.

Above all, those of us who have worked in Iran owe a great debt of gratitude to the officials and staff of the Iranian Ministry of Culture and Arts whose aid, understanding, and support have made our work in their country possible. I would like to express my appreciation in particular to those persons who were directly involved with the project: His Excellency M. Pahlbod, Minister of Culture and Arts; His Excellency A. A. Pourmand, Director General of Antiquities; Mr. S. M. Khorramabadi, Assistant Director General of Antiquities; Dr. H. Tayyeb-Naimi, Director of Excavations; and Mr. M. H. Khoshabi, Representative of the Ministry of Culture and Arts.

We arrived in the field on the 18th of September, 1970 and the actual work of the survey began shortly thereafter. It was to continue for the next eight months. We went into the field with the notes and maps produced by two previous surveys. I wish to thank Robert McC. Adams (The Oriental Institute of the University of Chicago) and Frank Hole (Department of Anthropology, Rice University) for their generosity in providing us with these unpublished materials.

Many people participated in the survey at various times and for various periods. For their valuable assistance I would like to thank: Ingrid Christensen, John Fritz, Joan Laubrends, William Laubrends, Richard Redding, Robert Schacht, Carol Scheffer, Charles Scheffer, Nancy Talbot, Harvey Weiss,

LOCAL EXCHANGE AND EARLY STATE DEVELOPMENT

Aileen Wenke, Robert Wenke, Susan Wineberg, and Frances Wright. Thanks must also go to Mr. Ahmed Iliosi, our skillful driver, who can take a jeep into and out of places where the laws of nature indicate it could not go.

Throughout the survey and other programs of the project Mr. Khoshabi provided continual assistance with much understanding and tolerance of our perhaps bizarre activities and way of life.

Ours was not the only archaeological project on the Susiana during the fall and winter of 1970-71. We received gracious hospitality and enjoyed profitable discussions on visits to the Chogha Mish project of The Oriental Institute of the University of Chicago, directed by Pierre Delougaz and Helene Kantor; and to the Haft Tepe project of The University of Tehran directed by Ezat O. Negahban. Shapur M. Shahmirzad graciously acted as our guide on a tour of the Haft Tepe excavations.

During the latter portion of the field season, my wife and I paid a three-day visit to the French Archaeological Mission at Susa where we were received with great hospitality by Jean Perrot, Director of the Mission, and his wife, Eva. Mr. Perrot was most generous in allowing us to examine and measure unpublished materials in the collections of the Mission, and in taking time from his busy end-of-season schedule to discuss various problems of the survey. While at Susa, I also profited from discussions with Alain Le Brun and Geneviève Dollfus who generously allowed me to inspect their material from the Acropole of Susa and Tepe Jaffarabad.

While still in Iran, we visited the offices of the Khuzistan Water and Power Authority. I would like to thank John Welton for his hospitality and permission to inspect photographs and maps in the KWPA collections.

Since returning from Iran, I have profited from discussions with a number of individuals. I would like in particular to thank Robert McC. Adams, Frank Hole, Helene Kantor, James Neeley (Department of Anthropology, University of Texas at Austin), Hans Nissen (Institut für Vorderasiatisches Altertumskunde, Berlin), and Ezat O. Negahban.

Most of the statistical analysis appearing in this dissertation was carried out with the aid of Constat, a user-prompter program package developed by the Statistical Research Laboratory of The University of Michigan. My interest in these analytical methods in archaeology is primarily due to my association with Robert Whallon Jr. of The University of Michigan Museum of Anthropology.

I would also like to thank George Stuber of the Museum of Anthropology who volunteered his time and labor for photographic reduction of the ceramic drawings and site maps presented here.

The original version of this report was submitted as a doctoral dissertation at The University of Michigan in 1972. The members of my Dissertation Committee deserve special thanks. I owe much to Henry T. Wright,

PREFACE

Director of the Southwest Iran Project, my principal Graduate Advisor and Chairman of my Dissertation Committee. Dr. Wright is primarily responsible for my interest in the development of the state as a research problem, and in the Middle East as a research area. He provided continual encouragement and assistance throughout the long period of research and preparation of this study. Occasionally he must have wondered if I had been built into his office along with its desks and bookshelves.

Special thanks must go to James B. Griffin, Director of The University of Michigan Museum of Anthropology. I received my introduction to Anthropological Archaeology from Dr. Griffin in 1965. Since then he has had a major influence in guiding my progress in the field, obtaining field work opportunities and graduate grants and fellowships. His personal interest in the staff and students associated with the Museum of Anthropology has been a major factor in providing an environment particularly conducive to learning and research.

My debt is also great to Kent V. Flannery and George Cameron, the remaining members of my committee, who suffered through initial drafts and revisions. They have lent their knowledge and experience to the transformation of assorted field notes and more or less vague ideas to a completed report.

Finally I would like to thank my wife, Mina. She can identify an Uruk bevel rim bowl rim at 20 paces among thousands of Elamite sherds. She worked with me throughout the survey making surface collections, processing survey material, carrying a stadia rod over innumerable tepes, and putting a shoulder to the back of our survey vehicle which under my control had a remarkable affinity for deep sand, loose gravel, mud, and small irrigation canals. She also executed most of the ceramic drawings and final copies of site maps presented here.

Many people have, then, contributed to the work reported here. Responsibility for any shortcomings or errors it contains is, of course, mine alone.

TABLE OF CONTENTS

I. Introduction
   Operational Definition of the State 1
   Decision Hierarchies and General Societal Complexity 4
   Theories of the Origin of the State 12
   Central Place Theory, Functional Hierarchies, and State Settlement
      Patterns 13

II. The 1970–71 Susiana Survey
   Geomorphology, Hydrology, and Environment of the Susiana Plain ... 17
   Survey Method 24
   Method of Metrical Analysis of Ceramics 27
   Uruk Relative and Absolute Chronology 29
   Areal Size and Population Estimates for Terminal Susa A and
      Uruk Settlements 64
   Settlement Pattern Maps 81

III. Analysis of the Settlement Patterns
   Terminal Susa A 87
   Early Uruk 90
   Middle Uruk 101
   Late Uruk 143

IV. Summary and Conclusions

Appendices
I.   Type Counts: 1970–71 Survey 163
II. Grid Coordinates for Determination of Site-to-Site Distances ... 175
III. Ceramic Measurements 177

BIBLIOGRAPHY 199

PLATES I–XX 206

LIST OF TABLES

1. Time Requirements for Systematic Surface Collection of Susiana
   Terminal Susa A and Uruk Sites: 10% Areal Sample 26

2.	Weighted Presence-Absence Coding for the 1970–71 Uruk Surface Collections	32–37
3.	Seriation of Ceramic Types: 1970–71 Susiana Survey	38
4.	Type Counts of Uruk Ceramics from the Acropole Sondage (1969–) at Susa	39–40
5.	Weighted Presence-Absence Coding for Susa, Acropole Ceramic Type Counts	42–43
6.	Seriation of Uruk Ceramic Types: Susa, Acropole Sondage	44
7.	Susa, Acropole Sondage: Interpretation of Stratigraphy	45
8.	Type Counts of Uruk Ceramics from Excavation B, Tepe Farukhabad	47
9.	Seriation of Uruk Ceramic Types: Tepe Farukhabad, Excavation B	48
10.	The Uruk Ceramic Sequence at Tall-i-Ghazir (Step Trench)	49
11.	The Uruk Ceramic Sequence at Uruk-Warka (Deep Sounding)	50
12.	Proposed Chronological Divisions of the Warka Deep Sounding	52
13.	The Uruk Ceramic Sequence at Nippur (Deep Sounding)	53
14.	Uruk Stratigraphic Correlations	60
15.	Impressed Strip Bowls: Student's t Tests	61
16.	Absolute Chronology	65
17.	Area of Susa: Terminal Susa A to Late Uruk	71
18.	1970–71 Survey: Estimated Site Areas	74–78
19.	Distribution of Early Uruk Neckless Ledge Rim Jars	94
20.	Estimation of Center and Village Sustaining Areas—Early Uruk	97
21.	First Order Nearest Neighbor Distances for Potential Middle Uruk Centers	111
22.	Cross Hatch Bands: Student's t Tests	117
23.	Cross Hatch Bands: Chi Square on Type and Area	117
24.	Wide Strap Handles vs. Other Strap Handles: Student's t Test	118
25.	Wide Strap Handles: Student's t Test	121
26.	Wide Strap Handles: Chi Square on Type and Area	121
27.	Wide Strap Handles and Ceramic Wall Cones: Yates' Corrected Chi Square	123
28.	Mid Width Strap Handles: Student's t Tests	124
29.	Mid Width Strap Handles, Partioned by Area Collected: Student's t Test	125
30.	State Redistribution to Gurus Workers	129
31.	Estimated Volumes of Uruk Bevel Rim Bowls: Histograms	133
32.	Estimated Volumes of Uruk Bevel Rim Bowls: Histograms	134
33.	Distribution of Uruk Bevel Rim Bowl Modal Volumes	136
34.	Caloric Value of Possible Uruk Barley Ratios on the Susiana Plain	138
35.	Type Counts: 1970–71 Survey Surface Collections	165–173
36.	Grid Coordinates for Determination of Site-to-Site Distances	176
37.	Impressed Strip Bowl Measurements	179–180
38.	Uruk Neckless Ledge Rim Jar Measurements	182
39.	Uruk Cross Hatch Band Measurements	184–185
40.	Uruk Strap Handle Measurements	187–188
41.	Uruk Bevel Rim Bowl Measurements	190–195
42.	Uruk Twisted Handle Measurements	197

LIST OF FIGURES

1.	Development of Decision Hierarchies—Scatter Plot	11
2.	Lower Mesopotamia Location of the 1970–71 Susiana Survey Area	16
3.	1970–71 Susiana Survey Area—Khuzistan, Iran	18
4.	Monthly Precipitation: Shush Meteorological Station	20
5.	Ancient Settlements and Watercourses	23
6.	Impressed Strip Bowls—Scatter Plot	62
7.	Proposed Stylistic Development of Impressed Strip Bowls	63
8.	Susa: Reported Distribution of Uruk Ceramics	69
9.	Site Map of Chogha Mish	72
10.	Settlement Areas—Histograms Definition of Settlement Areal Size Classes	79
11.	Terminal Susa A Settlements	82
12.	Early Uruk Settlements	83
13.	Middle Uruk Settlements and Special Function Sites	84
14.	Late Uruk Settlements	85
15.	Terminal Susa A Settlement Pattern	88
16.	Early Uruk Settlement System	91
17.	Early Uruk Neckless Ledge Rim Jars—Scatter Plot	93
18.	Early Uruk Local Exchange System Distribution of Neckless Ledge Rim Jars	95
19.	Middle Uruk Settlement System	102
20.	Dimensions of the Middle Uruk Site Typology	106
21.	Surface Evidence of an Uruk Ceramic Workshop (Abu Fanduweh—KS 59): Pace Map	108
22.	Uruk Cross Hatch Bands—Histograms	114
23.	Uruk Cross Hatch Bands—Scatter Plot	115
24.	Middle Uruk Local Exchange System Distribution of Early Cross Hatch Bands	119
25.	Uruk Strap Handles—Histograms	120
26.	Middle Uruk Local Exchange System Distribution of Wide Strap Handles	122
27.	Uruk Mid Width Strap Handles—Histogram	124
28.	Uruk Strap Handles—Scatter Plot	126
29.	Middle Uruk Local Exchange System: Ceramic Evidence	128
30.	Estimation of Uruk Bevel Rim Bowl Volumes	135
31.	Middle–Late Uruk Local Exchange System Distribution of Late Cross Hatch Bands	142
32.	Late Uruk Settlement System	144
33.	Uruk Twisted Handles—Histograms	148
34.	Uruk Twisted Handles—Scatter Plot	149
35.	Uruk Twisted Handles—Scatter Plot	151
36.	Impressed Strip Bowl Measurements	178
37.	Uruk Neckless Ledge Jar Rim Measurements	181
38.	Uruk Cross Hatch Band Measurements	183
39.	Uruk Strap Handle Measurements	186
40.	Uruk Bevel Rim Bowl Measurements	189
41.	Uruk Twisted Handle Measurements	196

LIST OF PLATES

(following page 205)

I.	Artifact Types.
II.	Artifact Types.
III.	Artifact Types.
IV.	Artifact Types.
V.	Artifact Types.
VI.	Artifact Types.
VII.	Artifact Types.
VIII.	Artifact Types.
IX.	Artifact Types.
X.	Site Maps.
XI.	Site Maps.
XII.	Site Maps.
XIII.	Site Maps.
XIV.	Site Maps.
XV.	Site Maps.
XVI.	Site Maps.
XVII.	Site Maps.
XVIII.	Site Maps.
XIX.	Site Maps.
XX.	Site Maps.

I

INTRODUCTION

OPERATIONAL DEFINITION OF THE STATE

KROEBER and Kluckhohn (1952) were able with apparent ease to devote 400 pages to a review and critique of the term "culture." In all probability a similar bulk could be assembled for the term "state." In recent years, however, there has been considerable convergence of opinion concerning the definition of a state. This convergence is seen in increasing emphasis on the organization of decision making in complex societies.

The organization of decision making, phrased in diverse ways, has been a primary definitional characteristic of states. Childe speaks of the differentiation of full-time specialist officials, priests, and rulers (among other groups) and "an effective concentration of economic and political power" (1951:158). Wittfogel states that "From the standpoint of human relations a state means government by professionals" (1957:239). Service emphasizes mechanisms of societal integration. In the case of the state he points to "bureaucratic governance by legal force" (1962:175). Wolf distinguishes primitive from civilized societies by the "crystallization of executive power" (1966:11). Adams stresses that a state is "hierarchically organized on political and territorial lines rather than on kinship or other ascriptive groups and relationships" (1966:14). While Fried defines the state as "a collection of specialized institutions and agencies, some formal and others informal, that maintains an order of stratification," he points out that state level societies concentrate "on the basic principles of organization: hierarchy, differential access to basic resources, obedience to officials and defense of [the state's] area" (1967:235). Sahlins emphasizes that a state is a society in which "there is an official public authority, a set of offices of the society at large conferring governance over the society at large" (1968a:6). Monopoly of force, power, or coercion is a second frequently cited characteristic of states (Service, 1962:175; Wolf, 1966:11; Adams, 1966:14; Fried, 1967:235; Sahlins, 1968a:6).

Wright has reduced these general administrative, managerial, or bureaucratic definitions to the level of basic decision making. "The state is a society in which there is a fully specialized decision making subsystem which mediates relations between other subsystems and which is itself internally specialized" (1970:19-20). Most recently, Flannery has concurred with this primary definitional emphasis on the organization of decision making. In a general discussion of the investigation of societies over a broad range of complexity, he concludes that ". . . the most striking differences between states and simpler societies lie in the realm of decision-making and its hierarchical organization, rather than in matter and energy exchanges" (1972:412). Naroll takes a similar position, considering "complexity of the structural ramification" of group decision communication channels to be a highly significant variable in social evolution (1956:696).

A state, for the purposes of the present discussion, will be defined as a *society* which is primarily regulated through a differentiated and internally specialized decision making organization which is structured in minimally three hierarchical levels, with institutionalized provision for the operation and maintenance of this organization and implementation of its decisions.

While brief, this definition involves a number of complex issues. A *state* is defined as a specific type of *society*. All states are societies, but only some societies are states. Others would argue that a state may be part of, but is distinct from, a given society (Krader, 1968:27). Here the state is *not* equated with the government or ruling class of certain complex societies. The presence of the state in all human societies is explicitly rejected.

A state is defined as being *primarily regulated* through a certain type of decision making organization. Wright speaks of mediation of subsystem relationships. The use of regulation implies aspects of active coordination and control in addition to the connection, linkage or channeling implied by mediation. The qualifying term "primary" emphasizes the importance of this organization while allowing for the presence of other regulatory mechanisms.

A state is defined as having a *differentiated* decision making organization of a certain level of complexity. This means that a decision making subsystem of the society is operational as a unit, and is constituted in an explicitly defined organization.

A state is defined as having an *internally specialized* decision making organization. Here specialization refers to horizontal specialization or simply division of work (Simon, 1944:17). The organization processes large amounts of information of a diverse nature in addition to the numerous other tasks it may perform. The amount of work involved exceeds the capacity of any individual. Numbers of individuals are required. The execution of specific tasks may involve a greater or lesser degree of expertise. Diversity of tasks may then require diversity of expertise beyond the capacity of an individual.

Task specialization reduces the amount of work and range of expertise required of individuals to a level at which the required work can be done. Increase in the workload on the organization can be met with expansion of its personnel and/or further specialization of its personnel.

A state is defined as having a *hierarchically structured* decision making organization. Hierarchy or vertical specialization allows coordination in horizontally specialized systems (Simon, 1944:17). As discussed above, horizontal specialization allows increases in the amount and diversity of work done by an organization. If the tasks performed by individual specialists are completely unrelated, hierarchical structure is not necessary. If, however, these tasks are related, as in the case of the decision making organization of a state, coordination between and among specialists is necessary. This coordination is provided by a specialist at a second structural level of the organization, and a two-level hierarchy is formed. Similarly, if the information processing capacity of this individual is exceeded, additional personnel will be required at this level. The activities of these personnel must also be coordinated and a third level of hierarchy is formed (Wright, 1969a:4). This process may continue to an undefined degree.

A state is defined as having a decision making organization of *minimally three hierarchical levels*. This is the most important specification in the present definition of the state. It is the only specification which explicitly distinguishes state level societies from a large number of less complex societies which have been called chiefdoms. Detailed exposition of this point will be deferred while less complex matters are discussed.

A state is defined as having *institutionalized provision* for the operation and maintenance of its decision making organization, and for implementation of this organization's decisions. The term, "institutionalized provision," is used in the sense of the presence of an established and functioning mechanism.

In a state there is institutionalized provision for the *operation* of the decision making organization. Operation is defined in terms of information processing which includes information collection and evaluation, decision making, and information dissemination. A greater or lesser degree of task specialization and hierarchical organization will be required depending on the volume of information processed and number of decisions made.

The amount of information processed is probably also the major determinate of the complexity of information storage and retrieval facilities used by a given society. A continuum of such facilities ranges from individual memory to modern data processing systems. The appearance of writing, for example, is viewed as one possible adaptive response to increase in the amount of information processed by the decision making organization of a society. Conversely the type of facilities used by the decision making organization of a society should provide a relative measure of the amount of information processed by that organization. Further, development over time of such facilities having increasingly large information storage capabilities should provide a measure of the increasing amount of information processed.

Increase in information processing has already been related to increase in task specialization and hierarchical organization in decision making organizations. Greater capabilities of information storage and retrieval facilities should then be directly related to increase in task specialization and hierarchical organization. The archaeological implications of this relationship will be brought out later in this study.

In a state there is institutionalized provision for *decision implementation*. Decisions may be made, but they might not be carried out: "... leaders can lead, but followers may not follow" (Fried, 1967:133). Decision implementation involves a number of structural requirements, and may of course fail.

Decisions must have the acceptance or acquiescence of the individuals or groups toward whom they are directed. Refusal of workers to work, soldiers to fight, priests to pray, or administrators to administrate is not conducive to getting things done. Acceptance may be conditioned by recognition of authority based on secular and/or sacred legitimation: "In the name of Her Majesty ..., by Grace of God, Queen ...." Acquiescence may be conditioned by the use or threat of use of secular and/or sacred sanctions: decapitation or excommunication, for example.

Implementation may require greater or lesser amounts of general or specialized labor derived from such sources as corvee, institutional workers, prisoners, slaves, and so on. Materials may be required and acquired from such sources as taxes, tribute, spoils or output of organizational holdings in agriculture, craft production, long range trade, or other sources. Finally implementation may require standardization of procedure of individual and group behavior. Such standardization may be institutionalized in custom and/or law.

In a state there is institutionalized provision for *maintenance* of the decision making organization. The continued functioning of the organization as the agent of primary societal regulation may require monopoly of authority and monopoly of sanctions. Monopoly of internal sanctions and security from extra-societal influence may be obtained through a variety of military or paramilitary organizations. Material support of organizational personnel and facilities may be obtained from the sources mentioned above. Finally recruitment and training of personnel may be organized through ascription and/or achievement, formal and/or informal instruction.

DECISION HIERARCHIES AND GENERAL SOCIETAL COMPLEXITY: SOME ETHNOGRAPHIC EXAMPLES

A society must have a differentiated decision making hierarchy of at least three levels to be considered a state. This implies that first, states may have more complex decision making hierarchies; and second, that societies organized below the state level have fewer hierarchical levels or none at all.

The presence and elaboration of such hierarchies have been related to problems of basic information handling and decision making. Increasing societal complexity over time (evolution), and variation in societal complexity at any given point in time can be related to differential requirements of information processing, decision making, and decision implementation.

At this point it would be appropriate to introduce a few ethnographic examples of what is meant by the structure of decision making and decision hierarchies. The societies selected for discussion cover a broad range of complexity and are intended to illustrate a continuum of decision making complexity, the upper end of which is occupied by states. The discussion emphasizes levels of decision making, not levels of social stratification. As the primary focus here is on states, the usual flow of discussion from the simple to the complex is reversed and examples of states are considered first. The treatment of individual societies is brief and primarily derived from secondary sources. The presentation is intended to illustrate and invidiously lend support to an argument, rather than to formally test a hypothesis. Having inserted what is, I hope, a sufficient disclaimer, let us proceed to the examples themselves.

Yoruba (Ifẹ)

Traditionally the Ana (Ifẹ), a Yoruba group of present Western Nigeria, had a complex decision making hierarchy of at least four levels. This highly simplified account is based on that of Bascom (1969) and refers to Ife organization of the early 19th century.

The territory of the Ifẹ covered an area of some 70 by 40 miles or about 7,250 square kilometers (Ibid.:29). The central administrative organization was located in Ile-Ifẹ, a settlement of several thousand, and was presided over by the king or Ọni and his assistants. The administration of this territory was divided under the Ọni between the capital and five provinces.

Each of the provinces, containing as many as 90 towns, was administered by a province chief who was directly responsible to the Ọni in the Ile-Ifẹ (Ibid.:29). Viewed from the capital, province chiefs were primarily responsible for collection of tribute from their areas. Fifty percent of this tribute was retained by province chiefs, the remainder being sent to the Ọni (Ibid.: 30). These provinces enjoyed considerable regional autonomy as long as provincial chiefs remained loyal to the Oni, and local affairs were run smoothly (Ibid.:30).

Individual towns within the jurisdiction of a province chief were administered by a town chief (Bale) (Ibid.:30). By analogy with the data presented from Ile-Ife, individual compounds within provincial towns were administered by the senior resident male. The duties of this official (Bale) will be outlined below in a discussion of Ile-Ife itself. Decision making in the provinces was then structured in four hierarchical levels represented by the Oni, province chiefs, town chiefs, and compound heads respectively.

Bascom provides a more detailed discussion of administration and decision making in Ile-Ife proper. The capital was divided into five wards, administered by a series of town chiefs (Ife) (Bascom, 1969:33). A series of palace chiefs (Woye) represented the interests of the Oni with these officials (Ibid.:34). The senior palace chief (Ijebe) acted as the Oni's treasurer, collecting tribute in his name (Ibid.:38). Various palace chiefs also acted as representatives of the Oni with the officials of outlying towns and with certain craft groups including blacksmiths, woodcarvers, and hunters (Ibid.:34). The Oni and these immediate representatives apparently functioned as the upper level of the decision making hierarchy.

Other major groups of officials attached to this level included the Emese, who acted as aids to the palace chiefs (Ibid.:35), and the Ogungbe who functioned as the Oni's bodyguard and town police. The latter group maintained a public executioner and dungeons for the incarceration of malcreants (Ibid.:36).

The ward chiefs (Ife) were responsible for the administration of the town (Ibid.:33). Each ward chief appointed a secondary chief (Bale) who was responsible for the behavior of the young adults within each ward (Ibid.:33). These officials appear to have been administrative assistants to the ward chiefs, and not to have constituted a separate level within the administrative hierarchy.

Compound heads (Bale) formed the base of this hierarchy. Compounds were large, housing up to several hundred individuals (Ibid.:30). The compound head provided direct articulation between the administrative organization and the administered population of the town. His duties included: adjudication of disputes within the compound; assignment of living quarters to residents; administration of resident farm lands; physical maintenance of the compound; and preparation of medicines and rituals to insure the physical and spiritual health of the residents (Ibid.:44).

The administrative organization of Ile-Ife was then parallel to that of the kingdom as a whole. The Oni and his immediate assistants administered the provinces and the capital through the hierarchy of chiefs outlined above. This rather elaborate organization was supported by a complex series of land grants, tributes, tolls on the movement of goods and traders, and labor levies (Ibid.:38). The Ife qualify as a state by virtually anyone's standards.

INTRODUCTION

Bulamogi

Traditionally the Bulamogi, a Basoga group of present day Uganda, had a clear three level decision making hierarchy. A fourth level was apparently emerging. This account refers to the period of the late 19th century.

The upper level of the hierarchy was occupied by the ruler (Zibondo), his primary administrative advisor (Kalikkiro), and an assortment of palace officials and functionaries (Fallers, 1965:136).

A second level was ideally composed of a series of district chiefs. These chiefs were recruited from commoner rather than from royal lineages (Ibid.:135) and were subordinate only to the Zibondo himself (Ibid.:136). Village and subvillage headmen were subordinate to district chiefs and occupied the lowest administrative level, directly articulating with the administered population (Ibid.:137).

Apparently in some periods an additional decision making level was interposed between the Zibondo and his district chiefs. This additional position was occupied by princes, sons of recent rulers, who had been given control of areas within the territory ruled by their fathers (Ibid.:134). The administrative position of these princes is ambiguous. Theoretically such princes were responsible to the Zibondo and subject to his decisions. In practice, however, it appears that they were frequently able to divorce themselves and their territories from the primary administrative organization. A prince, in such cases, became the administrative head of a virtually autonomous territory (Ibid.:134) which he might rule with an independent administrative organization (Ibid.:137). Princes can be viewed as constituting an emergent level in the decision making hierarchy.

The administrative hierarchy under a *de jure* ruler or effectively independent prince functioned in the adjudication of disputes, mobilization of military forces in time of war, and procurement of material and labor resources for support of communal projects and the hierarchy itself (Ibid.:137). Fallers terms the Bulamogi a state (Ibid.:126).

Hawaii

Administrative hierarchies in the Hawaiian Islands immediately prior to European contact had two clear administrative levels. A third level was apparently developing. Managerial control of land was, at least formally, divided into four categories as follows (Sahlins, 1958:14):

Level 1—An entire island; the usual autonomous political unit was controlled by a paramount chief (alii nui) and his principal advisor (kalaimoku).

Level 2—Island districts were controlled by high chiefs (alii).

Level 3—District tracts were controlled by stewards (konohiki).
Level 4—Small lots within tracts were controlled by commoners (makaainana).

Sahlins states that "Each manager was subordinate to the higher manager within whose domain he held stewardship prerogatives" (1958:14). Commoners were then subordinate to stewards, stewards to high chiefs, and high chiefs to the paramount chief and his advisor.

Stewards carried out a broad range of administrative functions. These included: mobilization of labor for construction projects; supervision of the construction and maintenance of irrigation works; direct supervision of household agricultural production; mobilization of military forces in time of war; and possibly settlement of disputes involving water rights (Sahlins, 1958:14-19).

These data suggest a three-level administrative hierarchy with stewards functioning as the primary link between the administrative organization and the administered population.

There is some question, however, about the position of high chiefs in island administrative organization. There appears to have been considerable overlap of administrative functions of high chiefs and stewards. Both groups directly initiated irrigation projects, supervised irrigation water allocation, and adjusted such allocations under conditions of water shortage.

Administrative directives, at least in some instances, were communicated from the paramount chief or his advisor directly to the stewards rather than through district high chiefs. Sahlins states that a paramount chief could mobilize labor *through the local stewards* (Ibid.:16). Wise points out that in time of war a paramount chief assembled the stewards to inform them of the number of men required for military service from their respective district tracts (1965:85). This would seem to suggest a two-level hierarchy of paramount chief and stewards with a developing third level represented by the district high chiefs. A basic two-level organization is confirmed by Handy who reports that, "Next to the Kalaimoku, probably the most important personage was the Konohiki. . . . He was the general executive upon whom the Kalaimoku depended to see that what he ordered was done" (1965:38). Sahlins calls the stewards a "primitive bureaucracy" (1958:16). The ambiguous administrative position of high chiefs indicates that examination of actual activities is more important here than examination of social roles. Administrative function and social position need not be coterminous.

Stewards, then, were the primary administrative officials of the paramount chief and his advisor. District high chiefs appear to have been moving in the direction of an intermediary administrative level. The Hawaiian system has been variously characterized as a chiefdom (Flannery, 1972:5), a centralized chiefdom (Sahlins, 1968a:43), and a crude state (Wittfogel, 1957:241).

INTRODUCTION

Tonga

The decision making organization of the Tonga was traditionally structured in two levels of hierarchy. There is no indication of the emergence of a third level as in Hawaii.

Traditionally there were three levels of social status in the Tongan Islands. The upper level was occupied by high chiefs and their immediate relatives (eike). The second level consisted of petty chiefs and chiefly attendants (matapule). The base of the *status* hierarchy was occupied by commoners (tua) (Sahlins, 1958:22). This hierarchy of social status partially paralleled the hierarchy of decision making. Three high chiefs and their immediate aids occupied the top level of this hierarchy. The highest ranking of these chiefs (Tui Tonga) had a position roughly equivalent to the paramount chief in Hawaii. The two remaining high chiefs (Tui Kanokupolo and Tui Haa Takalaua) acted as the Tui Tonga's advisors much as did the kalaimoku in Hawaii (Ibid.). Specially designated administrative assistants (falefa) were attached to the Tui Tonga (Ibid.). The other high chiefs also had aids or perhaps attendants who ranked as lesser chiefs (Ibid.:23).

The second level in the decision making hierarchy was occupied by petty chiefs. These officials provided the direct articulation between the high chiefs and commoners. They held a position equivalent to the stewards (konohiki) of Hawaii (Ibid.). These officials performed several functions. They transmitted orders from high chiefs to commoners (Ibid.:27). They had authority to initiate and direct a considerable amount of communal production, reaching down to the level of household production (Ibid.:24). These officials were apparently horizontally specialized. Some supervised communal shellfish collection. Others were in charge of such activities as the imposition of tabus for the conservation of agricultural land (Ibid.).

High chiefs also directly initiated communal projects. Directions from a council of high chiefs were communicated to the general population through petty chiefs. Labor for such projects was provided by commoners (Ibid.). Implementation of chiefly decisions was insured by physical sanctions including death and confiscation of property (Ibid.:26ff).

The Tonga then provide a clear example of decision making in two hierarchic levels. They are presented as an example of a chiefdom by Flannery (1972:5).

Lower Order Societies

The examples provided above illustrate the transition from chiefdoms to states in terms of decision hierarchies and, by implication, information processing. The Hawaiian case is particularly interesting because it provides an excellent example of an advanced chiefdom organized only slightly below the state level.

The organization of decision making becomes increasingly simplified in societies less complex than chiefdoms. If states minimally have a three-level decision hierarchy above the general population, and chiefdoms a two-level hierarchy, the next lower level would be expected to have a single decision level above the general population. This would appear to be a fair characterization of tribal societies.[1]

In tribal societies, decision making is differentiated in one structural level above the population as a whole. This level may be occupied by one or several persons. Such individuals may or may not occupy an "office." Witness the distinction between Melanesian "big men" and "petty chieftains" (Sahlins, 1968a:21; 1968b:161). In contrast to the cases discussed above, the scope of decision making by these persons is usually very limited while decision implementation is even more restricted. Sahlins refers to petty chiefs in his usual apt phraseology, "One word from him and everyone does as he pleases" (1968a:21).

Decision implementation is certainly not as weak as this in all tribal societies, and examination of the available ethnographic cases would probably reveal a continuum in the degree of decision making and implementation at this broad level of social complexity. The point here is the presence of a single-level, structurally differentiated, information handling institution, simple as it may be.

Descending to the lowest general level of societal complexity we find the band or egalitarian societies (Fried, 1967) in which hierarchical organization of decision making disappears. In these societies one can talk about leadership, but the role of leader is ephemeral indeed. Individuals of experience and recognized ability may make suggestions as to a course of action. Such suggestions may or may not be followed. Inidividuals who function as decision makers are probably those with a greater than average innate information processing capacity. Fried cites the Eskimo as perhaps the lower limiting case in this regard (1967:84).

It should be clear, then, that the ability to handle increasing amounts of information is here considered one of the primary factors of cultural evolution. This hypothesis is presented in graphic form in Figure 1, where the ethnographic cases discussed above serve as points in a scatter plot of information processing on levels of decision hierarchy. Note that no scale is indicated for information processing and thus the slope and even the basic shape

---

[1]Sahlins (1968a:20) considers chiefdoms and "segmental" tribes to be more and less complex versions of tribal society in general. Fried would abolish the term tribe (1967: 154). Here, however, Service's (1962) original distinction between tribes and chiefdoms is useful and is maintained.

INTRODUCTION

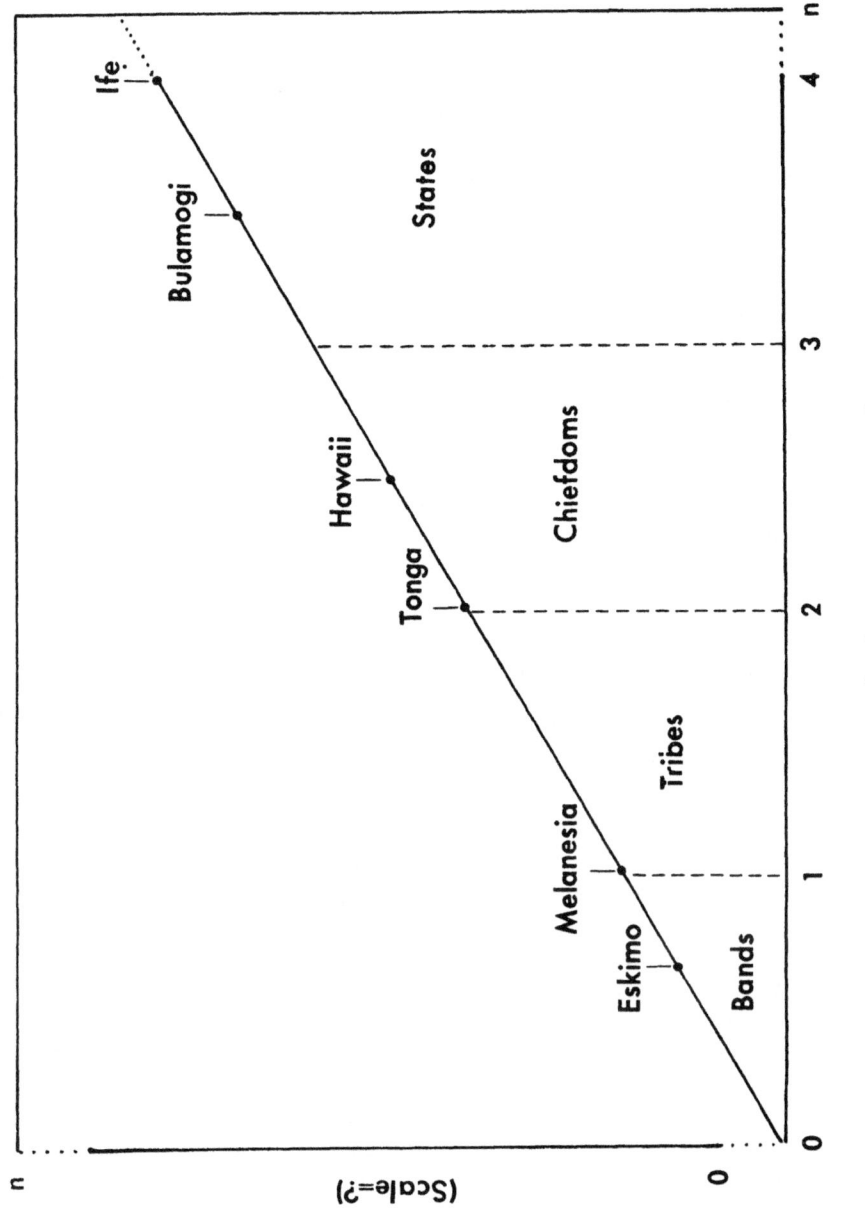

Fig. 1. Development of Decision Hierarchies – Scatter Plot

of the resulting curve is unknown. I would argue, however, that the structural requirements in a given society for information processing, decision making, and decision implementation are major determinates of the structure of the society as a whole. Note that in a recent paper Wirsing (1973) has been able to demonstrate a close positive relationship between hierarchic complexity of decision making organization and the degree of political power exercised in a sample of societies covering a wide range of social complexity.

In the following pages current theories of the origin of the state are briefly reviewed. These theories are evaluated in terms of a test case, namely the rise of the state during the fourth millenium B.C. on the Susiana plain of Khuzistan, Iran. A general information theory is adduced to explain this development and perhaps resolve the conflicting positions of other theories.

This monograph will attempt to show that increase in information processing requirements was a major determinant in the origin of the state in Khuzistan. Furthermore, it will argue that the relationship between information processing and societal complexity is equally applicable to explanation of primary states in general, and that factors resulting in increased information processing requirements may vary from case to case.

THEORIES OF THE ORIGIN OF THE STATE

Carneiro (1970), Wright (1970), and Flannery (1972) have presented critical reviews of current theories of the origin of the state, a number of which will be considered here. The positions of scholars who have utilized these theories in the recent literature will be summarized.

Diakonov (1969) and Carneiro (1970) are recent proponents of what Wright terms "conflict" theories. Their positions emphasize internal and external conflict respectively. Diakonov addresses himself specifically to the origin of the state in Southern Mesopotamia. Briefly, he argues that development of agricultural and craft specialization, occasioned by increase in irrigation and the general level of agricultural and craft production, led to wealth differentials and socio-economic class formation. Economic conflicts inherent in an emergent class society led to class conflict and ultimately to the formation of the state as the agent for maintenance of ruling class dominance (1969:185-88). Diakonov's argument is based primarily on textual sources and chronologically places the origin of the state during the Early Dynastic period of about 2950 to 2450 B.C. He places the beginning of this process in the preceding Jemdet Nasr period.

Carneiro sees the origin of early states as the result of increasing external conflict or warfare, under specified conditions. He argues that population increase within a geographically or socially circumscribed area resulted in increasing competition for land, warfare leading to subjugation of increasingly large social groups, eventual centralization of land control, and the emergence of the state (1970:734-36).

In an explicitly administrative theory, Wittfogel (1957) argues that in arid areas increases in the scale of irrigation and flood control works, providing stable productivity and wealth differentials, led to increasing leadership differentiation for coordination and control of hydraulic system construction, maintenance, and operation, and ultimately resulted in state formation.

Population increase was a major contributing factor to the development of warfare and the state as seen by Carneiro. Population increase assumes an even more central position in a recent theory proposed by Smith and Young (1969:72) in a much broader discussion of the relation of population and agricultural intensity in Greater Mesopotamia. They argue that increasing Late Ubaid population and population density led to intensification of agriculture, development of highly complex social and political structures for coordination and control of an increasing labor supply, development of competition for agricultural land, organized conflict, settlement fortification, population agglomeration, the emergence of urbanism, and presumably the state.

Another group of theories considers long range trade as a critical factor. Proponents hold that in the areas of primary state formation, local scarcity or absence of critical material resources led to long range trade, and the emergence of specialized administration and the state to regulate local production, export local produce, import and redistribute scarce and valuable materials. Sanders (1968:93) argues that regional trade and irrigation are the primary factors resulting in development of the state in the Valley of Mexico.

These theories indicate something of the range of factors considered important in primary state development. Each has been adduced as the primary cause of all early state origins as so-called "prime movers." Adams (1966) has proposed what Wright calls a synthetic theory of state origins. His position incorporates these and other factors in a multi-variant approach. I will argue that an even more highly generalized model is required for explanation of the origin of primary states as a specific cultural phenomenon.

CENTRAL PLACE THEORY, FUNCTIONAL HIERARCHIES, AND STATE SETTLEMENT PATTERNS

The primary data to be used in this study were derived from a settlement pattern survey of the Susiana plain in Khuzistan, Iran. Geographers have kindly developed a number of analytical techniques for the study of settlement patterns and models for the interpretation of analytical results. One such construct, or more properly, set of constructs, is known as Central Place

Theory. In his initial formulation of Central Place Theory, Christaller (1933) proposed ways in which a settlement system associated with a modern market economy could be spatially organized to perform certain types of work most efficiently. This work involved the production and distribution of goods and services. Briefly, in a settlement system organized according to Christaller's "Marketing Principle" central places or towns of the same functional size are equidistant from one another and, when most efficiently located, have a hexagonal distribution. Each town serves a surrounding, hexagonally shaped, complementary region. Smaller central places and associated complementary regions may be hierarchically nested within this system to form an intricate settlement lattice.

Within Christaller's model, the form of this lattice may be altered under conditions in which efficiency of transportation or administration are the primary factors in the determination of settlement locations. Christaller emphasized that the distribution of actual settlements should not be expected to conform exactly to any portion of his model. Deviations could result from the operation of a combination of his ordering principles or from the influence of variables not included in his theory.

Generalizing from this model, it may be suggested that settlement distributions similar to those proposed by Christaller should appear to the extent (1) that least effort considerations influence the spatial organization of the production and distribution of goods and services; and (2) that the operation of other factors does not obscure the influence of these considerations. Since effort minimization may appear to a greater or lesser extent in the context of market, redistributional or mixed economies, the application of the theory need not be restricted to the modern market situation for which it was designed.

The following assumptions are implicit above: (1) that there is a tendency toward agglomeration of human activities due to gains in efficiency obtainable by concentration of related activities at the same spatial locus; (2) that locational decisions are made in general to minimize energy expended in movement; (3) that all locations are accessible but some are more accessible than others; (4) that structural hierarchies within settlement systems may, but do not necessarily, appear as a function of the interrelation of activity agglomeration, movement minimization, and differential accessibility.

Central Place distributions do, in fact, occur on the ground, and not in theory only. Olsson (1965:7) concludes, on the basis of available studies, that Central Place hierarchies "... exist in many parts of the world, in spite of divergent levels of economic development and marked differences in culture." I have shown elsewhere (Johnson, 1972) that the Early Dynastic settlement pattern on the Diyala plains of Iraq conforms fairly well to a rhomboidal variation of the classic Central Place model. Similar distributions might then be expected to occur in the context of earlier states in which locational efficiency was a consideration in the organization of local exchange.

Christaller's construct proposes the best spatial ordering of a hierarchy of settlements. Strictly speaking, this is a functional size rather than a population or areal size hierarchy. Functional size refers to the number of types of activities carried out in a settlement. A number of field studies by geographers have confirmed not only hexagonal settlement distributions, but also a close relationship between settlement population and functional size. Haggett (1966:115-16) reviews a number of such studies in which linear correlations between functional and population size ranged from .75 for Snohomish County in the state of Washington, U.S.A., to .91 for southern Ceylon. Interestingly, the closest relationship was found in a non-western society.

There is then a very close cross-cultural relationship between functional size and population size. Data are not available to estimate the absolute functional sizes of the archaeological settlements to be discussed in this study. It will be assumed that functional size was directly proportional to population size. This assumption will be at least partially supported by data on relative functional size.

There has been considerable discussion in the geographical literature as to whether functional distributions are continuous or discontinuous. Given the assumption of direct proportionality between functional and population sizes, discontinuities in a distribution of population sizes will be taken to indicate discontinuities in a distribution of functional sizes. Population hierarchies indicate functional hierarchies. The thorny problem of population estimation will be discussed below.

The state was defined above as a society having a decision making organization of minimally three hierarchical levels. I would argue that a state should exhibit at least a three-level settlement hierarchy, each level of which corresponds to at least one level of a decision hierarchy. Problems of equifinality require that the number of levels in a settlement hierarchy be taken as an indicator variable only. Demonstration of state level organization will require evidence of administrative function at minimally three levels of a given settlement hierarchy.

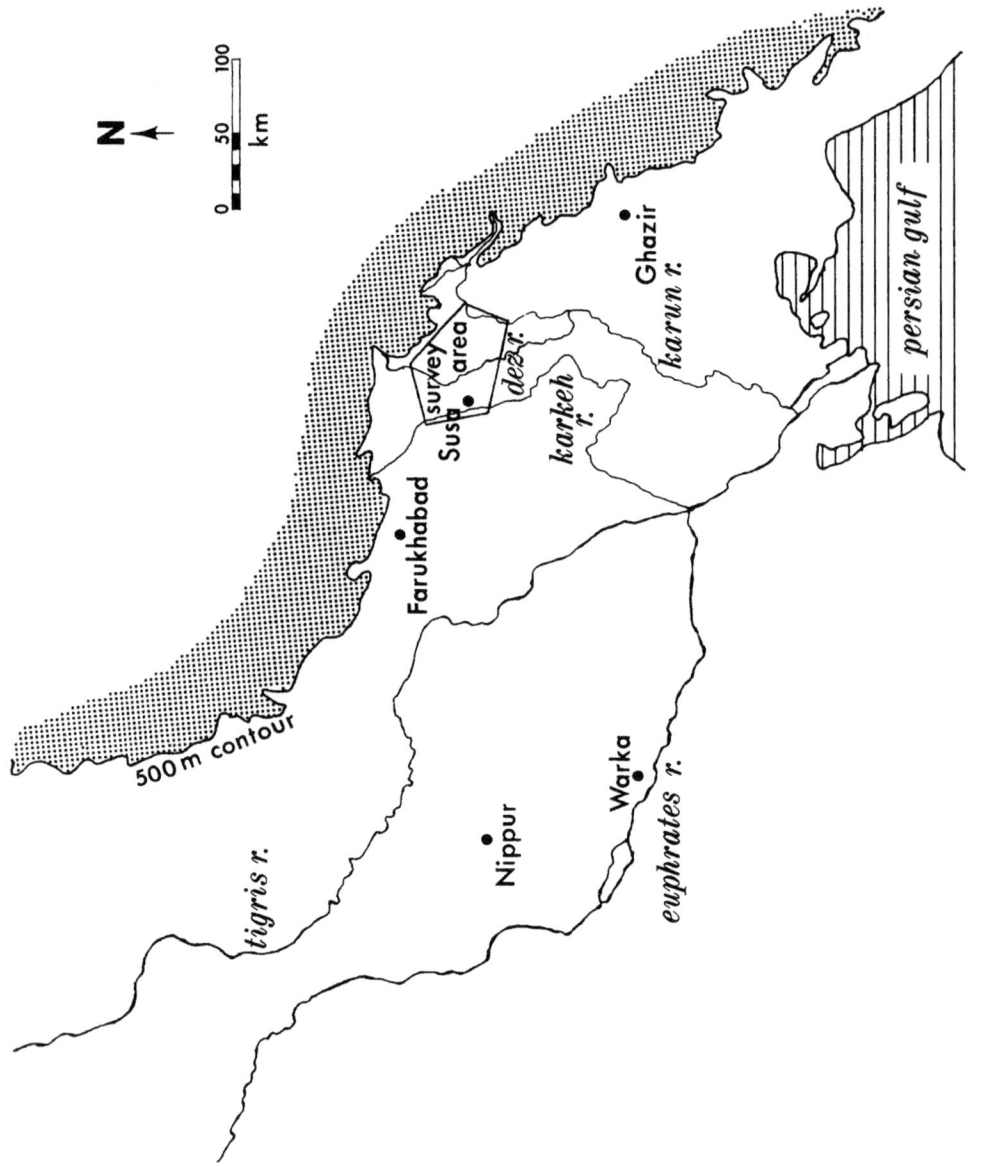

II

THE 1970-71 SUSIANA SURVEY

GEOMORPHOLOGY, HYDROLOGY AND ENVIRONMENT OF THE SUSIANA PLAIN

BROADLY speaking, the Susiana plain of Iran is an extension of the greater Mesopotamian plain of Iraq. The area was formed by massive tectonic movement caused by the relative approach of what is now Central Persia, and the Arabian massif. This process apparently reached a maximum during the Pliocene, but continues today. Movement involved massive geological folding and local depression resulting in the Zagros mountains and the Mesopotamian plains respectively (Lees and Falcon, 1952:27).

The plain has been slowly filled by erosional products originating in the Zagros range. Parallel to this filling, there has been a continued subsidence of the plain itself, allowing sedimentation to continue. This process is characterized as a continuing depression (Lees and Falcon, 1952:28).

The general location of the 1970-71 survey area is shown in Figure 2. The locations of major sites outside the survey area that will assume some importance below are also indicated. A more detailed map of the survey area is presented in Figure 3. The area is founded by the Karkeh river on the west, the Karun on the east, the Haft Tepe anticline on the south and the first low range of the Zagros on the north.

The most recent geological history of this area is not known in any detail. Apparently the latest phase of extensive sedimentation began by 6500 and possibly by 8000 B.C. During this period, river regimes were considerably different from those in effect in the area today. Aggrading river regimes were characterized by extensively braided, unstable, and frequently shifting courses (Kirkby and Kirkby:1969:2). Large areas around these channels were subject to frequent flooding. In some places rivers flowed on natural levees above the level of the surrounding plain.

This aggrading regime seems to have come to an end sometime between

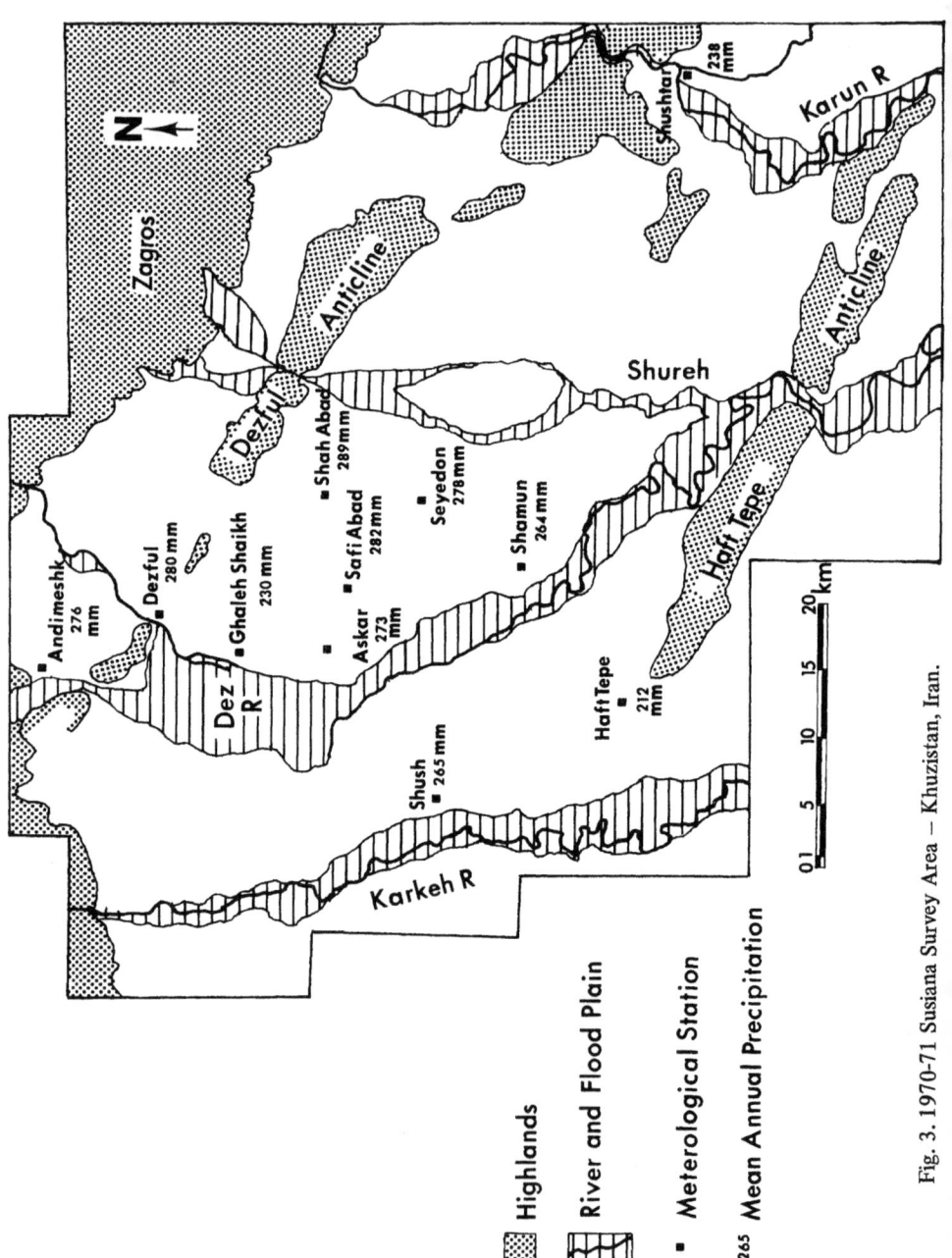

Fig. 3. 1970-71 Susiana Survey Area — Khuzistan, Iran.

3000 and 2000 B.C. with the development of a downcutting or degrading regime (Ibid.). The cause of this change is not known, but in any case rivers began to cut into the previously deposited alluvium yielding relatively stable channel positions. The present major channels and their floodplains are indicated in Figure 3.

The pattern of alluvial deposition over the plain is also not known, although it is probably quite complex. At least two meters of alluvium were deposited at Dar-i-Khazineh just southeast of Shushtar during the last period of sedimentation. Other portions of the plain have probably received at least twice this amount. In the future, determination of the sedimentation pattern will allow identification of areas where archaeological sites may be buried beneath the alluvium.

The modern soils of Khuzistan are primarily pedimental and fluvial deposits. Pedimental deposits are located on the northern edge of the Susiana plain and consist of gravelly alluvial fans. Gravels quickly merge with finer textured material on the plain itself (Veenenbos, 1958:28). Fluvial deposits cover most of the remaining portion of the plain and consist primarily of clay or clay loam. Major deposits of fluvial gravels are found immediately south of the Dezful anticline and in the Vale of Andimeshk between the Dezful anticline and the mountains (Veenenbos, 1958:31).

The major environmental characteristics of the area are primarily determined by temperature and rainfall. Seasonality is very marked in Khuzistan. The dry season usually extends from June through October and has no precipitation. Maximum daytime temperatures are high: 120°F (48.9°C) is not unusual, and temperatures as high as 138°F (58.9°C) have been reported (de Morgan, cited in Hole, Flannery and Neeley, 1969:15). During this period the unirrigated countryside is desolate, dessicated, and frequented at midday only by mad dogs and archaeologists.

The rainy season extends from November to May with an average of 250 mm of rain falling on the plain (Khuzistan Water and Power Authority nine-year records for 11 meteorological stations). Adams (1962:112) places the 300 mm isohyet just north of the Haft Tepe anticline. During the nine-year period for which detailed records are available, the 300 mm isohyet appears to have been located above the Dezful anticline (see Fig. 3).

Average yearly rainfall is misleading, however. Rainfall is actually very irregular, occurring in heavy showers (Veenenbos, 1958:49). Figure 4 presents monthly rainfall data for the Shush meteorological station. This graph illustrates both the seasonality and irregularity of rainfall in the area. Yearly figures range from 85.0 mm to 580 mm. Adams (1962:110) places the absolute lower yearly rainfall limit for dry farming in Mesopotamia at 200 mm. Less than 200 mm fell in two of the nine years for which data are available.

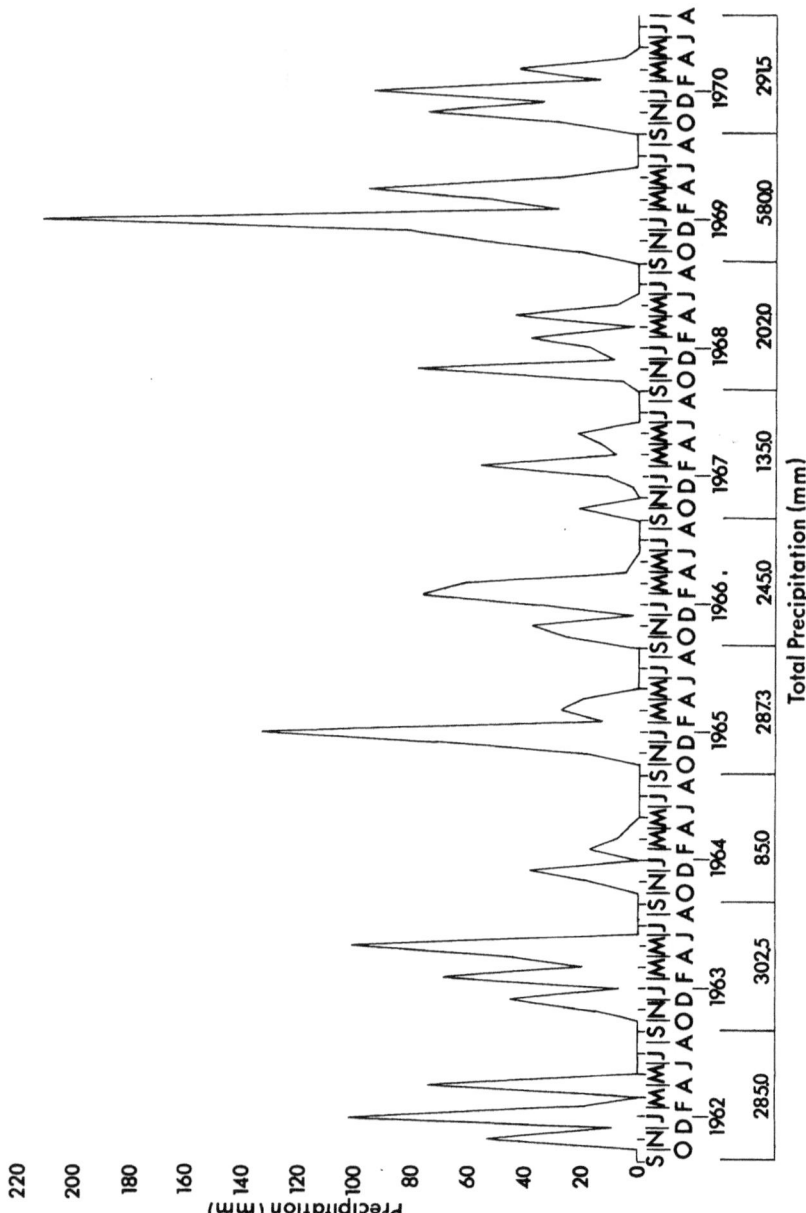

Fig. 4. Monthly Precipitation: Shush Meteorological Station.

Temperatures during the rainy season are mild, but may occasionally drop below freezing. Extended periods of cold weather have been known to occur.

The winter of 1963-64 was particularly severe:

> During the Fall and Winter Cropping season of 1963-64 (1342-43) precipitation was extremely low. Precipitation during Farvardin (March 21, to April 21) was so low that it would occur less frequently than one in a hundred years. Most of the dryland wheat in Khuzestan suffered severely, and a considerable amount was destroyed....
>
> High winds and heavy dust storms caused considerable damage to young irrigated crops. The heavy deposits of dust fully covered the plant leaves, and also caused a higher content of salt at the surface of the soil....
>
> Frost damage was also widespread in Khuzestan destroying most of the winter vegetable crops, and reducing the broadbean and berseem clover yields considerably.... Due to the very low precipitation river flows were at a very low level.... (KWPA, 1964:3-4)

While this year was exceptional, it does illustrate the adverse agricultural conditions which may prevail on the plain today. Such variability in weather probably occurred on the plain in the past. Other features of the visible environment may have changed.

The Susiana plain of 600 years ago probably bore only slight resemblance to the Susiana plain today. Man has been the largest contributor to degradation of the environment during this period. Pabot (1960:4) points to a number of human factors that have led to environmental deterioration. These include: destruction of forest trees by fire and overcutting; destruction of other woody plants by fuel collection; long term plowing of forest and pasture soils; depletion of soil organic material; overgrazing; trampling and compression of soils by herd animals, all resulting in streaming and final soil erosion (see Hole, Flannery, and Neeley, 1968, for a description of micro-environments in Khuzistan today).

Little is known about environmental conditions on the Susiana plain during the Uruk Period. Collection of floral materials by flotation of archaeological deposits and micromaterials in soil samples destined for pollen analysis has only begun recently. Good data of this sort are available for the Deh Luran plain for earlier periods, but as yet no analyzed sample exists from the Susiana plain proper. (The Deh Luran plain is located about 100 km west-northwest of the Susiana and is the location of Tepe Farukhabad, among other important sites; see Fig. 2.)

As discussed above, during the Uruk Period the rivers of Khuzistan had aggrading regimes resulting in levee formation, frequent flooding and shifting of channel locations. Virtually nothing is known, however, about specific channel locations during this period.

In some areas low ridges, running roughly northwest-southeast, probably represent pre-downcutting river levees. Channel locations are indicated in other areas by the presence of localized fluvial gravel deposits. Identification of these features on the ground or from air photographs is complicated by the absolute maze of Sassanian canals and other irrigation features that cover the plain (see Adams, 1962:117) for a simplified illustration of the Sassanian canal system). Identification is further complicated by construction of a major modern canal system and extensive land leveling in portions of the area between the Dez and Karkeh rivers. Archaeological sites and features of the area are rapidly disappearing in the face of necessary agricultural modernization.

Figure 5 illustrates the locations of known topographic and archaeological features probably indicating channel locations prior to downcutting. More and less certain channel courses are indicated by solid and dotted lines respectively. All archaeological sites on the plain to be discussed below are indicated and accompanied by their survey identification numbers. The channels indicated by dotted lines can be dated on geological grounds to the period roughly between 6000 and 2000 B.C. Channels indicated by solid lines were probably operative during the Uruk Period. There has been no attempt here to infer channel positions from linear site distributions on the assumption that all sites must have been located on or near a watercourse.

Pabot has reconstructed the theoretical climax vegetation for various zones of Khuzistan. Originally the plains between sea level and 300 meters in elevation, his "Dry Zone," were probably covered with scattered jujube trees (*Zizyphus*), Tamarix, and occasional pistachio (*Pistacia khunjuk*) (Pabot, 1960:7). During the rainy season abundant herbaceous vegetation provided excellent grazing for gazelle (*Gazella subgutturosa*) and onager or wild ass (*Equus hemionus*) (Hole, Flannery, and Neeley, 1969:17).

Moist areas next to stream courses probably supported a dense "jungle" of Tamarix and poplar (*Populus euphratica*) inhabited most notably by wild boar and lion in addition to a wide variety of smaller flora and fauna. In sum, the plain was probably a far less formidable place during the Uruk Period than it is today. The implications of these conditions for the human exploitation of the plain during the Uruk Period will be discussed below.

The plain, rich as it may have been, should not be considered as an isolated unit. The immediately adjacent mountain zone probably played an equally important role in the prehistory of the area. Here were stands of pistachio (*Pistacia atlantica*) and almond (*Amygdalus spartioides*) (Hole, Flannery and Neeley, 1969:19) as well as jujube (Pabot, 1960:7). Most importantly, highland valleys received more rain than the plains and during the summer months supported lush herbaceous vegetation providing excellent pasturage. Although this study deals mainly with settlement on the plain, the

THE 1970-71 SUSIANA SURVEY

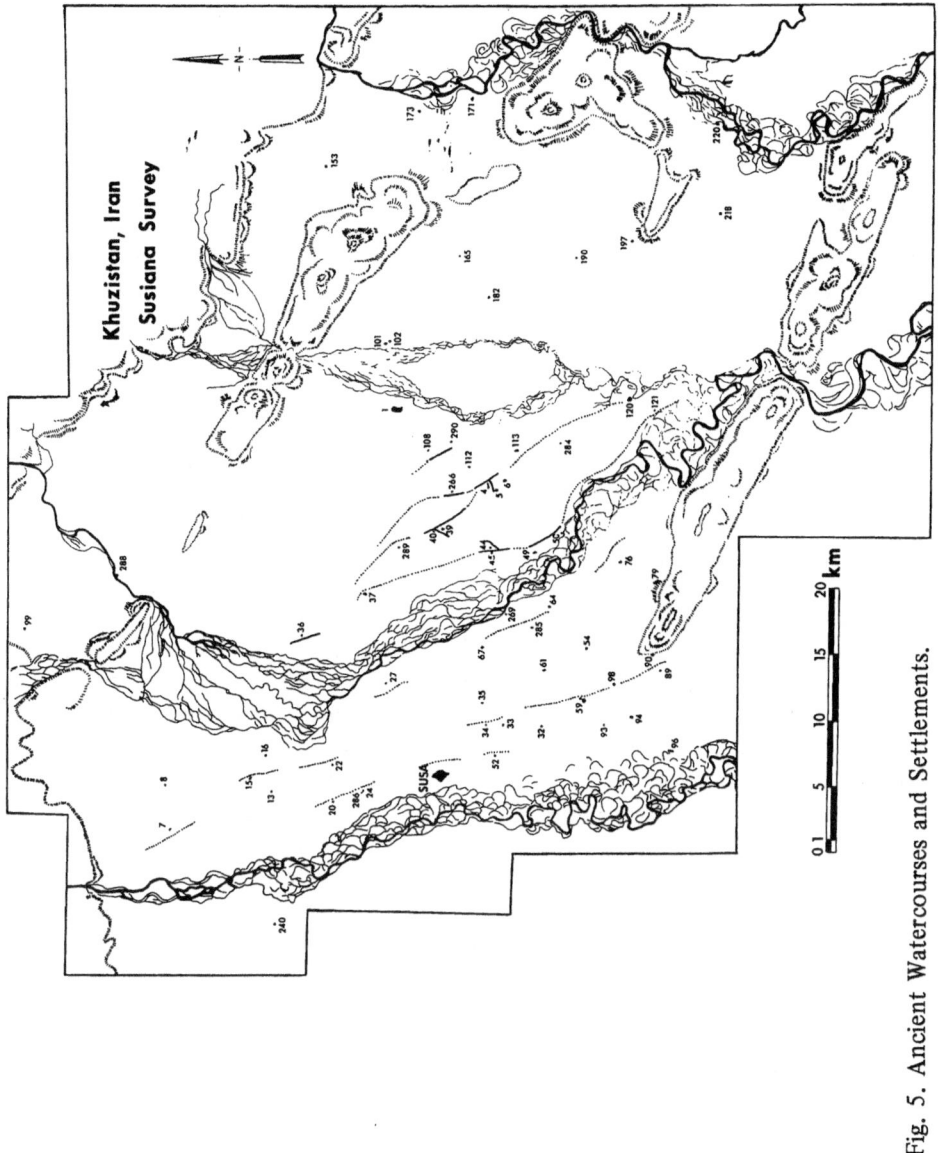

Fig. 5. Ancient Watercourses and Settlements.

mountains, intermountain valleys, and their inhabitants will occasionally be referred to.

SURVEY METHOD

The original survey plan called for a four-week operation during which the 39 sites noted by previous surveys as having Uruk occupations would be revisited. Each site would be mapped using a pace and compass technique. Additional surface collections would be made. Four selected sites would be studied more intensively. These sites would be mapped with an alidade and plane table. Surface collections would be made using a systematic, stratified, unaligned, random sampling design. It was expected that such rigorously drawn samples would provide additional data on chronological and functional variability within and between settlements.

The remaining survey period would be used to recheck sites not included among the 39 known Uruk settlements and for laboratory work on the surface collections. During the remaining months of the project I would participate in the excavation of a small Uruk site, Tepe Sharafabad, KS-36.

It became necessary to alter this plan considerably. During the initial survey period it was discovered that some settlements previously described as having Uruk occupations had none. The serious possibility then arose that some number of Uruk occupations might have gone previously undetected. A systematic program of resurvey of all fourth and fifth millenium sites was begun. Eventually this was expanded to include all sites of noticeable elevation within the survey area.

It also became clear that the topographic complexity of many sites was such that they could not be effectively mapped by the pace and compass technique. An effort was made to map all Uruk sites with a plane table and alidade, increasing measurement accuracy considerably.

Finally it became clear that many Uruk sites had been overlooked due to heavy overburdens of later material. Considerable time was often required to, first, determine the presence or absence of Uruk material and, second, to assemble a collection of Uruk ceramics sufficiently large for dating purposes. These factors combined to lengthen the time required for the basic survey.

Seven months were devoted to survey and laboratory work on the surface collections. Survey was discontinuous throughout depending upon the availability of equipment and personnel also required for other parts of the project, the progress of laboratory work, and on the relative accessibility of parts of the survey area during the winter rainy season.

As a result of this and previous surveys, 67 sites having Uruk or Terminal Susa A ceramics among their surface materials have been identified. This probably represents at least an estimated 95 percent of all Uruk sites projecting above the alluvium, and most probably includes all such sites one hectare or larger in area.

It is not possible at present to estimate the number of sites which are represented only by sherd scatters at the present plain level, or which are covered by alluvial deposits. Single house mounds, herding camps, and various special functional sites potentially fall into this category. Recent construction of large irrigation canals near Haft Tepe (KS-98) revealed the presence of several previously unknown Susiana period sites (E. O. Negahban, personal communication, 1972). It should not be assumed that Uruk sites of this type do not exist. However, at present only one site (KS-286) represented by a plain level sherd scatter has been located.

The systematic surface collection technique mentioned above has been used to advantage in the Near East (Redman and Watson, 1970; Whallon, 1969). The logistics of extensive use of such a sampling design are complex. For example, it would be ideal to have systematic samples for each of the Terminal Susa A and Uruk sites known on the Susiana plain. Such samples would undoubtedly increase our knowledge of occupational extent, chronological and functional variability within and among these sites. The collection and analysis of this material would, however, require a considerable investment of time and labor.

The total area of known sites having Terminal Susa A or Uruk occupations within the survey area is 203.22 hectares or 2,032,200 square meters. Redman and Watson recommend a 10 percent sample for an acceptable level of statistical reliability (Redman and Watson, 1970:281). In this case, the sample would amount to 203,220 square meters. Our experience indicates that an average of 13 man/minutes is required to completely collect one square meter of site surface. Collection of a 10 percent sample would require 44,031 man/hours. Table 1 presents estimated time requirements for collection of this sample by field crews of varying sizes. The estimates are based on eight-hour working days, and six-day working weeks. Only actual surface collecting times are included.

It has also been our experience that the average square meter of site area in Khuzistan contains about two kg of material. The estimated amount of material expected from this hypothetical 10 percent sample would be on the order of 400 metric tons or roughly 900 English tons, some 894,542 pounds. Reduction of the sample to a statistically unreliable 1.0 percent would still yield an expected 41 metric tons of material.

Despite the favorable results obtained with this technique by Whallon and by Redman and Watson, extensive use of this method was not considered fruitful during the 1970-71 survey. Two sites, KS-108 and KS-36, were collected using this technique. Limitations of time only allowed collection of a two percent sample from KS-108. This sample was sufficiently large to allow

TABLE 1
TIME REQUIREMENTS FOR SYSTEMATIC SURFACE
COLLECTION OF SUSIANA TERMINAL SUSA A AND
URUK SITES (10% AREA SAMPLE)

Crew Size	Time Required (years)	Crew Size	Time Required (years)
1	19.1	5	3.8
2	9.5	10	1.9
3	6.4	20	1.0
4	4.8	40	0.5

statistical definition of erosional features on the site, if little else. The results of the systematic collection of KS-36, where excavations were undertaken by other members of the project, are expected to appear in the site report.

The recovery technique employed for nearly all sites surveyed may be called an "area pickup." In this method a site is divided into topographically distinct areas on the assumption that topographic differences reflect occupational differences within the site. Diagnostic artifacts are then collected within each of these areas. The relative density of the material, presence of unusual sherd concentrations, special features such as kilns, and material from previous and subsequent occupations are noted.

The operational research design for the survey did not call for detailed studies of functional variability within sites, or estimation of relative amounts of Uruk material versus other material present. The data sought were the following: sufficiently large and diverse samples for relative dating; preliminary estimation of the extent of Uruk occupation through estimates of the areal distribution of Uruk ceramics; and sufficiently large samples of individual ceramic types for use in local exchange studies.

Surface collection was concentrated specifically on Uruk material. This narrow focus was adopted for several reasons. Concentration on material of one period allows greater speed and reliability in collection. With some experience an individual making a collection is able to scan the surface material of a site quickly, locating perhaps infrequent Uruk sherds among vast numbers of sherds of earlier or later periods. The surface density of Uruk ceramics may not exceed .0025 per square meter on some Uruk sites with heavy overburdens of later materials.

In addition to these considerations, collection of earlier and later materials as well as Uruk sherds would have duplicated previous work. Frank Hole of Rice University has surveyed the area specifically for sixth and fifth millenium sites; Elizabeth Carter of the University of Chicago has surveyed the area specifically for second millenium sites.

Our area pickup has disadvantages. It must be assumed that our collection are representative of the Uruk pottery discarded on any particular site. The quality of a collection, given the surface conditions of a particular site, is a direct function of the person or persons making the collection. During the course of the 1970-71 survey, the members of the survey crew became increasingly familiar with the types of Uruk ceramics present in the area and increasingly proficient in their collection. Sites visited early in the survey were revisited later to provide at least some control on differential collecting proficiency.

Resampling of specific sites using randomized collection techniques in conjunction with subjective pick up will be required in the future to test hypotheses generated by analysis of the present survey and excavation programs. At present the 1970-71 survey provides the most extensive extant body of data on the Uruk Period in the Khuzistan.

METHOD OF METRICAL ANALYSIS OF CERAMICS

Much of the analysis to follow deals with spatial and temporal variability in Terminal Susa A and Uruk ceramics. Investigation of spatial variability faces one particularly difficult problem. We know virtually nothing about Uruk workshops beyond their mere existence. Presently there is no way to assess directly the degree of variability in a particular ceramic type produced within a single workshop. This problem could be most reasonably solved by detailed excavation of an actual workshop area. Such excavation has not been undertaken.

If our present control of variability in Uruk ceramic material is highly restricted, our control of Uruk lithic variability is virtually nonexistent. Recently James Phillips of the University of Illinois began work on the problem with lithic material from a site on the Susiana plain.

With these qualifications in mind, a few comments on the theory and method of ceramic measurement are in order. A virtually unlimited series of measurements could be taken on any given sherd, stone, or bone. Normally numbers of possible measurements are grouped into categories called attributes. Sherd thickness, for example, is a commonly-measured ceramic attribute. The number of thickness measurements that could be made on a given sherd is obviously very large, and is effectively limited only by the area of the sherd and the area of the contact surface on the measurement instrument used.

Use of an attribute system allows combination of a large number of possible measurements into a much smaller measurement series. It should be recognized that this combination may result in the masking of significant variability. One solution to this type of problem is to measure a given attribute several times, to sample a category of possible measurements. This sample may be averaged to obtain a "representative" measurement or analyzed for significant internal variation, or both. While this approach is probably preferable, it can also be extremely time-consuming. For example, in the case of the bevel rim bowls discussed below, 10 attributes were measured for each sherd; the sample consists of 278 examples and each attribute was measured once, resulting in 2,780 individual measurements. An averaging approach, with, for instance, five measurements of each attribute, would result in 13,900 individual measurements. Measurement accuracy of this sort is usually precluded by limits of time, money, and sanity. These limitations apply to the present study. Each attribute was measured once. A subjective if conscientious effort was made to obtain a representative or modal measurement for each attribute on each sherd.

Attribute selection is a second problem in ceramic measurement. What do you measure? Attribute definition depends upon the particular problem or problems dealt with in a given study. The classical distinction here is between functional and stylistic studies, which implies that stylistic and functional attributes can be differentiated. This is not always as simple as it might seem. Surface decoration is easily identified as stylistic variation. How much of the variability in jar rim form is functional and how much is stylistic is another matter.

With the exception of a study of bevel rim bowls, ceramic measurement in the present work is not specifically aimed at either functional or stylistic variability, but at spatial variability. Is it possible to distinguish vessels made in one workshop from those made in another in those cases where the same basic form is being produced? An argument that such distinction is possible is made below.

The specific attributes measured in each case were selected for a variety of reasons. Some were selected because they had been used previously and found valuable by Wright (personal communication) in his studies of Uruk ceramics from Tepe Farukhabad. Use of a comparable attribute system allows initial comparison between samples. Such comparison would obviously be precluded if different systems were used.

Wright's attributes were selected to include the subjectively-defined, basic, formal characteristics of each ceramic type. This selection procedure constitutes the "art" of ceramic measurement. Eventually this "artistic" component may be reduced by experimental studies in the modern duplication of specific ceramic types. Once it is known how these vessels were made, or perhaps how they could have been made, it will be possible to construct a more objective attribute system directly keyed to individual operations of ceramic production. New attributes defined for this study were defined either because particular ceramic types had not been previously measured, or because they were considered potentially valuable additions to attributes already defined.

The attributes finally included are virtually all reflected in linear or angular measurements that could be made on a continuous scale. Interval and ordinal measurements are also occasionally used. Unless otherwise specified, all ceramic measurements included in this study were made by the author. Measurement by a single person is suggested whenever possible to insure that observer error will at least be constant. Automated measurement should resolve this problem in the future.

Appendix III contains tabulated ceramic measurements used in this study. Each table is prefaced by a line drawing illustrating the measurement of each attribute included in the analysis of each ceramic type. The tables should provide valuable comparative material for future studies.

This discussion has received a liberal scattering of qualifications, disclaimers, and general hedges. Even so, many readers may feel that much of the data analysis in the following pages is pushed beyond all reasonable limits. This criticism would have considerable merit. However, if our understanding of primary states, in general, and of the Uruk Period in Khuzistan, in particular, is to be advanced, data will have to suffer a little strain. An effort has been made to present complete data sets upon which conclusions are based to enable readers to examine the basic data for themselves.

URUK RELATIVE AND ABSOLUTE CHRONOLOGY

It is not difficult to identify Uruk ceramics per se in surface collections and thereby determine that a series of sites was occupied during the Uruk Period. It is doubtful, however, that all Uruk sites on the Susiana plain were occupied simultaneously. At various times during the Uruk Period some sites were probably abandoned, others were founded, while still others were occupied continuously. The investigation of economic and political processes operative during the Uruk Period on the Susiana plain and reflected in changes in the Uruk settlement pattern requires chronological distinctions that facilitate identification of the Uruk settlement pattern during several broad time intervals.

In the following pages a corpus of Uruk ceramic types from the surface collections is presented and the collections analyzed for temporal variation. Early, Middle, and Late Uruk ceramic assemblages are defined and compared with stratified Uruk ceramic sequences from the Acropole of Susa, Excavation B of Tepe Farukhabad, the Step Trench of Tall-i-Ghazir, the Deep Sounding in the Eanna precinct of Warka, and the Deep Sounding in the Inanna precinct of Nippur. In addition an early ceramic phase is proposed which is equivalent to late Susa A in Khuzistan.

The chronological system proposed and the stratigraphic correlations made are tentative. Undoubtedly further excavation and more complete reporting of the presently excavated material will enable considerable refinement of this system. At present, however, it is internally consistent and based upon the most complete data that I have been able to assemble.

Plates I-IX present illustrations of the corpus of Uruk ceramics from the 1970-71 survey collections to be discussed in this study. Supplementary references to recent publications of the French Mission at Susa are included for various ceramic types. There is really no satisfactory way to present a corpus of ceramic material in a form other than the sherds themselves. Ceramic types are illustrated as sherds such as were collected on the survey. No attempt has been made to reconstruct vessel forms. At best I hope that the illustrations will strike a spark of recognition in readers familiar with Uruk ceramic material.

Relative Chronology of Ceramic Types
From the 1970-71 Survey Surface Collections

The ceramic type counts from the survey surface collections are presented in Appendix I. Each site or site area from which Uruk ceramics were collected is listed individually, identified by a site number, and, if applicable, a letter indicating a collection area within each site. The location of collection areas within individual sites is indicated on the site maps (Pl. X-XX).

The type counts are affected by several sources of variability. The collections from some sites are relatively large due to the fact that the Uruk occupation was the last occupation or that rich ceramic deposits were revealed by erosion or recent human activity. Other collections are relatively small due to poor collecting conditions, erosional destruction of the Uruk deposits, or heavy overburden of later materials.

The specific types found on any given site are affected by chronological and/or functional differences as well as by the condition of the remaining Uruk deposits.

The type counts were coded in a weighted presence-absence system for the purpose of analysis of temporal variation. This system reduces variability in the sample due to sample size or functional differences. A histogram of type counts was constructed for each site or collection area. All types present in the collection from a site or area and represented by one example were included in the first interval of the histogram. All types represented by two examples were included in the second interval of the histogram, and so on. These histograms were *inspected* for modal divisions, and the types included within each mode were coded according to the number of modes present. For example, a histogram might have three modes and be coded as follows: all types not present are coded "0"; all types represented by one to three examples are coded "1"; all types represented by four to eight examples are coded "2"; all types represented by nine to 11 examples are coded "3." Each site or collection area included in the analysis was coded separately. Certain sites were eliminated from the analysis due to the low number of types represented in their surface collections. Table 2 presents a list of the sites or areas included and the coding system for each.

Table 3 presents the results of this analysis in the form of an ordered correlation matrix of ceramic types. (See Hole and Shaw, 1967, for an extended discussion of matrix ordering for seriation.) It is assumed that the primary axis of variation within the ordered matrix is time or that the types are ordered relative to their chronological relationships. The method emphasizes the modal position of a type in a temporal series, not its first appearance in that series. Three ceramic clusters corresponding to three assemblages are indicated. The assemblages are proposed as characteristic of Early, Middle, and Late Uruk ceramic assemblages on the Susiana plain.

Having proposed a tripartite division of the Uruk on the basis of the surface collections, it is necessary to provide supporting evidence from stratigraphic contexts. This evidence is presented below.

The Uruk Ceramic Sequence at Susa, Acropole Sondage 1969

A small stratigraphic excavation was undertaken on the Acropole of Susa in 1969 (see Fig. 2). The preliminary report of these excavations provides a detailed consideration of the architectural stratigraphy (Le Brun, 1971).

During a three-day visit to Susa in March of 1971 I was very kindly permitted to study the then unpublished material from levels 16 to 27 of this excavation. At that time, type counts were made of the available ceramic material of levels 17 to 24 which encompass the Uruk deposits in the area. These counts are presented in Table 4. Inspection of the table reveals that most of the material was from Level 17 where the primary excavations had been carried out. At that time, very little material was available from levels 18 to 24. It must also be stressed that the type counts were made in haste, using the survey type system. Undoubtedly they contain many errors and oversights which will be corrected with full publication of the French report. At present, however, they are the best data available.

TABLE 2
WEIGHTED PRESENCE-ABSENCE CODING FOR THE 1970-71
URUK SURFACE COLLECTIONS

Site	Frequency	Coding
KS-4 Area E	0	0
	1-3	1
	4-7	2
	8+	3
KS-8 Area A	0	0
	1-4	1
	5-8	2
	9+	3
KS-8 Area B	0	0
	1-3	1
KS-16	0	0
	1-3	1
	4-5	2
	6-8	3
	9+	4
KS-22 Area B	0	0
	1-3	1
	4-5	2
	6-7	3
KS-24	0	0
	1-4	1
	5-8	2
	9+	3
KS-27	0	0
	1-2	1
	3-6	2
	7+	3
KS-32	0	0
	1-2	1
	3-4	2
	5-8	3
	9+	4
KS-34 Area A	0	0
	1-2	1
	3	2
	4+	3

TABLE 2 (continued)

Site	Frequency	Coding
KS-34 Area B	0	0
	1-4	1
KS-34 Area C	0	0
	1-2	1
	3-4	2
	5+	3
KS-35 Area A	0	0
	1-2	1
	3-5	2
	6+	3
KS-35 Area B	0	0
	1-2	1
	3+	2
KS-36 Area A	0	0
	1-2	1
	3+	2
KS-36 Area B	0	0
	1-2	1
	3-4	2
	5+	3
KS-36 Area BP	0	0
	1-2	1
	3+	2
KS-36 Area C	0	0
	1-2	1
KS-36 Area G	0	0
	1-2	1
	3-6	2
	7+	3
KS-39 Area A	0	0
	1-4	1
	5+	2
KS-39 Area C	0	0
	1-3	1
	4+	2

TABLE 2 (continued)

Site	Frequency	Coding
KS-39 Area C	0	0
	1-2	1
	3-5	2
	6+	3
KS-49 Area C	0	0
	1-3	1
	4+	2
KS-52 Area A	0	0
	1-3	1
	4+	2
KS-54	0	0
	1-3	1
	4-7	2
	8+	3
KS-59 Area B	0	0
	1-2	1
	3-4	2
	5+	3
KS-59 Area C	0	0
	1-3	1
	4+	2
KS-59 Area D	0	0
	1-3	1
	4+	2
KS-59 Area F	0	0
	1-3	1
	4-6	2
	7+	3
KS-59 Area G	0	0
	1-3	1
	4-6	2
	7+	3
KS-59 Area I	0	0
	1-3	1
	4+	2

TABLE 2 (continued)

Site	Frequency	Coding
KS-61	0	0
	1-3	1
	4-5	2
	6+	3
KS-64	0	0
	1-2	1
	3-5	2
	6+	3
KS-76	0	0
	1-2	1
	3-5	2
	6+	3
KS-79		0
	1-3	1
	4-6	2
	7+	3
KS-90	0	0
	1-2	1
	3-4	2
	5+	3
KS-93	0	0
	1-3	1
	4+	2
KS-94	0	0
	1-2	1
	3-4	2
	5+	3
KS-96 Area B	0	0
	1-3	1
	4-6	2
	7+	3
KS-96 Area H	0	0
	1-2	1
	3-6	2
	7+	3
KS-108 Area A+B	0	0
	1-2	1
	3-4	2
	5-7	3
	8-9	4
	10+	5

TABLE 2 (continued)

Site	Frequency	Coding
KS-108 Area C	0	0
	1-2	1
	3-5	2
	6-10	3
	11+	4
KS-108 Area F	0	0
	1-2	1
	3-7	2
	8+	3
KS-113 Area A	0	0
	1-3	1
	4-5	2
KS-121	0	0
	1	1
	2-4	2
	5-8	3
	9+	4
KS-153 Area A	0	0
	1-2	1
	3-5	2
	6-8	3
	9+	4
KS-153 Area B	0	0
	1-4	1
	5+	2
KS-165 Area B	0	0
	1-3	1
	4-6	2
	7+	3
KS-171 Area B	0	0
	1-5	1
	6+	2
KS-171 Area A	0	0
	1-4	1
	5-9	2
	10+	3
KS-173	0	0
	1-2	1
	3-6	2
	7+	3

TABLE 2 (continued)

Site	Frequency	Coding
KS-197	0	0
	1-2	1
	3-5	2
	6+	3
KS-240	0	0
	1-2	1
	3+	2
KS-266	0	0
	1-3	1
	4-5	2
	6-8	3
	9+	4
KS-269	0	0
	1-2	1
	3-5	2
	6+	3
KS-284	0	0
	1-3	1
	4-7	2
	8+	3
KS-288	0	0
	1-2	1
	3-4	2
	5+	3
KS-289	0	0
	1-2	1
	3-4	2
	5+	3
KS-290	0	0
	1-2	1
	3-4	2
	5+	3

TABLE 3
SERIATION OF URUK CERAMIC TYPES: 1970-71 SUSIANA SURVEY

```
                #
                D #
                e D #
                - C C #
                - e D A #
                - - - D B #
                - - e D e B #
                - - C A A e A #              Early Uruk
                - - - e B A D C #
                e - - e D D - B A #
                - - e e - - D B B D #
                - - - e e - A D C e D #
                - - - - e - - D - B - e #
                - - - D e - - e - e - D C #
                - - - - - - - - - - D - - #
                - - - - - e e - - e - D B - - #
                - - - - - - - - - - - - D - #
                - - - - - - - - - - - - e A e #
                - - - - - - - - - - - D - e C #
                - - - - - - - - - - e D - e B #
                - - - - - - - e - - - e - e - e A #     Middle Uruk
                - - - - - - - - - - - - e C e C B A #
                - - - - - - - - - - - e e - D C - C D #
                - - - - - - - - - - - - - e - - e D A C D #
                - - - - - - - - - - - - - - - e - - D e B #
                - - - - - - - - - - - - - - - - - - D - D #
                - - - - - - - - e - - - - - - - - D C - - #
                - - - - - D - - - e - - - - - - - - B C B B #
                - - - - - - - - - - - - - - - - - - - e - - D #
                - - - - - - - - - - - - - - D - e - D - - B D #          Late
                - - - - - - - - - - - - - - - - e - - - - e C B #        Uruk
                - - - - - - - - - - - - - - - - - - - - - D C A A #
                - - - - - - - - - - - - - - - - - - - - - - B B A #
                - - - - - - - - - - - e - - e - - - - - - e e B A A A #
                - - - - - - - - - - - - - - - - - - - D - - - - - - A B A A #
                - - - - - - - - - - - - - e - - - e - - - - - - - - C D B A e C #
```

Symbol	r^1
#	1.00
A	.50
B	.45-.49
C	.40-.44
D	.35-.39
e	.26-.34
—	other

[1] Due to the coding system used here, the statistic p does not have a known sampling distribution. Associated probabilities are thus unknown.

Ceramic types (left to right): Beaded Lip Bowl, Impressed Strip Bowl, Heavy Lug, Neckless Ledge Rim Jar, Proto Bevel Rim Bowl, Round Rim Bowl, Ledge Rim Bowl, Flared Expanded Rim Jar, Flat Rim Bowl, Flared Round Rim Jar, Nose Lug, Straight Spout, Grooved Round Rim Jar, Rocker Stamp, Expanded Ledge Rim Jar, Punctate, Hatched Strip, Cross Hatch Band, Out-turned Expanded Jar, Low Expanded Band Rim Jar, Heavy Round Rim Jar, Strap Handle, Bevel Rim Bowl, Impressed Strip Jar, Expanded Ledge Rim Bowl, Sinuous Sided Cup Rim, Conical Spout, Ledge Rim Bottle, Beveled Rim Bowl, Full Twisted Handle, Band Rim Bottle, Groove and Oblique, Flat Twisted Handle, Droop Spout, Cross Hatch Triangle, Rim Lug

TABLE 4

TYPE COUNTS OF URUK CERAMICS FROM THE ACROPOLE SONDAGE (1969-) AT SUSA

Type	17A	17B	17	18	19	20	21	22	23	23-24	24
Groove and Oblique	31	4	7	3							
Late Straight Spout	120	1	49								
Ledge Rim Jar	44		17								
Hatched Strip	10	2	6	2							
Shoulder Groove	31	4	7	3							
Band Rim Bottle	29		16	6							
Impressed Strip Jar	3	1	7	2							
Rim Lug	16	4	10	5							
Droop Spout	53	8	41	48							
Full Twisted Handle	5		3	2							
Sinuous Sided Cup	175		97	36							
Chaff Tempered Round Rim Bowl	12		38	52							
Cross Hatch Band	11		19	11							
Ledge Rim Bottle	1		8	14							
Horizontal Reserve Slip					10		1				
Flared Expanded Rim Jar					16		1		8		
Beaded Rim Bowl								3			
Chaff Tempered Ring Base							1	1			
Proto Bevel Rim Bowl						1	11	60	3	2	
Unpainted High Neck Jar						1	1	6		1	
Grooved Flat Rim Bowl						1	1	8	2	1	
Impressed Strip Bowl							1	1		1	

TABLE 4 (continued)

Type	17A	17B	17	18	19	20	21	22	23	23-24	24
Wall Cone	13	4	14	9					1		
Bevel Rim Bowl	3	5	191	500		1	141	25	1	3	
Cross Hatch Square	5										
Incised Oblique Band	3		3								
Flat Rim Bowl	29		1			1	1				
Straight Spout						9	1				1
Susiana Painted Ware	12	4	23	6		3	4	25		8	
Low Expanded Band Rim Jar	5	2	4	2		8					
Diagonal Reserve Slip	2	2	3			6	1				
Chaff Tempered Tray	8	3	24	4							
Rocker Stamp	9	1									
Round Rim Jar	54	23	25	2							
Strap Handle	55	17	17	4		2	6	1			
Round Rim Bottle	11	19	4								
Nose Lug	21	44	19	7			1	1			
Cross Hatch Triangle	5	1	6								
Open Spout	4	1	6								
Straight Round Rim Jar	93	25	48								
Straight Flat Rim Jar	31	4	13								
Bevel Rim Bowl Variant	651	199	469								
Ledge Rim Bowl	57	42	33	1			1				
Round Rim Bowl	134	47	97	1							

The type counts were coded in a weighted presence-absence system to eliminate as far as possible variability due to differential sample size. The coding system is detailed in Table 5. Coding followed the same procedure used for the survey collections. The ceramic types were then seriated using the same method applied to the surface collections (see Table 6).

The first major break in the sequence appears in Level 24 with an increase in wall thickness and the beginnings of a transition from large Susa A to smaller Uruk type bricks (Le Brun, 1971, personal communication). This architectural change would seem to mark the transition from Susa A to Uruk. Susa A painted wares virtually disappear by Level 23, which is characterized by a large number of proto bevel rim bowls, and seems to be clearly within an Early Uruk range.

The next clear architectural change appears in Level 22 with a change in wall orientation (Le Brun, 1971, personal communication). Bevel rim bowls appear for the first time in quantity, although proto bevel rim bowls are still present, along with a number of other apparently early types. It is unclear whether this level should be assigned to Early or Middle Uruk, although the former is probably correct.

The next major change is in ceramics. A great many new types appear in Levels 18 and 17 (17, 17A, and 17B). Numerical tablets are present by Level 17 (Le Brun, 1971:211). It seems clear that these levels represent a Late Uruk occupation.

The Uruk sequence ends with Level 17. Level 16 represents a major break in the sequence both in architecture and in ceramics (see Le Brun, 1971). The level probably can be assigned to the Jemdet Nasr Period.

Examination of the ceramic seriation (Table 6) reveals two and perhaps three type clusters. The first corresponds to the Early Uruk Period represented by Level 23 and possibly Level 22. The cluster includes impressed strip bowls, grooved flat rim bowls, unpainted high neck jars, proto bevel rim bowls, chaff tempered thumb impressed ring bases, beaded rim bowls, and possibly flared expanded jar rims. The counts for Susa A painted sherds were analyzed but failed to show a significant association with any other type included. This suggests that while such forms as grooved flat rim bowls and high neck jars typical of Susa A are present, the levels in which they occur should be assigned not to that period, but rather to Early Uruk.

The second ceramic cluster contains all the remaining types in the seriation and represents a middle-late group. (The division indicated between Middle and Late Uruk in the seriation table is approximate only.) The Middle Uruk assemblage is represented only in Level 21, very little material having been recovered from Levels 20 and 19. Continuing French excavations of these levels promise to clarify this problem. The seriation indicates that there is a continual development from Middle to Late Uruk characterized primarily by proportional changes in ceramic types. New types appear, such as twisted

TABLE 5
WEIGHTED PRESENCE-ABSENCE CODING FOR SUSA,
ACROPOLE CERAMIC TYPE COUNTS

Level	Frequency	Coding
17A	0	0
	1 - 7	1
	8 - 17	2
	18 - 31	3
	32 - 57	4
	58 - 172	5
	173 - 651	6
17B	0	0
	1 - 8	1
	9 - 25	2
	26 - 47	3
	48 - 199	4
17	0	0
	1 - 7	1
	8 - 10	2
	11 - 20	3
	21 - 25	4
	26 - 49	5
	50 - 97	6
	98 - 496	7
18	0	0
	1 - 7	1
	8 - 11	2
	12 - 19	3
	20 - 52	4
21	0	0
	1 - 5	1
	6 - 12	2
	13 - 21	3
22	0	0
	1 - 4	1
	5 - 12	2
	13 - 21	3
23	0	0
	1 - 3	1
	4 - 8	2

TABLE 5 (continued)

Level	Frequency	Coding
	9 - 25	3
	26 - 60	4
24	0	0
	1 - 2	1
	3 - 8	2

TABLE 6
SERIATION OF URUK CERAMIC TYPES: SUSA, ACROPOLE SONDAGE

```
#
A #
- b #
- b b #                      Early Uruk          Symbol         r¹
- b A # #                                           #          1.00
- b b A A #                                         A          .83-.99
- - - - - - #                                       b          .71-.82
- - - - - - b #                                     -          other
- - - - - - - #
- - - - - - - A #                             ¹ See note, Table 30
- - - - - - - A A #              Middle Uruk
- - - - - - - b A A #
- - - - - - - A A A A #
- - - - - - - A A A A A #
- - - - - - - - A b b A #
- - - - - - - - b - b A A #
- - - - - - - - b b A A A b - #
- - - - - - - - b b b A A A A A #
- - - - - - - - b - b A A A - A #
- - - - - - - - - b b b - - A A - #
- - - - - - - - - b b b b - A A - A #
- - - - - - - - - - b b - b b A b b b #
- - - - - - - - - - b b A b A A b A A b #
- - - - - - - - - - b A b b A b b A b A #        Late Uruk
- - - - - - - - - - b A b b A b A A b A A #
- - - - - - - - - - b b - A A - A A b A A A #
- - - - - - - - - - b b A A b A A b A A A A #
- - - - - - - - - - - b b - b b b b A A A A A #
- - - - - - - - - - - b b - b b b b A A A A # #
- - - - - - - - - - - b b - b b - b b A A A A A A #
- - - - - - - - - - - - - b - - b b b b b A A A #
- - - - - - - - - b - - - - b b - A A b A b A A A b b A b #
- - - - - - - - - b - - - - b - - b b - b b b b b - - b - A #
- - - - - - - - - - - - - - A b - A A A b b b A A - - - - b b #
- - - - - - - - - b - - - - - - - - - - - - - - - - - - b b - #
- - - - - - - - - - - - - - - - - - - - - - - - - - - - - b - - #
- - - - - - - - - - - - - - - - - - - - - - - - - - - - - - b b #
```

Impressed Strip Bowl, Flat Rim Bowl, Unpainted High Neck Jar, Proto Bevel Rim Bowl, Chaff Tempered Ring Base, Beaded Rim Bowl, Flared Expanded Rim Jar, Horizontal Reserve Slip, Ledge Rim Bottle, Cross Hatch Band, Chaff Temp. Rnd. Rim Bowl, Sinuous Sided Cup, Full Twisted Handle, Droop Spout, Rim Lug, Impressed Strip Jar, Band Bottle, Groove Shoulder, Hatched Strip, Ledge Rim Jar, Late Straight Spout, Groove and Oblique, Round Rim Bowl, Ledge Rim Bowl, Bevel Rim Bowl Variant, Straight Flat Rim Jar, Straight Round Rim Jar, Open Spout, Cross Hatch Triangle, Nose Lug, Round Rim Bottle, Strap Handle, Round Rim Jar, Rocker Stamp, Chaff Tempered Tray, Diagonal Reserve Slip, Low Expanded Band Rim Jar

handles, band rim bottles, and cross hatch triangles. When reliable proportional data are not available as is the case in most survey situations, Middle Uruk is identified by the absence of diagnostic Early and Late types rather than by the presence of diagnostic Middle types. Difficulties of this sort can be expected when a developmental continuum is divided for purposes of analysis into discrete segments. Table 7 presents a correlation between the provisional stratigraphy of the Acropole Sondage suggested by Le Brun (1971), and the interpretation presented here.

TABLE 7
SUSA, ACROPOLE SONDAGE: INTERPRETATION OF STRATIGRAPHY

Le Brun (1972:211)	Level	Johnson
Period III	16	Jemdet Nasr
	17	Late Uruk
	18	Late Uruk
	19	Middle Uruk (?)
Period II	20	Middle Uruk (?)
	21	Middle Uruk
(Early Phase)	22	Early Uruk
	23	Early Uruk
(Late Phase)	24	Transitional or Terminal Susa A
Period I (Middle Phase)	25	Susa A
	26	Susa A
(Early Phase)	27	Susa A, Early (?)
	Virgin Soil	

The Uruk Ceramic Sequence at Tepe Farukhabad

Tepe Farukhabad is situated on the Deh Luran plain on the Memeh river, 12 km south of the village of Deh Luran in Khuzistan. The site was tested during March and April of 1968 by Henry T. Wright of The University of Michigan Museum of Anthropology. Three excavations were made; Excavation B contained the most complete Uruk sequence and will be discussed here (Wright, 1969b:172).

Of the 47 layers defined in Excavation B, levels 30 to 35 were originally designated as Uruk (Wright, 1969b:173). Subsequent analysis of the material has led to a redefinition of the Uruk stratigraphy as follows: Levels 29 Upper to 31, Late Uruk; Levels 32 to 34, Middle Uruk; and Levels 35 to 36, Early Uruk (Wright, 1970: personal communication). The architectural sequence consists primarily of a series of small structures, probably private housing, dump, and courtyard areas. This sequence changes only in Level 30 where the first of a series of massive riemchen walls was found (Wright, 1969b:173), indicating the presence of a major building.

The ceramic type counts for Levels 29 Upper to 36, made available by Wright, are presented in Table 8. The Early Uruk levels contain primarily Sargarab ware, a ware containing a large proportion of straw temper. This ware is largely restricted to the Deh Luran plain, and the Zagros highlands. Middle Uruk is defined by the appearance of an increased number of sandy Uruk ware types. These include fine bases, sinuous sided cups, and low expanded band rims. Late Uruk is defined by the appearance of twisted handles, band rim bottles, and numbers of droop spouts. Bevel rim bowls are present throughout the sequence, although they show a marked increase in the first Middle Uruk level (34).

A seriation of the type counts in Table 8 is presented in Table 9. Inspection of the table reveals a clear definition of the Early Uruk Sargarab ware assemblage. As was the case in the analysis of the material from Susa, the division between Middle and Late Uruk is less obvious. Twisted handles and band rim bottles are defined as unambiguous Late Uruk types. Other types, while occurring at the late end of the seriation, first appear during the Middle Uruk period.

The Uruk Ceramic Sequence at Tall-i-Ghazir

Tall-i-Ghazir is located on the Ram Hormuz plain, Khuzistan. Excavations were carried out here in 1948 and 1949 by Donald and Garnet McCown of the Oriental Institute of the University of Chicago. The most complete Uruk sequence from the site occurred in the "Step Trench" excavated in 1949 and are briefly described by Caldwell (1968:348-355).

TABLE 8

TYPE COUNTS OF URUK CERAMICS FROM EXCAVATION B, TEPE FARUKHABAD

Type	29U	29L	30	31	32	33U	33L	34	35	36
Ledge Rim Bowl	2	2	1	1			1			1
Groove and Oblique		2		2			1			
Out-turned Expanded Rim Jar	1	1	3	1		1				
Droop Spout	4	3	1	5	1					
Round Rim Bowl	9	12	23	9	6	2	3		1	1
Band Rim Bottle	2	4	6	5						
Full Twisted Handle	1		1	1						
Low Expanded Band Rim Jar	3	2	10	6	4	1	1	1		
Conical Cup	13	5	14	21	10	7	3	4		
Beveled Lip Bowl	2	2	3	6	3					
Fine Base	1	3	6	8	6	4	3	2		
Small Expanded Jar	2	2	3	8	3	3		2	2	1
Cross Hatch Band	2		3	5	4	2	3			
Flared Expanded Rim Jar			2	7	8	4		4		1
Strap Handle	2	1	2	5	7			2	1	1
Nose Lug	1	1	1	3	4	3	1		2	
Ledge Rim Jar	2	1	2	1	8	2	1			
S-Coarse Bowl					2	3	1	4	5	
Flared Found Rim Jar			1	1	2	4	2		1	1
Incurved Beaded Rim Bowl		1		1	2	4	2	2		
S-Thick Ware	2		1	3	4	3	10	8	7	4
S-Flared Round Rim Jar				1	5	1	2	2		
S-Incurved Beaded Rim Bowl		2	3	5	2	11	5	4	8	
S-Flared Rim Jar				2	1	7	1	3	8	
S-Fine Jar				4	3	5	5	2	4	
S-Incurved Rim Bowl			2		2		1	3		
S-Straight Spout			1		1	1		2		
S-Nose Lug				1	1	1		1		
S-Strap Handle			1		2	1			2	
S-Round Rim Jar		3	3	2	2	6				
S-Beveled Lip Bowl	2			1		3				

S = Sargarab Ware

48 LOCAL EXCHANGE AND EARLY STATE DEVELOPMENT

TABLE 9
SERIATION OF URUK CERAMIC TYPES: TEPE FARUKHABAD, EXCAVATION B

```
#
B  #
-  d  #
B  B  B  #
C  C  B  B  #
-  C  A  C  A  #                           Early Uruk
-  -  d  B  -  d  #
-  d  -  d  -  d  d  #
-  -  d  C  C  B  C  B  #
-  -  -  -  d  B  d  d  A  #
-  -  -  -  -  -  d  C  C  B  #
-  -  -  -  -  -  -  -  -  d  d  #
-  -  -  -  -  -  -  -  -  -  -  -  #
-  -  -  -  -  -  -  -  -  -  -  -  -  #
-  -  -  -  -  -  -  -  -  -  -  -  -  d  #
-  -  -  -  -  -  -  -  -  -  -  -  -  d  B  #
-  -  -  -  -  -  -  -  -  -  -  -  -  d  d  -  #         Middle Uruk
-  -  -  -  -  -  -  -  -  -  -  -  -  B  d  B  #
-  -  -  -  -  -  -  -  -  -  -  -  -  -  d  -  -  #
-  -  -  -  -  -  -  -  -  -  -  -  -  -  -  d  -  #
-  -  -  -  -  -  -  -  -  -  -  -  -  -  d  B  d  #
-  -  -  -  -  -  -  -  -  -  -  -  -  -  d  -  d  B  C  #
-  -  -  -  -  -  -  -  -  -  -  -  -  -  -  C  B  C  A  #
-  -  -  -  -  -  -  -  -  -  -  -  -  -  d  -  d  d  C  #
-  -  -  -  -  -  -  -  -  -  -  -  -  -  -  -  -  d  B  C  #
-  -  -  -  -  -  -  -  -  -  -  -  -  -  -  -  -  d  d  B  D  #
-  -  -  -  -  -  -  -  -  -  -  -  -  -  -  -  -  -  B  d  B  #         Late Uruk
-  -  -  -  -  -  -  -  -  -  -  -  -  -  -  -  d  -  B  C  -  d  d  -  #
-  -  -  -  -  -  -  -  -  -  -  -  -  -  -  -  -  -  B  d  B  A  -  #
-  -  -  -  -  -  -  -  -  -  -  -  -  -  -  -  -  -  d  d  -  d  -  -  #
-  -  -  -  -  -  -  -  -  -  -  -  -  -  -  -  -  -  -  -  -  d  -  -  #
```

Symbol	r	p
#	1.00	.01
A	.90–.99	.01
B	.80–.89	.01
C	.76–.79	.01
d	.63–.75	.05
–	other	

r = Linear Product-Moment Correlation

p = Probability

Columns (left to right): S-Beveled Lip Bowl, S-Round Rim Jar, S-Strap Handle, S-Straight Spout, S-Incurved Rim Bowl, S-Flared Rim Jar, S-Nose Lug, S-Fine Jar, S-Incurved Beaded Rim Bowl, S-Flared Round Rim Jar, S-Thick Ware, Incurved Beaded Rim Bowl, S-Coarse Bowl, Ledge Rim Jar, Flared Round Rim Jar, Nose Lug, Strap Handle, Flared Expanded Rim Jar, Cross Hatch Band, Small Expanded Rim Jar, Fine Base, Beveled Lip Bowl, Conical Cup, Low Expanded Band Rim Jar, Full Twisted Handle, Band Rim Bottle, Round Rim Bowl, Droop Spout, Out-turned Expanded Rim Jar, Groove and Oblique, Ledge Rim Bowl

TABLE 10
THE URUK CERAMIC SEQUENCE AT TALL-I-GHAZIR
(STEP TRENCH)

Levels	Proto Bevel Rim Bowl	Beaded Rim Bowl (Club Rims)	Straight Spout	Nose Lug	Cross Hatch Band	Bevel Rim Bowl	Reserve Slip	Punctate	Strap Handle	Pear Shaped Jar	Droop Spout	"Teapot"
36-38			?	?	351	?	?	?		351	351	351
28-35			?	?	350	350	350	352	351			
16-27	350	350	350	350	350	350	350	350				
11-15	350	350	350	350	350							
7-10	(marked decrease in proportion of painted wares—349)											

Note: Numbers in the body of the table indicate the presence of a given ceramic type. They are also page references to Caldwell (1968).

Caldwell's data on Uruk ceramic stratigraphy are summarized in Table 10. He interprets the stratigraphy as follows: Levels 7-10 Transitional; Levels 11-27, Early Uruk; Levels 28-38, Late Uruk (1968:349ff). On the basis of the data presented, Early Uruk would be defined by the presence of proto bevel rim bowls, beaded rim bowls, and straight spouts. Middle Uruk at Ghazir would be defined by the presence of strap handles, pear shaped jars, droop spouts, and Warka "teapots."

Both periods share ceramic types, indicating a continual development. The presence of a number of unshared types, however, would seem to justify Caldwell's division of the sequence.

The Uruk Ceramic Sequence at Uruk-Warka

Although Warka is the type site for the Uruk period, an apparently complete Uruk sequence has been obtained only from the Deep Sounding of 1931-32 reported by Nöldeke, et al. (1932). Table 11 presents the Uruk

TABLE 11
THE URUK CERAMIC SEQUENCE AT URUK-WARKA (DEEP SOUNDING)

Level	Ceramic Wall Cone	Cross Hatch Triangle	Punctate	Band Rim Bottle	Conical Spout	Droop Spout	Twisted Handle	Fingernail Impressed	Shoulder Groove	False Spout	Cut Spout	Surface Combed	Chaff Tempered Tray	Cross Hatch Band	Strap Handle	Bevel Rim Bowl	Nose Lug	Pointed Base Bottle	Impressed Strip Bowl	Straight Spout
IV	?	****	45	45	43	43	?	?	45	?	?	?	43	45	?	41	43			
V	?	?	?	44	43	43	?	44	?	?	?	40	?	44	?	41	43			
VI	44	45	39	44	***	?	?	40	43	42	44	40	42	39	39	41	42			
VII			43	43	**	*	?	?	43	43	43	39	42	39	39	41	39			
VIII							?	39	?	42	42	39	42	?	39	41	?			
IX							39		42	42	42	42	?	42	?	41	?	42		
X												38	42	?	?	41	?	42		
XI												38	42	?	?	41	?	42		
XII														42	38	?	?		41	
XIII																41	38		41	41
XIV																				41

(marked decrease in Ubaid painted wares—first considerable amounts of red and gray wares—37)

Note: Numbers in the body of the table indicate the presence of a given ceramic type. They are also page references to Nöldecke, et al. (1932).

Additional references:
* Pl. 18: Figure Du'
** Pl. 18: Figure Dg
*** Pl. 19: Figure Bc'
**** Pl. 20: Figure Al'

ceramic types which can be consistently identified from von Haller's descriptions rather than from his illustrations alone. Early Uruk seems to be represented only by Level XIII which is characterized by long spouted jars. Impressed strip bowls, early pointed base bottles, and nose lugs also occur.

Bevel rim bowls are first mentioned in Level XII. It seems that they first appear in quantity in this level, although they may have been present earlier. Their appearance in quantity suggests the beginning of the Middle Uruk period. Early long spouted bottles are present in only one example in this level, further suggesting a significant change from Level XIII. Strap handles and cross hatch bands also appear in Level XII.

Late Uruk appears to begin in Level VII with the introduction of a number of new ceramic types. These include droop spouts, conical spouts, and band rim bottles. The distribution of twisted handled cups is unclear. They are first mentioned in Level VIII and probably occur through Level IV. The first substantial Uruk architecture appears in Level VI (Nissen, 1972:794) and continues through an elaborate building series in Level IV (Lenzen:1968). It is generally recognized that Uruk ends with Level IV, and that Jemdet Nasr begins in Level III (Lenzen, 1968:13). Middle Uruk would then appear to be represented by Levels XII through VII.

A large number of stratigraphic systems have been proposed for the Deep Sounding, of which that suggested here is only the latest. Several of these systems are presented in order of their appearance in Table 12. Inspection of the table reveals that there has been general agreement on at least one division of the sequence somewhere around Level VIII. The system proposed here is in closest agreement with that presented by Adams and Nissen (1972), with the exception of the addition of Transitional and Early Uruk phases in Levels XIV and XIII respectively. It is important to note that Adams and Nissen (1972:100) do not feel that there are grounds for identification of a Middle Uruk Phase at Warka based on the material available. The system proposed above, however, seems to be most consistent with the other stratified Uruk sequences discussed here.

The Uruk Ceramic Sequence at Nippur

Hanson (1965) presents the available published data on the Uruk ceramic sequence from the Deep Sounding in the Inanna Precinct of Nippur. These data are rearranged in tabular form in Table 13. Hanson divides his sequence into Middle Uruk (Levels XX-XVII) and Late Uruk (Levels XVI-XV) phases. Inspection of the data reveals, however, that such apparently diagnostic Late Uruk types as droop spouts, twisted handles, bottles and cross hatch triangles appear as early as Inanna XVII. On the basis of ceramic consideration alone, it would seem reasonable to assign Inanna Levels XX-XVIII to Middle

TABLE 12
PROPOSED CHRONOLOGICAL DIVISIONS OF THE WARKA DEEP SOUNDING

Level	Lloyd 1948	Perkins 1949	Eliot 1950	LeBreton 1957	Nagel 1963	Hanson 1965	Porada 1965	Mallowan 1965	Steve & Gasche 1971	Adams & Nissen 1972	Johnson
IV											
V	Late Uruk 50	Proto-literate 97	Late Uruk 6	Late Warkan 95	Early Sumerian 17	Late Uruk 204	Late & Middle Uruk 153-154	Late Uruk 12	Uruk Récent 205	Late Uruk 100	Late Uruk
VI											
VII			Middle Uruk ? 6	?	Late Warka 16	Middle Uruk 201		?		?	
VIII	Early Uruk 50	Warka 97	Early Uruk 6		Early Warka 11		Early Uruk 153	Early Uruk 12	Uruk Ancien 205	Early Uruk 100	Middle Uruk
IX											
X											
XI											
XII											Early Uruk
XIII											
XIV											Transitional

Note: Numbers in the body of the table are page references to the sources cited. Dashed lines indicate uncertainty of stratigraphic division.

TABLE 13
THE URUK CERAMIC SEQUENCE AT NIPPUR (DEEP SOUNDING)

Levels	Cross Hatch Triangle	Bottle	Twisted Handle	Droop Spout	Cross Hatch Band	Nose Lug	Reserve Slip	Bevel Rim Bowl	Strap Handle	Combed Surface	Sinuous Sided Cup	Red Ware	Gray Ware	Chaff Tempered Tray	Punctate	Hatched Strip	Rocker Stamp
XV	?	202	202	206	?	205	202	202	202	202							
XVI	205	202	202	205	205	205	202	202	202	202	202	202		202			
XVII		202	202	204	?	204	202	202	202	202	202	202	202	202			
XVIII					203	203	202	202	202	202	202	202	202	202	203	204	203
XIX						203	202	202	202	202	202	202	202	202	203	?	201
XX										202	202	202	202	202	203	203	202

Note: Numbers in the body of the table indicate the presence of a given ceramic type. They are also page references to Hanson (1965).

54 LOCAL EXCHANGE AND EARLY STATE DEVELOPMENT

Uruk and Levels XVII-XV to Late Uruk. There may, of course, be compelling architectural evidence to the contrary.

Comparison of the Seriation of Uruk Ceramic Types from 1970-71 Survey Surface Collections with the Excavated Sequences

Early Uruk
1. Beaded Rim Bowls

Beaded rim bowls which are early in the surface collections (Table 3) are also early at Susa (Table 6), Tepe Farukhabad (Table 9), and Tall-i-Ghazir (Table 10). The bowls at Farukhabad occur on straw tempered, Sargareb ware which is typical of Early Uruk ceramics in Deh Luran. Beaded rim bowls are not reported from Warka or Nippur.

2. Impressed Strip Bowls

Impressed strip bowls are early in the surface collections as well as at Susa, Tepe Farukhabad, and Warka (Table 11). The examples at Farukhabad occur on a Sargarab paste. Impressed strip bowls are not reported from Tall-i-Ghazir or Nippur.

3. Heavy Lugs

Heavy jar lugs are apparently early in the survey collections. They are not, however, reported from any of the excavated sequences considered here.

4. Neckless Ledge Rim Jars

Neckless ledge rim jars are early in the surface collections. This rim type is not reported from any of the stratified sequences considered here.

5. Proto Bevel Rim Bowls

Proto bevel rim bowls are early in the surface collections as well as at Susa and Tall-i-Ghazir. They are not reported from Tepe Farukhabad, Warka, or Nippur.

6. Round Rim Bowls

Round rim bowls as a general type have a very wide chronological distribution. They are generally early in the surface collection, although they show a close association with ledge rim bottles, a probable late type. They are also reported from Susa in a late context and from Tepe Farukhabad, primarily in a late context. The type is not reported from Tall-i-Ghazir, Warka, or Nippur.

7. Ledge Rim Bowls

While ledge rim bowls seriate early in the surface collections, they are late at Susa and generally late at Tepe Farukhabad. It would appear that the type is generally late, and appears to be early in the surface collections through sampling error. This type is not reported from Tall-i-Ghazir, Warka, or Nippur.

8. Flared Expanded Rim Jars

Flared expanded rim jars are early in the surface collections and at Susa.

This type occurs primarily in a Middle Uruk context at Tepe Farukhabad, but is also present in early levels. The type is not reported from Tall-i-Ghazir, Warka, or Nippur. It appears that flared expanded rim jars are primarily characteristic of early Uruk although they continue into Middle Uruk.

9. Flat Rim Bowls

Flat rim bowls are early in the surface collection and are also early at Susa. They are not reported from Tepe Farukhabad, Warka or Nippur.

10. Flared Round Rim Jars

Flared round rim jars are early in the surface collections. At Tepe Farukhabad they are early on a Sargarab paste and primarily middle on an Uruk paste. The type would appear to be primarily early. Flared round rim jars are not reported from Susa, Tall-i-Ghazir, Warka, or Nippur.

11. Nose Lugs

While nose lugs seriate early in the surface collections they have a wide chronological distribution. A larger sample of these lugs will be required to develop a chronologically sensitive typology.

12. Straight Spouts

Straight spouts are early in the surface collections as well as at Susa, Tepe Farukhabad, Tall-i-Ghazir, and Warka. They are not reported from Nippur. The spouts of this type at Farukhabad occur on a Sargarab paste. The type may be considered highly diagnostic for Early Uruk.

13. Grooved Round Rim Jars

Grooved round rim jars are known only from the survey collections, where they are early.

14. Rocker Stamping

Rocker stamping is a rare type in the survey collections. It appears early in the seriation. At Susa the type is very late, while at Nippur (Table 13) it is Middle Uruk. The type is not reported from Tepe Farukhabad, Tall-i-Ghazir, or Warka. Rocker stamping thus appears to have a wide chronological distribution and cannot be used as a diagnostic type for any particular period.

15. Ledge Expanded Jar Rims

Ledge expanded jar rims were only identified in the surface collections, where they are a transitional type between Early and Middle Uruk.

16. Punctate

Punctate shoulder decoration is a transitional type in the surface collections between Early Uruk and Middle Uruk. It is also identified as an Early and Middle Uruk type at Tall-i-Ghazir. The type is middle and late at Warka and Nippur. Punctate decoration has a wide chronological distribution and cannot be assigned to any particular period.

Middle Uruk

17. Hatched Strips

Hatched strip shoulder decoration appears in the Middle Uruk assemblage in the seriation of the surface collections. The type occurs in a late context at Susa and a middle context at Nippur. The type appears to be primarily Middle Uruk although it continues into Late Uruk.

18. Cross Hatch Bands

Cross hatch band jar shoulders appear as a Middle Uruk type in the seriation of the ceramic types in the surface collections. At Susa they appear in a late context, while at Tepe Farukhabad, Warka, and Nippur they occur in both middle and late contexts. At Tall-i-Ghazir the type is early and middle. This distribution suggests that incised cross hatch bands are characteristic of Middle Uruk although they occur in other contexts. It will be shown below that it is possible to make temporal distinctions within the type.

19. Out-turned Expanded Rim Jars

Out-turned expanded rim jars are assigned to the Middle Uruk assemblage in the surface collections; at Tepe Farukhabad they occur in Middle Uruk but are primarily found in Late Uruk contexts. The type has not been identified at Susa, Tall-i-Ghazir, Warka, or Nippur. The type would appear to be transitional between Middle to Late Uruk.

20. Low Expanded Band Rims

Low expanded band rim jars also appear in the Middle Uruk assemblage in the survey collections, while appearing in a late context at Susa. At Tepe Farukhabad the type is primarily late but it also occurs in Middle Uruk levels. The type then seems to have appeared in Middle Uruk but to have been most popular in Late Uruk. These rims have not been identified at Tall-i-Ghazir, Warka, or Nippur.

21. Heavy Round Rim Jars

Heavy round rim jars are defined only from the survey collections where they are primarily a Middle Uruk type. They do, however, show some association with full twist handles, a late type discussed below, and probably continue into Late Uruk.

22. Strap Handles

Strap handles are defined as a Middle Uruk type in the survey collections, although they are known to occur in Early and Late Uruk contexts. At Susa they are concentrated in Late Uruk levels, but will doubtless be found in Middle Uruk levels as well. At Tepe Farukhabad, Tall-i-Ghazir, and Warka strap handles are primarily found in Middle Uruk levels. At Nippur they occur in both Middle and Late contexts. Strap handles can then be defined as primarily a Middle Uruk type which continues into Late Uruk.

23. Impressed Strip Jar Shoulders

Impressed strip jar shoulder decoration is defined as a transitional middle-late type in the surface collections. At Susa they occur in late levels. The type is not included in the material from the other sites considered here.

Impressed strip jar shoulders are probably a middle-late type not as yet found in Middle Uruk deposits at Susa due to the small amount of Middle Uruk material excavated to date.

24. Expanded Ledge Rim Bowls

Expanded ledge rim bowls are also defined as transitional middle-late type in the surface collection. They have not been identified in the material from the other sites considered here.

25. Sinuous Sided Cups

Sinuous sided cups appear to be another transitional middle-late type as defined in the surface collections, at Susa, Tepe Farukhabad, and Nippur. The type is not reported from Warka or Tall-i-Ghazir.

Late Uruk

26. Conical Spouts

Conical spouts are defined only from the surface collections where they appear to be primarily late.

27. Ledge Rim Bottles

Ledge rim bottles are defined as a late type in the seriation of ceramic types from the surface collections. They are also a late type at Susa. They are rare at Farukhabad and have not been identified at Tall-i-Ghazir, Warka, or Nippur.

28. Beveled Lip Bowls

Beveled lip bowls are late in the surface collections as well as at Tepe Farukhabad. They have not been identified at Tall-i-Ghazir, Susa, Warka, or Nippur.

29. Full Twisted Handles

Full twisted handles are late in the surface collections as well as at Susa, Tepe Farukhabad, Warka, and Nippur. They are not reported from Tall-i-Ghazir. This is a diagnostic Late Uruk type.

30. Band Rim Bottles

Band rim bottles are a late type in the surface collections. The type is also late at Susa, Tepe Farukhabad, Warka, and Nippur. Band rim bottles are not reported from Tall-i-Ghazir. The type is diagnostic Late Uruk.

31. Groove and Oblique

Incised groove and oblique jar shoulder decoration is a late type in the surface collections, at Susa, and at Tepe Farukhabad.

32. Flat Twisted Handles

Flat twisted handles are defined only from the survey collections, where they are a Late Uruk type.

33. Droop Spouts

Droop spouts are late in the surface collections and are also a late type at Susa, Tepe Farukhabad, Warka, and Nippur. They are not reported from

Tall-i-Ghazir. Droop spouts appear to be a primarily Late Uruk type which first appears in late Middle Uruk.

34. Cross Hatch Triangles

Incised cross hatch triangle jar shoulders are a late type in the surface collections as well as at Susa, Warka, and Nippur. They are extremely rare at Tepe Farukhabad, but occur in Late Uruk contexts (Wright, 1970; personal communication). Cross hatch triangles are not reported from Tall-i-Ghazir. The type would appear to be diagnostic Late Uruk.

35. Rim Lugs

Rim lugs are apparently late in the surface collections as well as at Susa.

36. Bevel Rim Bowls

Bevel rim bowls apparently occur at all Middle and Late Uruk sites.

Chronological Position of Ceramic Types Not Included in the Seriation

37. High Expanded Band Rim Jars

High expanded band rim jars are an ill-defined type at present. They seem, however, to be primarily a transitional early-middle type.

38. Reserve Slip

Reserve slip has a wide chronological distribution. The type occurs in Early and Middle Uruk contexts at Tall-i-Ghazir, Middle and Late Uruk contexts at Nippur, and in Late Uruk contexts at Susa. Data from Susa and the survey suggest that horizontal reserve slip is generally earlier than diagonal reserve slip. The available samples are too small, however, to confirm this suggestion.

39. Grooved Shoulders

Grooved jar shoulders occur late in the sequence at Susa, and apparently in Middle and Late Uruk contexts at Warka. The type is probably primarily Middle Uruk, although it occurs with groove and oblique jar shoulder decoration in Late Uruk.

40. Combed Surface

Surface combing is found in both Middle and Late Uruk contexts at Warka and Nippur. It probably has a similar chronological distribution in the surface collections.

41. Oblique Bands

Incised oblique band jar shoulder decoration has been found in Late Uruk levels at Susa.

42. Chaff Tempered Trays

Crude chaff tempered trays are found in Middle and Late Uruk levels of Warka and Nippur. They occur in late levels at Susa. It seems probable that the type appears in Middle Uruk and continues through Late Uruk. It may, however, be more characteristic of Middle Uruk.

Summary

The evidence presented above indicates that the seriation of ceramic types recovered on the survey corresponds remarkably well to the reported stratified sequences discussed here. This is especially the case for Early and Late Uruk, Middle Uruk being defined more on the basis of proportional changes in type counts than on the presence of diagnostic Middle Uruk types. As discussed above, identification of Middle Uruk in surface collections is often done on the basis of the absence of diagnostic Early and Late Uruk types.

The primary purpose of this discussion has been to evaluate the chronological significance of the Uruk ceramics in the survey collections. It also permits, however, general correlation of the individual stratigraphic sequences discussed. Table 14 presents what appear to be the most reasonable correlations, given the data available. The primary advantage of this exercise is that it presents a general picture of Uruk ceramic development in Khuzistan and southern Sumer. This is not to imply that Uruk ceramic assemblages are the same everywhere. There are significant local differences. Given the present low level of our knowledge of Uruk in Greater Mesopotamia, however, it is the similarities rather than the local differences which are of greater practical interest. The fact that such detailed correlations can be made over such a broad area would appear to speak to the question of the development of close and wide ranging cultural connections. We will return to this point below.

Definition of the Terminal Susa A Period

The preceding discussion dealt with the division of the Uruk period into Early, Middle, and Late Uruk. One additional period will be considered in this study. Terminal Susa A, immediately prior to Early Uruk on the Susiana plain, is defined primarily on the basis of heavy bowls with applied thumb impressed strip decoration (see Pl. II, Fig. b). The type, broadly defined, has a wide chronological range, from Terminal Susa A through at least Elamite on the Susiana plain. Sherd temper and paste may, however, be used to differentiate the bowls of each period. Terminal Susa A bowls have a fine mineral temper. Uruk bowls have a coarser, typically Uruk, mineral temper. Elamite bowls have a considerable amount of vegetal material added to their temper.

Terminal Susa A impressed strip bowls are further distinguished from their Early Uruk counterparts by attributes of their rim and impression shapes. (A description and list of Impressed Strip Bowl measurements is presented in Appendix III.) Field observation of this material suggested the following stylistic developments of the type from Terminal Susa A to Early Uruk:

TABLE 14
URUK STRATIGRAPHIC CORRELATIONS

			Susa Acropole	Farukhabad Excavation B	Tall-i-Ghazir Step Trench	Warka Eanna	Nippur Inanna
Periods Defined from the Survey Collections		Late Uruk	17	29U		IV	XV
			18	31		VII	XVII
	Middle Uruk		19	32	38	VIII	XVIII
			21	34	28	XII	XX
			22	35	27		
	Early Uruk					XIII	
			23	36(7?)	11		
					10		
	Transitional		24			XIV	
					7		

1. Increase in rim thickness relative to side thickness
2. Increase in rim angle
3. Development of increasingly oval from essentially round impressions
4. Increase in impression angle
5. Change from a straight walled or slightly out-curved form to a basically in-curved form.

These observations are confirmed by statistical analysis of the material.

The available sample of impressed strip bowls of Uruk and probable Terminal Susa A age was stratified on the basis of sherd fabric differences described above. Student's t tests were run to evaluate significance of difference in variable means between the two proposed types. The results of these tests are presented in Table 15. Figure 6 presents a scatter plot of rim

TABLE 15
IMPRESSED STRIP BOWLS: STUDENT'S t TESTS

	Mean	t	df	p	at	adf	p	Variable
Fine	88.552	-2.532	56	0.014	-2.681	47.594	0.010	rim angle (degrees)
Coarse	98.552							
Fine	87.394	-4.647	56	0.000	-4.942	48.137	0.000	interior side angle (degrees)
Coarse	103.300							
Fine	13.868	-3.362	56	0.001	-3.502	45.423	0.001	impression angle (degrees)
Coarse	37.750							
Fine	1.373	-2.018	56	0.000	-6.200	31.485	0.000	rim shape index
Coarse	2.102							
Fine	1.211		56	0.048	-1.752	27.730	0.091	impression shape index
Coarse	1.339							

Key:
t = student's t statistic (assumes equal variances)
df = degrees of freedom
p = probability associated with the test statistic
at = approximate student's t statistic (does not assume equal variances)
adf = approximate degrees of freedom

Note: These abbreviations will be used throughout the remainder of this study.

and impression shape indices for fine temper versus coarse temper bowls. Though the two groups show some interdigitation on the plot, they are distinct, as demonstrated above. Figure 7 illustrates these proposed stylistic developments.

The remaining content of the Terminal Susa A assemblage is poorly defined. It includes grooved flat rim bowls, unpainted high neck jars, ring bases, and an apparently small amount of painted material. Thus far only one painted type has been associated with the assemblage. This is a small jar having rudimentary nose lugs and a band of horizontal wavy lines set between a pair of straight lines (see Pl. IX, Fig. d). Excavation of a small Terminal Susa A site would do much to improve our knowledge of the ceramic assemblage of this period.

Absolute Chronology

In a sense, our present control of the relative chronology is superior to our control of the absolute chronology. There are very few carbon dates available for the Uruk period as a whole. This is generally true for the other periods of the Susiana sequence. Given the uncertain status of the MASCA correction curve and the limited number of determinations available, the time is not yet appropriate to undertake an extended discussion of the absolute chronology. A large series of new determinations should soon be available

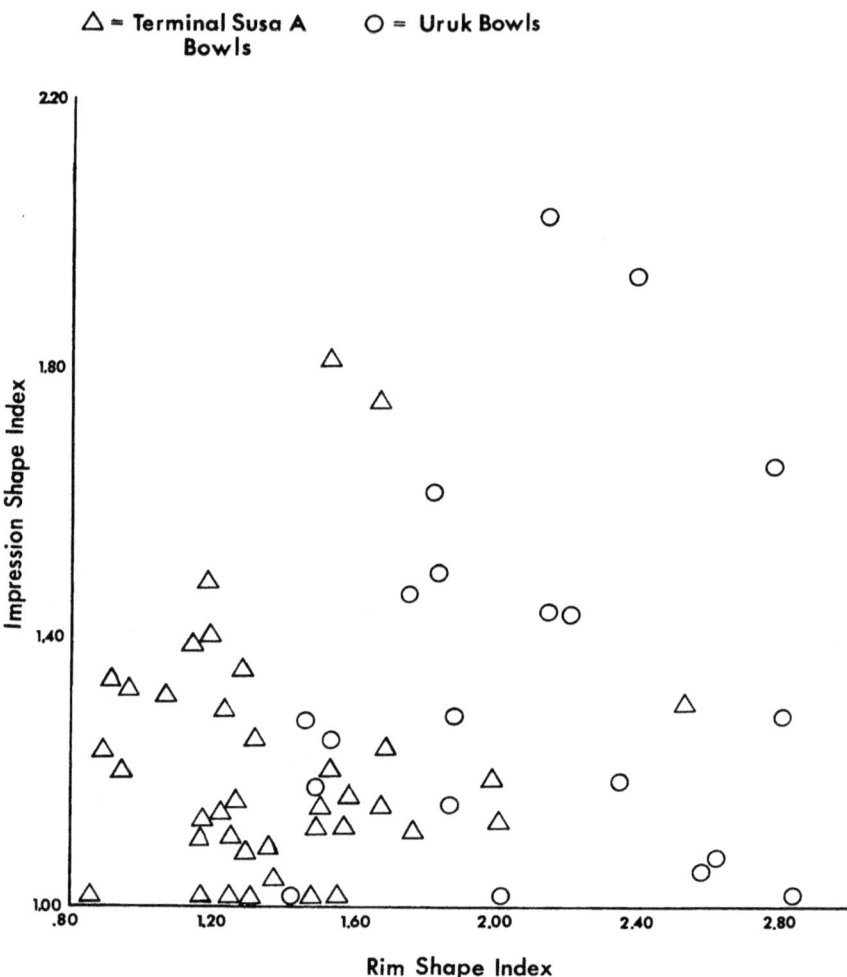

Fig. 6. Impressed Strip Bowls – Scatter Plot

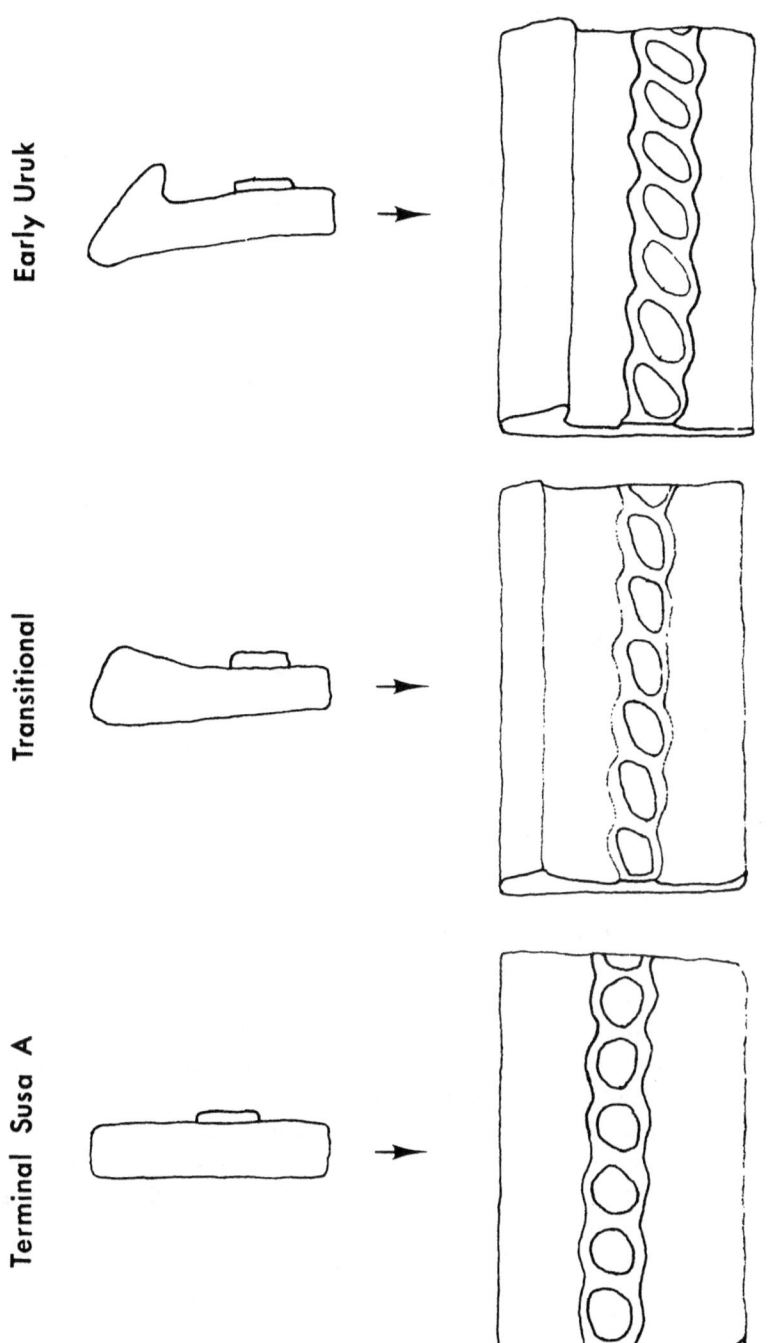

Fig. 7. Proposed Stylistic Development of Impressed Strip Bowls.

64 LOCAL EXCHANGE AND EARLY STATE DEVELOPMENT

from Susa, Chogha Mish (KS-1), Tepe Sharafabad (KS-36), and Tepe Jaffarabad (KS-20).

Until a larger series of determinations is available and the MASCA correction has been fully evaluated, the absolute chronology remains very uncertain. Table 16 presents our current working guesses of the absolute dates involved. The lower end of the series is set almost 1000 years earlier than would be indicated by use of a Libby half-life calculation. Hole, Flannery, and Neeley, using uncorrected dates (their publication of the dates preceded publication of the latest correction curve), place the Deh Luran equivalent of Susiana d at about 4000 B.C. (Hole, Flannery, and Neeley, 1969:9). The absolute chronology presented in Table 16 should thus be considered as a hypothesis which requires future testing.

AREAL SIZE AND POPULATION ESTIMATES FOR TERMINAL SUSA A AND URUK SETTLEMENTS

Having defined the ceramic assemblages of Terminal Susa A through Late Uruk, settlements included in the 1970-71 survey and occupied during one or more of these periods can be identified. Problems of population and areal size estimation will be discussed; areal size estimates at each relevant period of occupation will be presented for each site, along with basic settlement pattern maps for the survey area during the Terminal Susa A through Late Uruk periods.

Population Estimation

Population estimation has been and remains a difficult problem in Near Eastern archaeology. This is particularly unfortunate because population plays such a large role in many theories of state origins. The problems involved in population can be divided into two general categories: estimation of individual settlement population and estimation of regional population.

Population estimation for individual settlements includes two critical components: estimation of population density in a settlement and estimation of the areal size of a settlement. The former ideally requires at least a sample of residential architectural plans from a sample of sites at each level of a settlement size hierarchy. It is unlikely that population density in villages was the same as in major centers. Similarly, excavation samples should be available for non-residential land use within settlements: public buildings, workshops or work areas and so on. Data of this sort are virtually nonexistent for the Uruk period in Khuzistan. Village architectural plans were expected from Tepe Sharafabad (KS-36) excavated during the 1970-71 project, but the Uruk

TABLE 16
ABSOLUTE CHRONOLOGY FOR THE SUSIANA PLAIN

Years B.C.	Periods
2800	
2900	Early Dynastic I
3000	
3100	Jemdet Nasr
3200	
3300	Late Uruk
3400	Middle Uruk
3500	
3600	Early Uruk
3700	
3800	
3900	Terminal Susa A
4000	
4100	
4200	
4300	Susa A
4400	
4500	
4600	Susiana d
4700	
4800	

architecture had been largely destroyed by erosion and Elamite terracing. An important body of residential plans from a major center will become available with the publication of the preliminary report on Chogha Mish (KS-1) (H. Kantor, 1972; personal communication). This difficulty is usually overcome by assuming that residential density for archaeologically known settlements in Khuzistan was about the same as it is for traditional settlements in the area today.

Gremliza (1962) provides demographic data on 53 traditional villages in the survey area. A linear correlation analysis reveals the following relationships between population size and four potentially archaeologically observable variables.

Correlation of village population with:
1. Area of village in hectares $r=0.85$
2. Area occupied by houses $r=0.86$
3. Number of houses in village $r=0.98$
4. Number of rooms in village $r=0.98$

All coefficients are statistically significant above the .01 level.
The mean values for these four variables are:
1. 202 persons per hectare of village area
2. 748 persons per hectare of house area
3. 5 persons per house
4. 3.85 persons per room

It has been customary to use the figure of 200 persons per hectare for population estimates of archaeological sites in the area. There are obvious problems with this figure. First, as discussed above, there is really no archaeological evidence to support this estimate. Second, the settlement sample upon which the estimate is based is biased in favor of small settlements. The relationship between settlement size and population size need not be linear.

The present study contributes little to the solution of this problem except to provide improved areal estimates for Terminal Susa A and Uruk sites. Since population estimates in this study will be based on settlement area, the problems of regional population estimation have already been discussed in the description of methodology.

I will stress the point here and reiterate it later that population figures suggested in this study must be taken as order of magnitude estimates only. The proportional relationships between estimates are probably far more reliable than the absolute values of the estimates themselves.

Estimates of Terminal Susa A and Uruk Settlement Areal Sizes

Estimates of Terminal Susa A, Early, Middle, and Late Uruk settlement areal sizes are presented in the following pages. Brief discussions of the relevant occupations of Susa and Chogha Mish (KS-1), the two largest settlements to be discussed here, are presented individually along with modified reductions of maps of these sites published by their excavators. Available plane table or pace maps of the remaining sites are also presented. Unless otherwise specified these maps were made during the 1970-71 survey. All such sites were mapped at a scale of 1:20. Maps presented here are reductions of the originals. An effort has been made to present all maps on the same scale. This has not been possible in three cases: the maps of Susa, Chogha Mish, and KS-96 are presented at variant scales and are thus not visually comparable to the rest of the series.

Most sites are identified by a survey number: Chogha Mish is KS-1 for example. These numbers were initially assigned by Adams during his 1961 survey of the Susiana plain. They have been retained in subsequent surveys by Hole, Wright, Carter (University of Chicago), and myself. New numbers were assigned to additional sites as they were found. Such assignment has been coordinated among the individuals listed above to insure that no two sites carry the same number.

The survey settlement maps present a variety of coded data (Pl. X-XX). Surface collection areas are indicated by a letter code. Type counts for ceramics collected from these areas are presented in Appendix I. A two meter contour interval is used for most maps. Elevations are indicated in meters above surrounding plain level. Some sites have been partially destroyed through river erosion or other causes. The original extent of such sites could be estimated in some cases. This areal reconstruction is indicated by a line composed of dots and dashes superimposed over the contours of the site as it existed at the time of mapping. Occasionally field estimates could be made of the extent of the Terminal Susa A or Uruk occupation of a site that are more accurate than could be determined by later examination of the surface collections. Such estimates are presented by a dotted line enclosing the estimated occupational area. It is hoped that these maps will prove useful to those who wish to reanalyze the data presented here or who plan to do their own field work in the area. A series of additional notes on selected sites is included below.

Susa: Areal Size Estimates

Although excavation at Susa has been virtually continuous since 1897, except for the periods of World Wars I and II, little is known about the Uruk occupation of the site. This is primarily due to the preoccupation of excavators with painted pottery. Uruk ceramics, which are seldom painted and which can rarely be said to be aesthetically pleasing, have received little attention. This fact, in addition to a certain lack of clarity and completeness characteristic of the earlier excavation reports, makes discussion of the Uruk at Susa difficult indeed. Fortunately the importance of the Uruk occupation has been recognized by recent investigators who have devoted considerably more skill and attention to the study of this period.

It is the purpose of this section to provide estimates of the areal size of Susa during each broad occupational phase, from Terminal Susa A through Late Uruk. The treatment provided here is brief and may be supplemented by reference to Dyson's extensive discussion of the excavation data (1966). The site of Susa covers some 100 hectares, of which only two areas are significant here: Acropole and Apadana. Individual excavations mentioned in the present discussion can be located on the map of these two areas (Fig. 8).[2]

Having previously discussed the Uruk ceramic chronology at Susa, the stratigraphy of individual excavations to be mentioned below need not be a matter of great concern. Areal size estimates require only discussion of the areal distribution of diagnostic ceramic types reported from the site. This material can then be treated as a surface collection.

Terminal Susa A

No definite Terminal Susa A assemblage has been reported from the site. It appears, however, to be present on the Acropole: the small collection from Level 24 of the current Acropole sondage will probably prove to be Terminal Susa A. Dyson may have material of this period from his 1954 stratigraphic sounding (1966:334ff) and a few examples of Terminal Susa A types have been recently illustrated by Steve and Gasche (1971). These latter examples, all apparently redeposited, include a typical impressed strip bowl (Steve and Gasche, 1971:141, Fig. 27). Finally Terminal Susa A materials may have been included among those recovered by de Morgan from Gallery C, where he notes a transition from fine painted wares to coarser, predominantly unpainted wares (de Morgan, 1900:83).

Possible Terminal Susa A materials are then reported from roughly the southern one-half of the Acropole. A conservative estimate would place the area of the site at perhaps five hectares during this period.

Early Uruk

Early Uruk material has been recognized primarily from the Acropole. The Early Uruk levels of the current Acropole sondage were discussed earlier. As mentioned above, Gallery C may have contained Early Uruk material as well as that of Terminal Susa A. Steve and Gasche (1971) illustrate numerous

---

[2]This composite map was prepared from: Jéquier (1900:70); Eliot (1950:29); Ghirshman (1954: Plan 1); Dyson (1966:143); LeBrun (1971:Fig. 31); Steve and Gasche (1971: Plan 1).

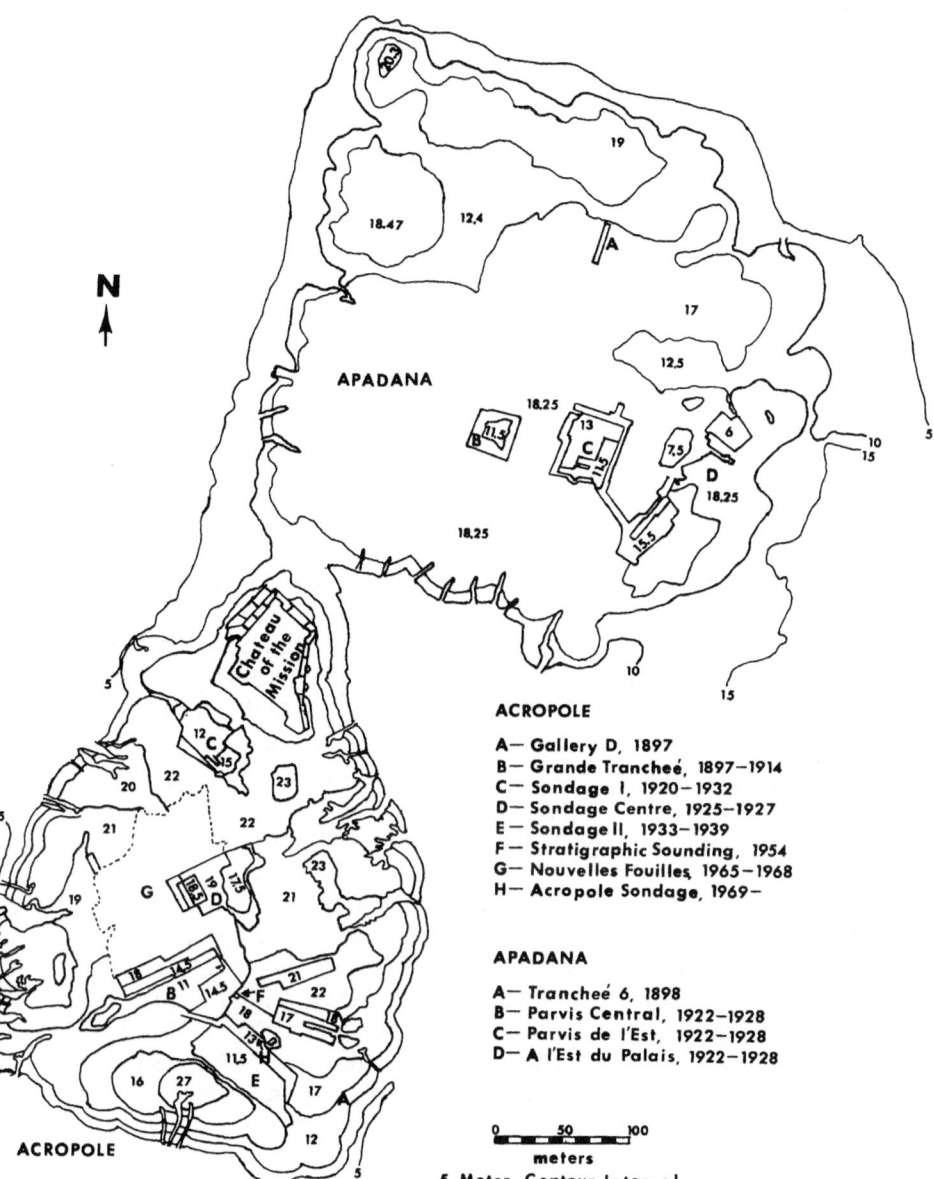

Fig. 8. Susa: Reported Distribution of Uruk Ceramics

examples of Early Uruk ceramic types including proto bevel rim bowls (139, Figs. 9,11), straight spouted jars with flared expanded rims (141, Figs. 9,10), impressed strip bowls (141, Figs. 25,26), and chaff tempered thumb impressed ring base bowls (141, Fig. 19). Dyson (1966) reports the presence of proto bevel rim bowls in his sondage (344) and illustrates an early straight spout (335) similar to one illustrated by de Mecquenem from Acropole Sondage I (de Mecquenem, 1928:103, Fig. 2).

It appears, from this admittedly miniscule evidence, that during Early Uruk all of the Acropole was occupied. This amounts to some nine hectares of site area. This occupation probably extended to parts of Apadana where possible Early Uruk straight spouts are reported from the Parvis de l'est (de Mecquenem, 1928:112). The best current estimate for the size of Susa during the Early Uruk is then on the order of 12 hectares.

Middle and Late Uruk

It is frequently difficult to specifically identify Middle Uruk levels at Susa from the excavation reports, which often makes it necessary to assume their presence. It appears, however, that the entire Acropole was occupied during both periods.

Clear middle and late assemblages from the current Acropole sondage were discussed above. Dyson (1966) reports Middle Uruk material from his 1954 sondage (348), followed by diagnostic late types (349) including band rim bottles (330), droop spouts, and twisted handles (335). Similarly diagnostic Late Uruk types are reported by Steve and Gasche (1971). The late types present include cross hatch triangles (155, Fig. 18) and droop spouts on band rim bottles (155, Fig. 29). No twisted handles are reported from their excavations.

De Morgan (1972) reports five to eight meters of deposit in the Grand Tranchee (22-23) containing a great quantity of bevel rim bowls (97). Presumably both Middle and Late Uruk levels are represented. Clear Late Uruk twisted handles are reported from both Sondage I (de Mecquenem, 1928:101-103) and Sondage II (de Mecquenem, 1934:196-197). In addition droop spouts, nose lugs and incised decoration are reported from Sondage I (de Mecquenem, 1928:101). A portion of a massive mud brick platform from the 'Sondage Centre apparently pertains to both periods (Dyson, 1966:223).

While Apadana was apparently occupied during the Middle Uruk period there is no available evidence of Late Uruk occupation in the area. Middle Uruk material, primarily bevel rim bowls, is reported from Sondage six (Jèquier, 1900:74-75), Parvis central (de Mecquenem, 1928:105), the Parvis de l'est (de Mecquenem, 1928:112), and the excavation "a l'est du palais" (de Mecquenem, 1928:112). An unpublished excavation by Ghirshman on the

THE 1970-71 SUSIANA SURVEY 71

western flank of the tell contains large numbers of bevel rim bowls (E. Carter 1972, personal communication). Other materials are less frequently reported, but include strap handled cups and clay sickles (de Mecquenem, 1928:112).

Allowing nine nectares for Acropole and 16 hectares for Apadana, the size of Susa in Middle Uruk is estimated at 25 hectares, and in Late Uruk as nine hectares. The sizes of these areas were estimated from a topographic map of the site (Ghirshman, 1954: Plan 1) with a correction for enlargement of the site by extensive back dirt piles.

Table 17 summarizes the size estimates for Susa during each of the four periods discussed. These estimates must be considered first approximations.

TABLE 17
AREA OF SUSA (in hectares):
TERMINAL SUSA A TO LATE URUK

Period	Acropole	Apadana	Total
Terminal Susa A	5	–	5
Early Uruk	9	3	12
Middle Uruk	9	16	25
Late Uruk	9	–	9

Chogha Mish[3]

The Uruk occupation of Chogha Mish (KS-1) would appear to span the Middle and Late Uruk periods. Terminal Susa A impressed strip bowls have not been found either in surface collection or excavation of the site. Terminal Susa A painted material is also absent.

This is also the case for Early Uruk ceramic types. None of the following common types have been recognized at the site: proto bevel rim bowls, chaff tempered thumb impressed ring base bowls, early straight spouts, flared expanded rim jars, or high expanded band rim jars. It may be concluded that neither Terminal Susa A nor Early Uruk materials are represented in the available collections from Chogha Mish.

Estimation of the areal size of the site during the Middle and Late Uruk periods is difficult at present. Figure 9 presents a map of the site (adapted from Delougaz, 1967:32-33). The exposure of the site above the level of the

[3] Unless otherwise specified, all data contained in this discussion were kindly provided by Dr. Helene Kantor, co-director of the Chogha Mish project.

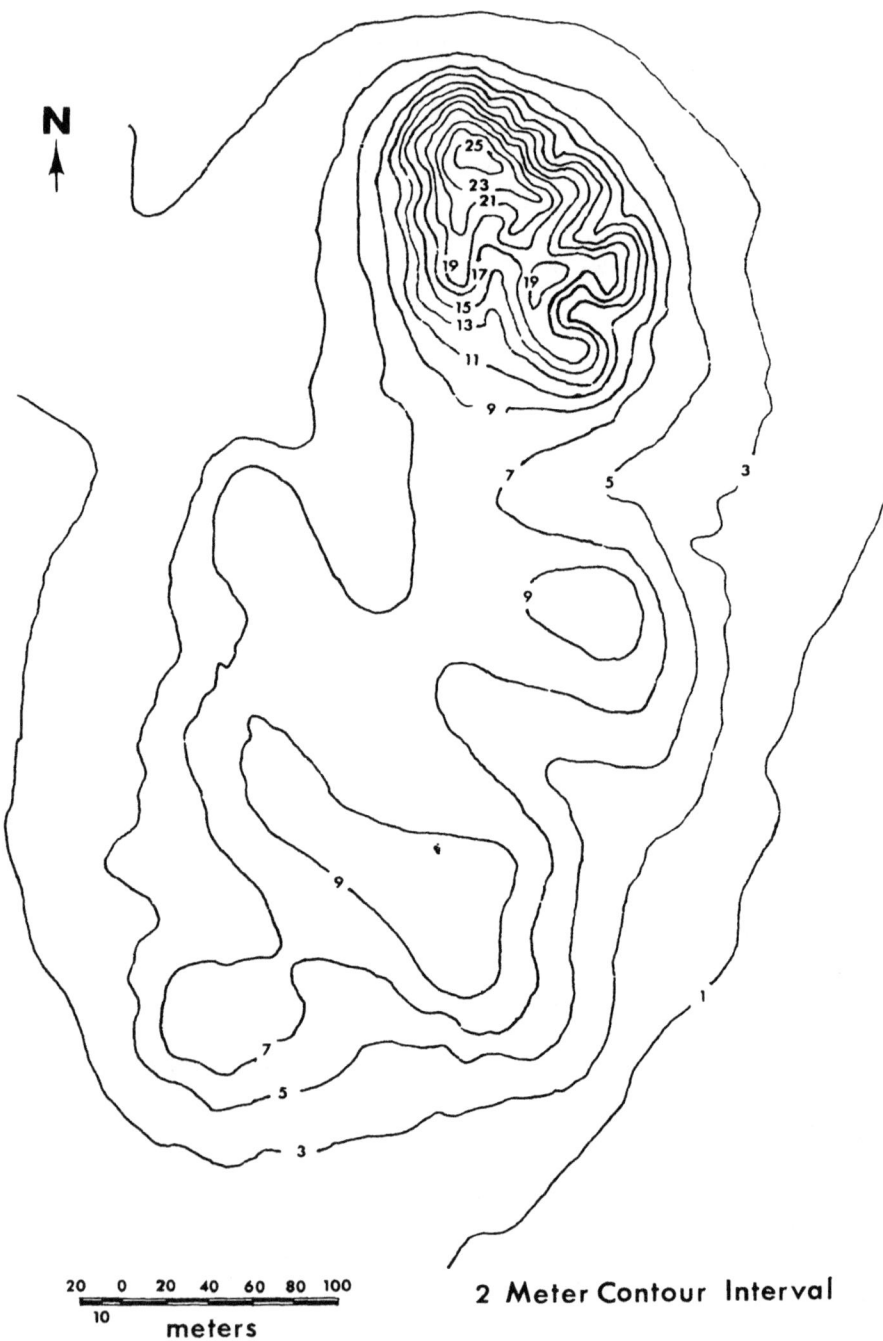

Fig. 9. Site Map of Chogha Mish, KS-1.

present alluvium covers some 18 hectares. The excavators feel, however, that much of the site may now be covered by alluvial deposits and that originally it may have covered as much as 60-70 acres or 24-29 hectares (Delougaz, 1966:31).

Characteristic Late Uruk ceramic types are distributed over the entire present site surface. These types include twisted handles, band and ledge rim bottles, and cross hatch triangles. The areal size of the site in Late Uruk will be considered for present purposes as 18 hectares.

The extent of the Middle Uruk occupation of the site has not been determined. It would seem unreasonable to propose the appearance of an 18 hectare site somewhat ex nihilo during Middle Uruk. Then for present purposes the size of the Middle Uruk occupation will be arbitrarily set at 10 hectares.

Areal size estimates for the remaining sites to be considered in this study are presented in Table 18. The areal size estimates presented above were used to define the settlement size hierarchy for each of the four periods to be discussed. Figure 10 presents histograms of the size distribution for each period. The histogram for each period is broken into two or more "modes" defining size classes. As in most archaeological settlement pattern studies, the sample size for any given period is too small to permit statistical definition of multimodality. Divisions were made at "natural breaks" in the size distributions. While this method lacks analytical elegance, it is a pragmatic solution to necessary partitioning of the data.

Each mode in each histogram is then classified as one of four settlement size types ranging from villages to large centers. The statistical characteristics of any particular settlement type vary from histogram to histogram or period to period. Villages in one period are not necessarily the same size as villages of another period. This would seem a justifiable approach when dealing with diachronic change in a single system. It allows investigation of changes within and between individual settlement types over time. Such changes will prove to have important implications later in this study.

Assignment of names to each settlement type posed theoretical problems. Few readers will probably dispute designation of village and large village settlement types. The two remaining size types were called small centers and large centers. Ambiguous and theoretically loaded terms such as town, city, and urban center were assiduously avoided. This study does not directly concern itself with the emergence or characteristics of these settlement types, whatever they may be, and thus it was thought best to avoid possible confusion by use of the center designations. The term center also has definite theoretical implications, some of which have already been discussed.

74 LOCAL EXCHANGE AND EARLY STATE DEVELOPMENT

TABLE 18
1970-71 SURVEY: ESTIMATED SITE AREAS

Site Number	Site Name	Height (m)	Total (ha)	Terminal Susa A (ha)	Early Uruk (ha)	Middle Uruk (ha)	Late Uruk (ha)	Alidade Map	Pace Map	Comment
004	Ishan Abu Diyyayyat	16	6.88		2.76	1.12		x		
005		13	2.40			.80		x		
006		5	4.84	1.84	1.84			x		
007	Tepe Senjar	12	-13.00			1.00			x	
008	Tepe Saiyeh	4	1.08		.42	.76		x		
013	Tepe Band-i-bal	9	1.70			?				Special Function
015		2	2.00			.02			x	Special Function
016	Tepe Mohammed Ahga	12	.68	.68	.68	.68		x		
020	Tepe Jaffarabad	7	.20			?				Special Function
022		10	1.51	.50	1.51	1.51		x		
024	Tepe Suleiman	16	.84		.40	.40		x		
027	Tepe Jardari	12	.60		.60	.60		x		
032		6	1.50		1.50	1.50	1.50	x		

TABLE 18 (continued)

Site Number	Site Name	Height (m)	Total (ha)	Terminal Susa A (ha)	Early Uruk (ha)	Middle Uruk (ha)	Late Uruk (ha)	Alidade Map	Pace Map	Comment
033	Ishan Rud	6	1.24		1.24			x		
034		7	1.88		1.88	1.88	.92	x		
035		5	1.04		1.04	1.04		x		
036	Tepe Sharafabad	10	1.30		1.04	1.04	.31	x		
037	Tepe Galeh Bongoon	6	3.50			.80				
039	Tepe Rahimeh	10	1.96		.68	1.50	1.38	x		
040		6	.92			.56		x		Special Function
044N		5	.80			.80		x		
044S		3	1.28		1.28	1.28		x		
045		9	.60			.08		x		Special Function
049	Bugga Ishan	12	4.28		3.48	1.00		x		
050	Tepe Alvan	11	1.20		.75	.75		x		
052		5	1.52	.96	1.36	.96		x		
054		4	2.48		2.48	2.48	2.48	x		
059	Abu Fanduweh	14	9.94	5.16	6.92	9.56	8.16	x		

76 LOCAL EXCHANGE AND EARLY STATE DEVELOPMENT

TABLE 18 (continued)

Site Number	Site Name	Height (m)	Total (ha)	Terminal Susa A (ha)	Early Uruk (ha)	Middle Uruk (ha)	Late Uruk (ha)	Alidade Map	Pace Map	Comment
061		8	1.28	.60	1.28	1.28	.68	x		
064		5	1.72	1.48	1.72	.64		x		
067		8	2.00	2.00				x		
076		10	2.62		2.62	2.62		x		
079	Tepe Sayed Nabih	12	3.20		3.20	2.32	1.84	x		
089		7	1.64			?		x		
090	Kasanet Sabeh	15	3.88		2.28	2.28		x		
093		6	2.52		1.12	1.12		x		
094		6	2.40	2.40	2.40	2.40		x		
096	Tepe Keihf	13	10.76		.50	5.20	4.00	x		
098	Haft Tepe	8	.80			.80				
099		4	2.76	2.00	2.00	2.00		x		
101	Chogha Pahn	3	1.20		1.20			x		
102		9	1.20			1.20		x		
108	Chogha Kabire	14	2.80	1.00	1.56	2.80	.56	x		

THE 1970-71 SUSIANA SURVEY

Site Number	Site Name	Height (m)	Total (ha)	Terminal Susa A (ha)	Early Uruk (ha)	Middle Uruk (ha)	Late Uruk (ha)	Alidade Map	Pace Map	Comment
112	Tepe Twaim	6	3.00	1.50	1.50					
113	Tepe Sanjar	20	5.16		1.28	3.58	1.12	x		
120	Tepe Deh Now	16	9.00		6.00	6.00				
121		7	1.33		1.33	1.33			x	
153		5	6.44		6.44	6.44		x		
165	Chogha Pahwandeh	13	2.00		1.01	2.00		x		
171		4	2.80		2.80	2.80	2.80	x		
173		2	2.08		2.08	2.08		x		
182		3	1.36	1.36				x		
190		4	.56	.56				x		
197	Burj-i-Bazazi	7	1.00		1.00	1.00		x		
218		4	2.00			1.50		x		
220	Tepe Sadarabad	12	1.75			1.12				
240	Tepe Imam Atuyi	8	2.20		2.20	2.20				
266		9	1.44	1.44	1.44	1.44		x		

TABLE 18 (continued)

Site Number	Site Name	Height (m)	Total (ha)	Terminal Susa A (ha)	Early Uruk (ha)	Middle Uruk (ha)	Late Uruk (ha)	Alidade Map	Pace Map	Comment
269		6	.40	.40	.40			x		
284		4	.84	.84	.84	.84		x		
285		5	.36		.36	.36		x		
286		.3	1.12		1.12	1.12		x		
288		—	.50		.50	.50				
289		4	.38		.38	.38				
290		6	2.75		2.00	2.00		x		

THE 1970-71 SUSIANA SURVEY

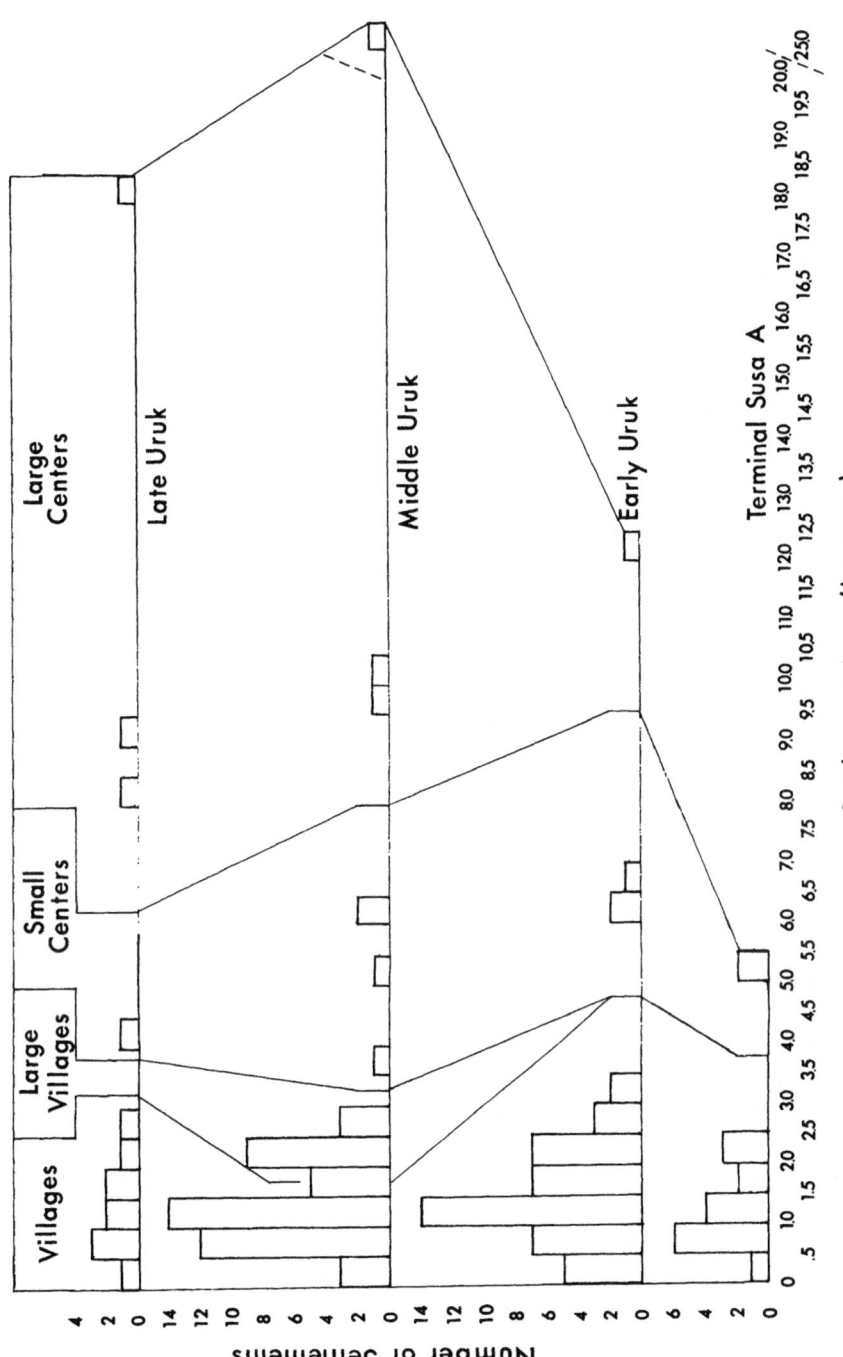

Fig. 10. Settlement Areas – Histogram Definition of Settlement Areal Size Classes.

Additional Notes on Selected Sites

KS-4 (Pl. X). The area mapped is a portion of the site as originally defined by Adams in his 1961 survey. A second 2.08 hectare mound is located 200 meters east-southeast of the area indicated. As there was no evidence of Terminal Susa A or Uruk occupation of this second mound, it was deleted from the map presented here. In Appendix I type counts are presented from area east of KS-4. This material was recovered from a possible Uruk canal exposed by construction of a modern canal 300 meters south-southeast of the site as mapped here.

KS-8 (Pl. XI). Half of this site would appear to have been destroyed in modern times. The original area is reconstructed from surface evidence.

KS-44 (Pl. XIII). The original contours of the southern mound on this site have been greatly altered by construction of the two canals indicated on the site map. The original shape of the site has been reconstructed from surface evidence.

KS-49 (Pl. XIV). Some portion of this site has been destroyed, probably by erosional action of the Dez river. A conservative reconstruction of the original extent of the site is presented.

KS-54 (Pl. XIV). This site has been largely destroyed in the recent past as a source of fill dirt. The original extent of the site has been reconstructed from visible surface traces.

KS-76 (Pl. XV). This site has been recently damaged as a source of fill dirt.

KS-96 (Pl. XVII). This large site presented considerable survey difficulties. The Uruk occupation of portions of the site, in particular the northern area, is covered by a massive overburden of later materials. Large-scale earth moving in antiquity probably also resulted in a wider distribution of Uruk material than was originally present. The areal size estimates for this site must be considered very tentative.

KS-89 (Pl. XVI). As indicated by the map, this site was in danger of destruction at the time of survey. The site has been completely leveled since this map was made.

KS-93 (Pl. XVI). This site has served as the source of materials for a modern brick kiln. The original extent of the site has been reconstructed from surface evidence.

KS-197 (Pl. XX). This site has been largely destroyed as a source of material for construction in a nearby modern village. The original extent of the site has been reconstructed from surface evidence.

KS-290 (Pl. XX). This site has been largely destroyed by an unknown agency. The reconstructions of its original areal extent must be considered highly tentative.

Comments on Selected Sites for which Maps are Not Available

KS-98. This site was a major Elamite center of some 30 hectares. Only the portion of the site occupied during the Uruk period is listed in Table 18.

KS-120. This 9.5 hectare site was apparently another major Elamite center. The Uruk occupation is covered by perhaps 15 meters of Elamite and later deposits. The areal extent of the site during the Uruk period was estimated from the distribution of a handful of sherds. This estimate is the most tenuous of any presented in this study.

SETTLEMENT PATTERN MAPS

Settlement pattern maps for the Terminal Susa A, Early Uruk, Middle Uruk, and Late Uruk periods (Figs. 11-14) are presented in the following four pages. The maps are reductions of tracings made by Adams of 1:25,000 air photographs. Presentation of area maps is a difficult problem when format requirements strictly limit the scale of reproduction possible. These maps present the basic locational data of the 1970-71 survey and thus are of some importance. An attempt has been made to circumvent the scale problem by providing grid coordinates for each site discussed in this study (see Appendix II). While the coordinates were taken from a 1:50,000 reduction of the original map, they provide a far higher degree of accuracy than is possible in a small map presentation.

The remaining maps presented in this study are very schematic and intended for illustration rather than data presentation. Some readers may wish to undertake their own analysis of the data presented here and require site to site distances not specifically mentioned in this text. Such distances would best be calculated from the coordinates provided. The following four maps should be used should anyone feel a compulsion to take distance measurements directly from the mapped settlement distributions.

These maps also provide a more realistic impression of settlement density on the plain. Sites are indicated as closely as possible to the same scale as topography and river systems.

82 LOCAL EXCHANGE AND EARLY STATE DEVELOPMENT

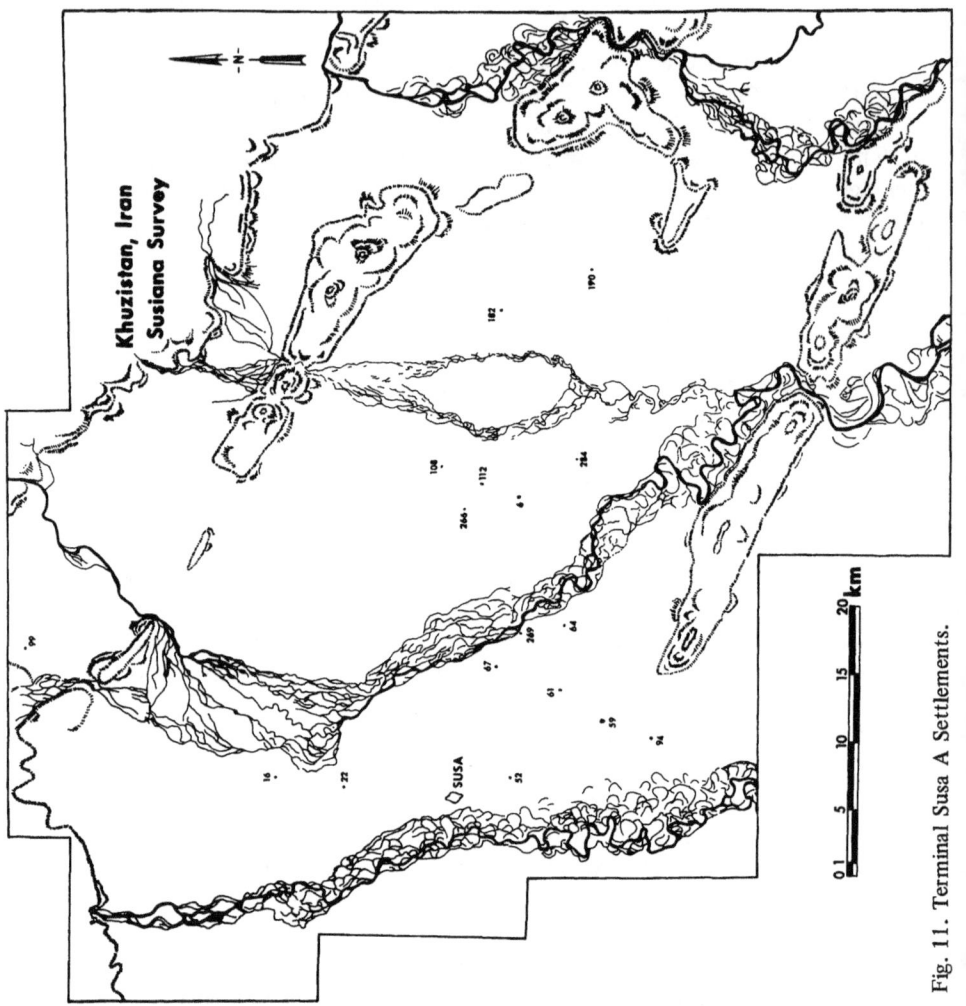

Fig. 11. Terminal Susa A Settlements.

THE 1970-71 SUSIANA SURVEY

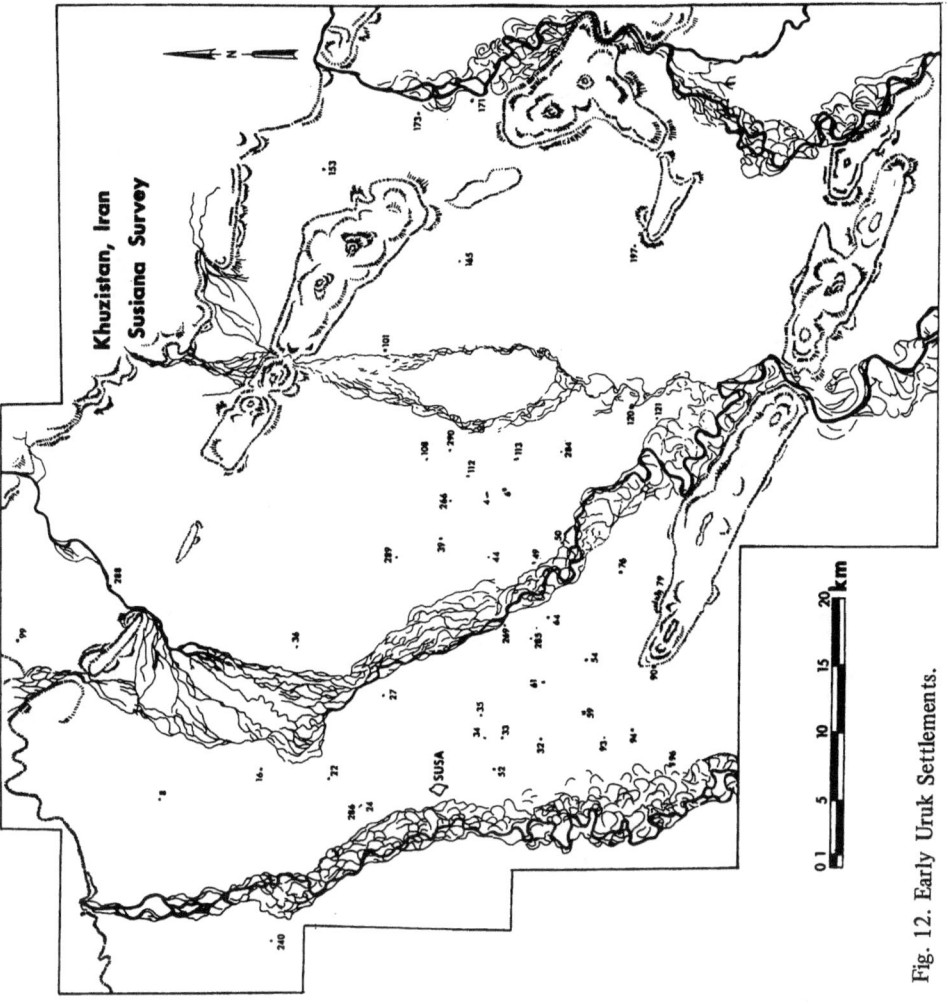

Fig. 12. Early Uruk Settlements.

84 LOCAL EXCHANGE AND EARLY STATE DEVELOPMENT

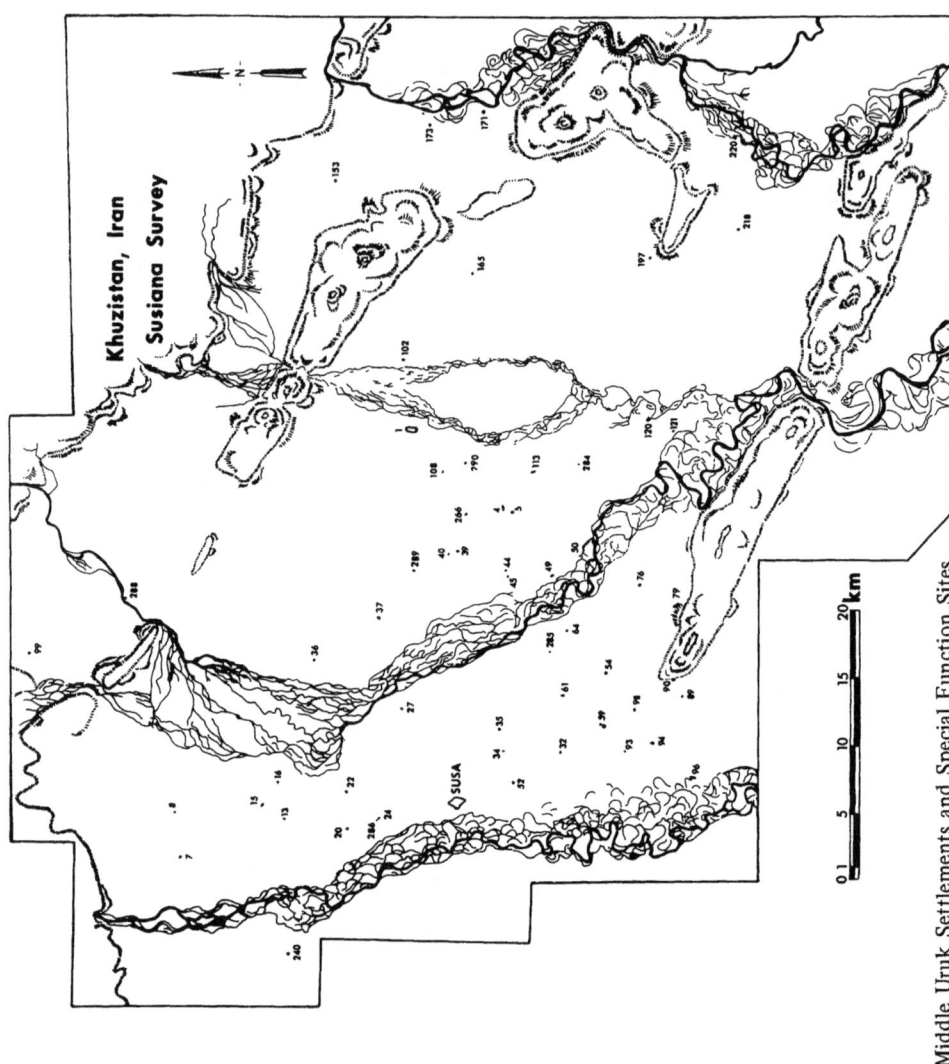

Fig. 13. Middle Uruk Settlements and Special Function Sites.

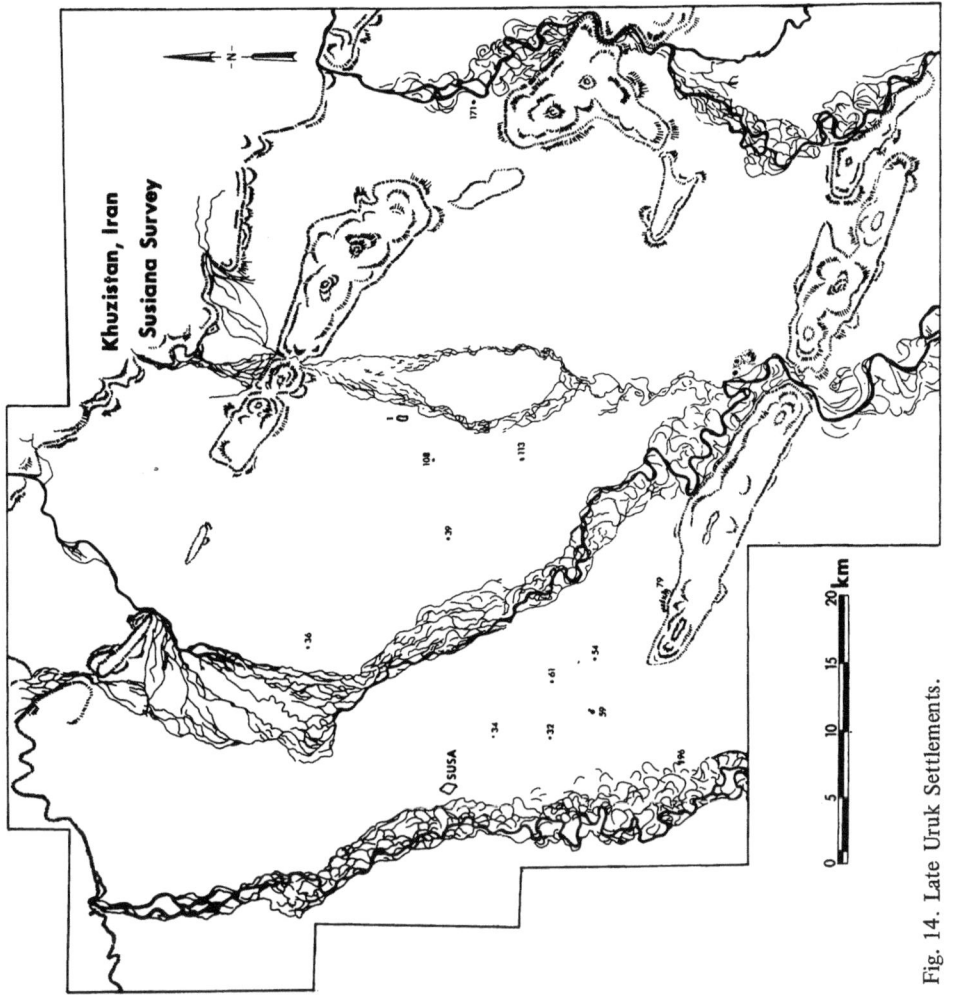

Fig. 14. Late Uruk Settlements.

III

ANALYSIS OF THE SETTLEMENT PATTERNS

TERMINAL SUSA A

THE Terminal Susa A settlement pattern is included in this study for two reasons: first, to provide a base point for a discussion of the Uruk occupation of the plain; and second, because its newly defined ceramic assemblage provides some stylistic transition between Susa A and Early Uruk. There has appeared, in the past, to be a complete stylistic hiatus between Susa A and Uruk. The definition of Terminal Susa A helps to fill this gap.

The most remarkable feature of the Terminal Susa A settlement pattern is its low density. Eighteen sites are known, with an estimated total of 29.72 (30) hectares of occupied area. This may represent something on the order of 6,000 people.

With so few sites a histogram of settlement area (Fig. 10) is not very impressive. Two modes are relatively clearly indicated. Settlements in the first mode are defined as villages. The modal value for settlement area is .75 hectares and the mean is 1.22 hectares. An argument could be made for an additional division at 1.75 hectares although, given the small sample size and method of measurement, such a division would be difficult to justify. The second mode defined here is comprised of Susa and Abu Fanduweh (KS-59). Both settlements had an estimated area of about five hectares during Terminal Susa A. They are classified as small centers.

The settlement pattern was not only very thin, but disjointed as well (see Fig. 15). At least three roughly linear clusters of sites are discernible. The first includes Susa as a small center and three villages: KS-16, KS-22, and KS-52. The second cluster includes Abu Fanduweh as a small center and five villages: KS-61, KS-64, KS-67, KS-94, and KS-269. The third cluster lacks a dominant settlement and includes five villages: KS-6, KS-108, KS-112, KS-266, and KS-284.

88 LOCAL EXCHANGE AND EARLY STATE DEVELOPMENT

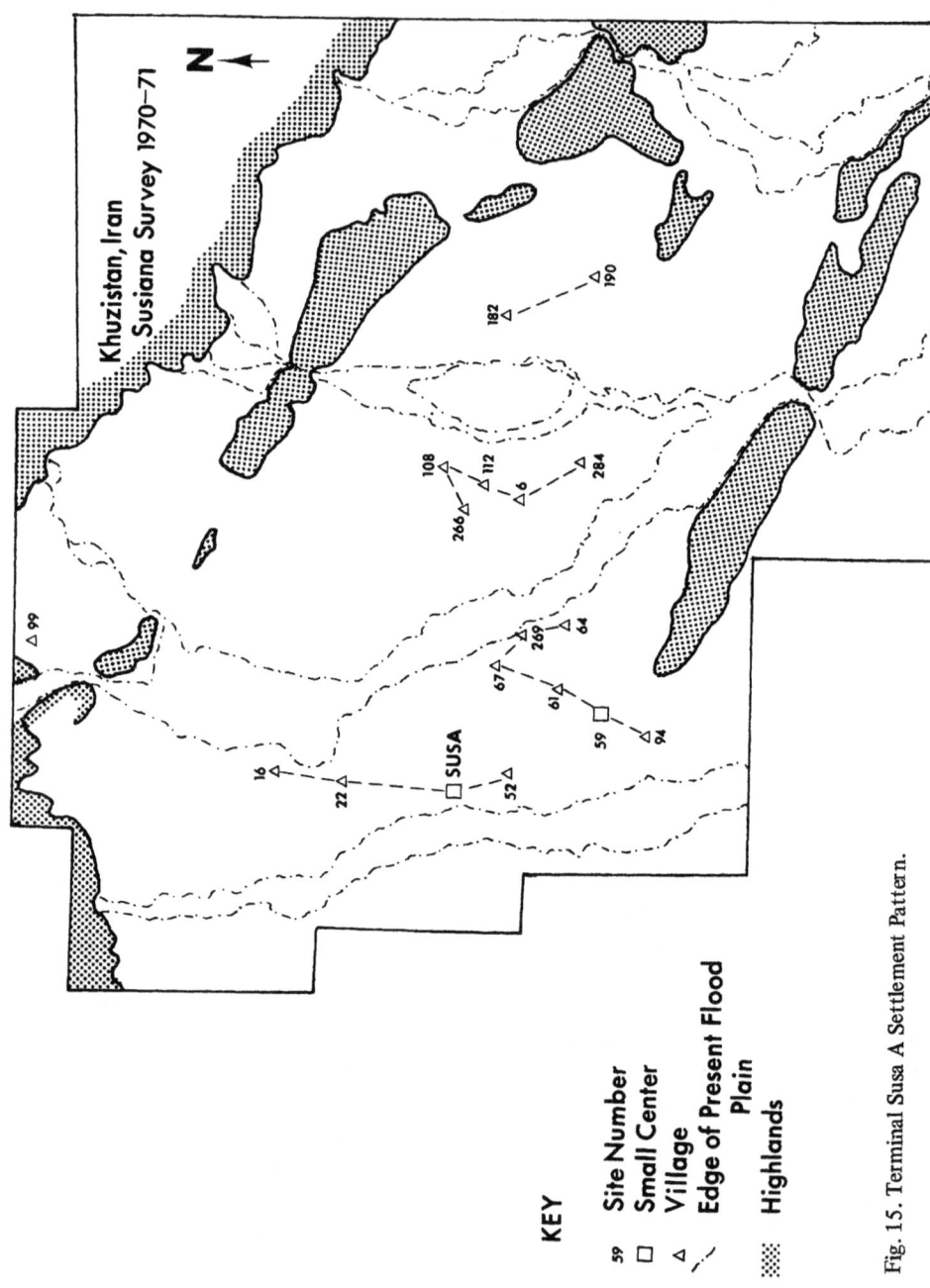

Fig. 15. Terminal Susa A Settlement Pattern.

ANALYSIS OF THE SETTLEMENT PATTERNS

Three settlements remain unaccounted for: of these three, KS-99 is isolated on the far northern margin of the plain. KS-182 and KS-192 on the eastern portion of the plain may constitute a fourth cluster, though a cluster of two sites is not very convincing. These settlements and KS-99 will be deleted from the remainder of this discussion as unknowns.

Little can be said about the locational structure of the three remaining settlement clusters. Their roughly linear distributions may indicate location on or near natural or artificial watercourses. The settlements do, however, show some regularity in spacing. The dashed lines connecting sites in Figure 15 define the extent of each cluster, indicate possible watercourse locations, and suggest site-to-site relationships.

Average site-to-site distance was calculated for each cluster. Only first order, nearest neighbor distances along possible watercourses were used. Reflexive nearest neighbor pairs were ignored. In the Susa cluster, for example, KS-16 and KS-22 are a reflexive nearest neighbor pair. The 5.21 kilometers between these sites was entered only once rather than twice into calculation of the mean for the cluster. Cluster means are: Susa cluster, 5.93 kilometers; Abu Fanduweh cluster, 3.99 kilometers; and the eastern cluster, 3.70 kilometers. F and t statistics do not indicate significant differences in variance or mean of site-to-site distance between any two of these three clusters.

Site-to-site distances within clusters are thus rather uniform, having an average of 4.54 kilometers. This can be contrasted to between-cluster distances, defined as the distance between nearest settlements belonging to each of two neighboring clusters. This is equal to 7.27 kilometers between KS-52 of the Susa cluster and KS-59 of the Abu Fanduweh cluster. The closest settlements of the Abu Fanduweh and eastern clusters were KS-64 and KS-6, which are 10.29 kilometers apart. So defined, the average between-cluster distance is 8.78 kilometers, based on a sample of two. Mean within-cluster distance is thus roughly one-half (51.7 percent) of mean between-cluster distance. This difference in means may indicate that each settlement cluster represented a discrete economic and political system.

The interpretation of the Terminal Susa A settlement pattern is made more difficult by two factors. First, the ceramic assemblage is not well defined and thus there may be more Terminal Susa A sites on the plain than are now known. Second, an interpretation must lean heavily on the classical Susa A settlement pattern(s), discussion of which is beyond the scope of this study.

Whatever future research may indicate about the late Susiana and Susa A periods, it is likely that the relatively large ranked societies of the late Susiana period were becoming smaller and more fragmented, reaching a low point in the Terminal Susa A period. It is possible that intense competition, similar to that proposed below for Late Uruk, was responsible for this decline.

It is not possible at present to test any of these hypotheses. Later in this study, various Uruk ceramic types will be used to investigate the locational structure of local exchange in preliminary tests of hypotheses concerning state formation. A similar approach should be equally applicable to the Terminal Susa A period. Unfortunately the impressed strip bowl is the only Terminal Susa A type for which a relatively large sample is available. A large proportion of these bowls were recovered from KS-67 and KS-269. Both of these sites are located in the Abu Fanduweh cluster and thus the data are not amenable to a local exchange study. The important point about the Terminal Susa A settlement pattern is not so much what it may indicate, but what it does not indicate. Its two-level hierarchy and disjointed locational structure do not indicate the presence of state level organization.

EARLY URUK

The transition from Terminal Susa A to Early Uruk involved a number of important developments. The most noticeable change was a considerable increase in the number of occupied settlements. The 18 sites occupied during Terminal Susa A increased to 49 sites in Early Uruk. Occupied settlement area increased from a total of 30 to 95.18 (95) hectares in Early Uruk. Assuming that population was directly proportional to settlement area, population trebled in this period. Perhaps 20,000 people are represented, indicating a density over the whole plain of seven persons per square kilometer. Similar densities were attained at least as early as Susiana d. (This estimate is based on survey data currently under analysis by Frank Hole of Rice University.)

Perhaps the most important feature of the Early Uruk population increase was that it involved considerable expansion of the occupied area of the plain (see Fig. 16). The three linear settlement clusters of Terminal Susa A were merged into a more or less continuous settlement distribution. This change in the settlement pattern would in itself imply an increasing scale of political and economic organization.

Processes other than population increase were, however, more important, though less obvious, in early Uruk. The first of these was the development of a third level of the settlement size hierarchy marked by the emergence of Susa as a large center of some 12 hectares. The average size of villages and small centers increased slightly: villages from 1.22 to 1.45 hectares and small centers from 5.08 to 6.45 hectares. Thus there was not only population increase, but also population agglomeration.

As predicted, there is locational evidence for an increasing scale of political and economic organization of Early Uruk settlements on the plain. This evidence consists of the emergence of spatial settlement distributions which approximate Christaller's theoretical Central Place distributions. These patterns

ANALYSIS OF THE SETTLEMENT PATTERNS

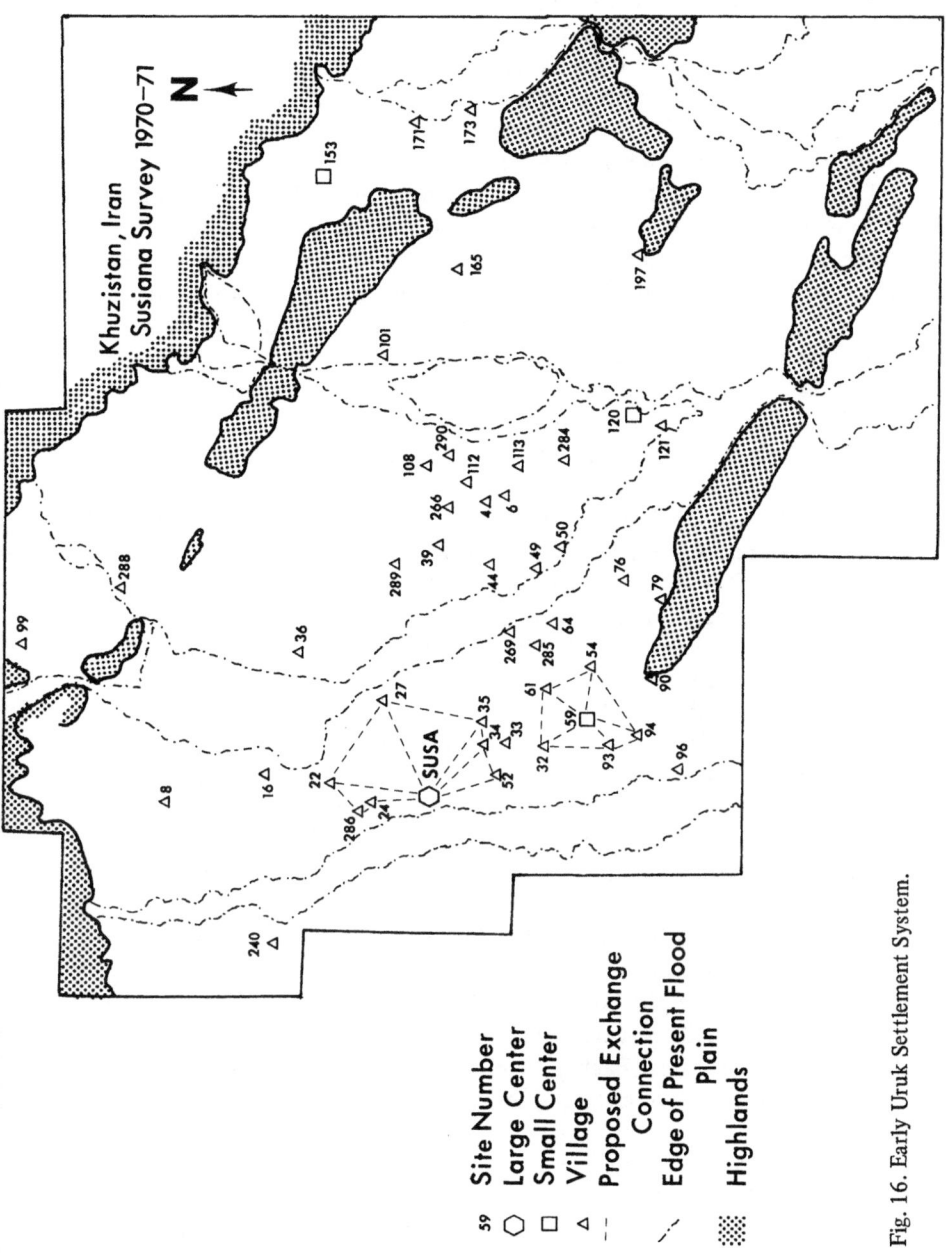

Fig. 16. Early Uruk Settlement System.

were centered on Susa and Abu Fanduweh (KS-59) on the western portion of the plain.

Two possible Central Place systems are illustrated in Figure 16. Susa formed the center of a distribution including KS-24, KS-286, KS-22, KS-27, KS-35, KS-34, and KS-52. Abu Fanduweh formed the center of a distribution including KS-32, KS-61, KS-54, KS-94, and KS-93.

The development of these distributions theoretically indicates that considerations of distance to nearest center had become an important factor in the determination of settlement location for reasons of efficiency in travel and transport both to and from these centers. Presumably centers provided goods and services, in the broadest sense, unavailable in smaller settlements.

It appears, for example, that during the Early Uruk period production of many craft items became a spatially centralized rather than dispersed activity. Uruk ceramics were primarily wheel-made, in quantity and in specialized workshops. Although the relevant data are of the Middle Uruk period to be discussed below, it appears these workshops were restricted to the major settlements. Middle Uruk ceramic workshops are known from Susa, Abu Fanduweh, and Chogha Mish (KS-1). Presumably they were also present at Susa and Abu Fanduweh in Early Uruk. At the present time there is no clear evidence of Uruk ceramic production at any other site in the area.

Assuming that Susa and Abu Fanduweh were the major ceramic producing centers for the area in Early Uruk, ceramics produced in these centers, even if basically of the same form, should be distinguishable. This, of course, also assumes the availability of a sufficiently large sample.

The ceramics from the surface collections are not really equal to this task for the Early Uruk period. Only one type, neckless ledge rims, is present in sufficient quantity to make further analysis tempting. There are 29 measurable examples of this type in the surface collections. I am easily tempted.

A description and list of neckless ledge jar rim measurements is presented in Appendix III. It is not possible to statistically define subgroups within the available sample. Groups can be defined on a more subjective basis.

Figure 17 presents a scatter plot of interior rim angle against rim angle for 29 neckless ledge rims. Each plot point is accompanied by a number that identifies the site from which the sherd represented by the point was collected.

Clearly interior rim angle and rim angle are not closely related attributes (Pearson's $r = .23$, $R^2 = .05$). Inspection of the plot does, however, suggest two loose point clusters. If the sample is partitioned into these two possible groups, Type 1 and Type 2, interesting distributional observations can be made. Note the distribution by type and collection site in Table 19. This distribution is schematically mapped in Figure 18. Note that there are four sites

ANALYSIS OF THE SETTLEMENT PATTERNS

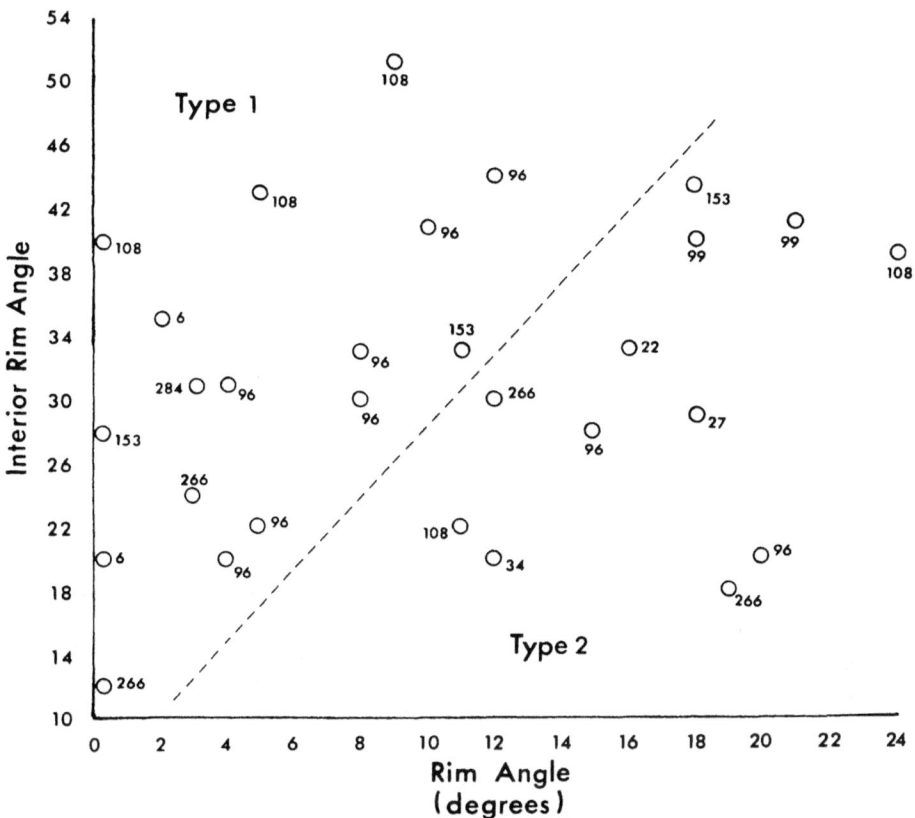

Fig. 17. Early Uruk Neckless Ledge Rim Jars — Scatter Plot.

TABLE 19
DISTRIBUTION OF EARLY URUK NECKLESS LEDGE RIM JARS

Site	Type 1	Type 2
KS-99	0	2
KS-34	0	1
KS-27	0	1
KS-22	0	1
KS-266	2	2
KS-153	2	1
KS-108	4	2
KS-96	6	2
KS-284	1	0
KS-6	2	0

where Type 1 rims were absent and Type 2 rims were present: KS-99, KS-34, KS-27, and KS-22. KS-99 is located on the far northern portion of the plain above Susa, while the remaining three sites are all dependent villages in the Susa Central Place system proposed above.

Type 1 rims are concentrated in the remaining sites which, with one exception, are located on the eastern portion of the plain. The exception is KS-96 located in the far southwestern corner of the plain below Abu Fanduweh. On the basis of the available data, I would suggest that jars with Type 1 rims were produced at Abu Fanduweh and distributed to settlements on the eastern side of the plain, as well as to those in the immediate area of the center. Susa would appear to have had a more restricted sphere of economic influence.

Though the local exchange evidence from the ceramics has been less than impressive, it is consistent with the hypotheses developed from the locational data. It could not be said to constitute a test of these hypotheses.

The basic spatial arrangement of settlements around Susa and Abu Fanduweh appears to have been largely determined by redistributional considerations. Specific center-to-village distances, however, seem to have been more related to agricultural requirements.

ANALYSIS OF THE SETTLEMENT PATTERNS

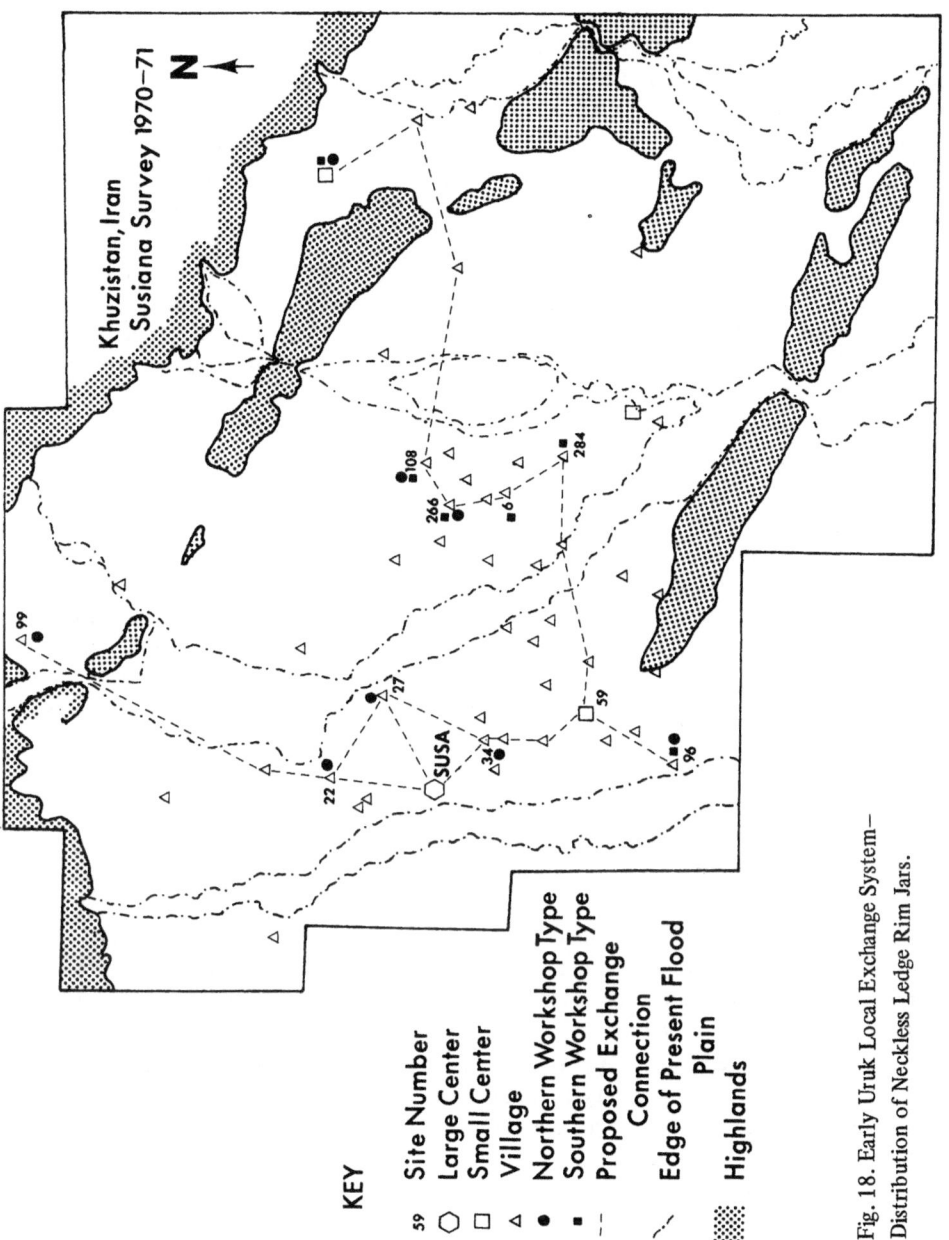

Fig. 18. Early Uruk Local Exchange System—Distribution of Neckless Ledge Rim Jars.

The average distance from central settlement to dependent settlements in the Susa system is 6.33 kilometers. The average for the Abu Fanduweh system is 3.80 kilometers. Size estimates for Susa and Abu Fanduweh in Early Uruk are 12.00 and 6.92 hectares respectively. Susa was 1.73 times larger than Abu Fanduweh. Average center-to-village distance in the Susa system was 1.67 times greater than in the Abu Fanduweh system. This suggests that in these individual Central Place systems, center-to-dependent settlement distance was proportional to center size.

This relationship might be explained through use of a simple agricultural sustaining area model. First, assuming that the immediate agricultural sustaining areas of a central settlement and each of its dependent settlements were immediately adjacent to one another, the eastern fields of Susa and the fields of KS-27, by implication, would have shared a boundary. Second, the assumption is made here that the placement of the boundary between sustaining areas reflected a simple relationship such that the distances from the boundary line to the central settlement and to a dependent settlement were directly proportional to their respective settlement sizes.

Estimates of the immediate sustaining areas of centers and surrounding villages may be made with these assumptions and one other to follow. As mentioned above, the average center-to-village distance in the Abu Fanduweh system was 3.80 kilometers. The estimated size of Abu Fanduweh was 6.92 hectares and the average estimated size of surrounding villages was 1.76 hectares. Given the assumptions stated above, the boundary of the center and average village sustaining areas was 3.02 kilometers from Abu Fanduweh and .78 kilometers from the "average" dependent village in the system.

Making the additional assumption of circular sustaining areas, these distances can be taken as radii for calculation of the size of these sustaining areas. Abu Fanduweh would then have had a sustaining area of 3,035 hectares and the average dependent village in the system a sustaining area of 191 hectares. Use of the 200 person per hectare of settlement area population estimate would provide an average sustaining area of 2.19 hectares per person for Abu Fanduweh, and .54 hectares per person for surrounding dependent villages.

Average center-to-dependent village distance in the Susa system was 6.33 kilometers. The area of Susa is estimated at 12.00 hectares in Early Uruk. Estimates for dependent villages average 1.31 hectares. As the Susa system appears to have been truncated to the west, perhaps by a river floodplain, one-half the estimated circular sustaining area was used for further calculations. With this exception the same procedure was followed as in the Abu Fanduweh case. This provides an estimated sustaining area for Susa of 5,080 hectares or 2.12 hectares per person. On the average, dependent villages had a 128 hectare sustaining area, or .49 hectares per person. The sustaining area

TABLE 20
ESTIMATION OF EARLY URUK CENTER AND VILLAGE SUSTAINING AREAS

	Susa System	Abu Fanduweh System
Center size (area)	12.00 ha	6.92 ha
Average village size (area)	1.31 ha	1.76 ha
Average center-to-village distance	6.33 km	3.80 km
Radius of center sustaining area	5.69 km	3.02 km
Center sustaining area	5,080 ha	3,035 ha
Radius of village sustaining area	.64 km	.78 km
Village sustaining area	128 ha	191 ha
Center population	2,400	1,384
Village population	262	352
Center sustaining area per person	*2.12 ha*	*2.19 ha*
Village sustaining area per person	*.49 ha*	*.54 ha*

estimates, per person, for the Susa and Abu Fanduweh systems are thus remakably similar. These calculations are summarized in Table 20.

The sustaining area estimates for villages may appear far too small. This, however, may not be the case. The estimates may be evaluated to some extent with data from traditional villages in the area today.

Traditional villagers in the Dez Pilot area consume about 3,000 calories per day. An average of 1,976 or 66 percent of these calories is derived from consumption of an average of .76 kilograms of bread per day (Gremliza, 1962:92). This rate of consumption would indicate a requirement of about 278 kilograms of bread per person per year.

Irrigated barley yields under traditional agricultural methods average 1.153 kilograms per hectare in this area (Schulze, 1959:50). Assuming a one-to-one, barley-to-bread weight ratio, the average person consumes the yield of about .25 hectares of barley per year.

The suggested Early Uruk village sustaining area per person was about .50 hectares. Assuming production and consumption levels comparable with the modern situation, maintenance of 50 percent of Early Uruk village lands in barley would have provided for a basic staple food supply. The remaining 50 percent would then have been available for gardens, orchards, other field crops, surplus barley production, fallow land, and so on. Surpluses would function as emergency supplies and may have functioned in exchange for nonhousehold-produced items. In sum, the .50 hectare per person estimate would appear to be more reasonable than one might initially assume.

The problem of the larger sustaining areas for Early Uruk centers remains. An average of 2.16 hectares per person was estimated for both Susa and Abu Fanduweh. I would suggest that this represents agricultural production far above subsistence levels for maintenance of Central Place craft production, administration, and other functions. Early Uruk centers may have been actually or potentially self sufficient, with production for maintenance of Central Place functions carried on largely by the agricultural population of the center alone. Villagers in Khuzistan today are engaged in surplus production for the support of central place functions. Gremliza (1962:38) gives the population density for villages in the Dez area as 52 persons per square kilometer. This provides a figure of 1.92 hectares per person. This figure compares rather favorably with the 2.12 and 2.19 hectare per person estimates for the residents of Susa and Abu Fanduweh during the Early Uruk period.

Agriculturalists on the Susiana today are producing at near capacity levels, given traditional agricultural methods. The same would appear to have been true for the resident agricultural population of the Early Uruk centers in the area. Further growth of these centers would then have required increasing involvement with outlying settlements. A major component of this involvement must have been extractive. Thus if these major settlements continued to expand after Early Uruk, one would expect to find archaeological evidence of increasing center involvement in, if not control of, village economies.

The development of apparent Central Place hierarchies in the Early Uruk period can be viewed as evidence of an increase in the elaboration of decision making organizations and an increase in information processing in general. The development of administrative hierarchies should be reflected by artifactual materials used in information storage and transfer. Artifacts of this type are available for the Uruk period in Khuzistan. Minimally, evidence of two processes of developing administration are expected: first, increasing amounts of information controlled by administrative organization; and second, increasing differentiation within administrative organization.

Preliminary data on Uruk seals and seal impressions constitute one line of evidence. Various containers such as jars, bales, and baskets could be closed with fine clay into which the impression of a seal could be made. The container could not then be opened without disturbing the seal. An intact seal impression would guarantee that the clay seal on a container had not been broken (Legrain, 1921:4). The seal impression probably indicated something of the origin, content, or quality, etc., of the material within a particular container.

Individual seals at various periods were probably specific to individuals, administrative offices, or institutions. These may be called sealing agencies. The responsibility for the reliability of the information conveyed by the presence of a particular seal could then be directly related to the particular sealing agency to which the seal belonged. The seal impression functioned as a mark of authenticity (Legrain, 1921:8).

In order for seals to function as a mark of identification of individual sealing agencies, seals in contemporaneous use must have differed from one another. Further, differences should have been readily discernible. Complexity of seal design should be directly related to the number of sealing agencies. Seal designs could be simple if few seals were in use. Increase in the number of sealing agencies, and thus in the number of seals in use, would require increase in the seal design corpus at a given level of complexity. Increase in the number of sealing agencies would require an increase in seal design complexity.

The simple use of seals implies not specialized administrative organization, but rather the transfer of certain types of information. The development of complex administrative organization in the context of an economic system in which seals were previously in use could be expected to result in a proliferation of sealing agencies. A marked increase in seal design complexity could be expected with this development.

The first seals and seal impressions in Khuzistan are known from the Susiana d period. Hole, Flannery, and Neely (1969:365) report sealed jar stoppers from the upper levels of Tepe Sabz. These occur in the Bayat phase which is roughly equivalent to Susiana d on the Susiana plain (Hole, Flannery, and Neely, 1969:9).

These bead seals carried simpler linear designs, no two of which were identical in the available sample. Le Breton (1957:92) reports two circular stamp seals from Tepe Band-i-bal (KS-13) on the Susiana plain. These seals can probably be dated to Susiana d.

Stamp seals are fairly common in Susa A levels at Susa. The designs are again relatively simple geometric motifs. Geometrically stylized figures of trees, men, animals etc. occur (Le Breton, 1957:92-93). Some increases in design corpus and complexity are evident.

Although ambiguous, the data suggest that the first marked increase in seal design complexity occurred in the Early Uruk period. Stamp seals become more numerous in Uruk deposits at Susa than in the previous Susa A levels (Le Breton, 1957:101). Motifs are still linear but show considerably increased elaboration in terms of the number of design elements used in a single seal. The use of figural elements in seal designs apparently increases (Amiet, 1961:223). This increase in seal complexity can probably be dated to the Early Uruk period.

Evidence provided by seals and seal impressions thus supports conclusions suggested from examination of the locational and ceramic data. Development of Early Uruk Central Place hierarchies was probably associated with the emergence of an administered local exchange system and an overall increase in administrative information processing requirements.

A number of problems are posed, however, by the emergence of Central Place hierarchies on the western portion of the plain. Why, for example, did not a similar system appear somewhere on the eastern portion of the plain, which was occupied almost completely by small settlements during the Early Uruk period?

Two small centers are indicated in the eastern area. KS-153 is estimated at 6.00 hectares and is located in the far eastern portion of the survey area. This and the two nearby settlements, KS-173 and KS-171, probably played a quite specialized role in the economy of the plain as a whole. We will return to these settlements later.

KS-120 is also estimated at about 6.00 hectares for Early Uruk. As discussed above, the site has a massive post-Uruk overburden making size estimation difficult. The remaining settlements on the eastern portion of the plain during the Early Uruk period were all in the village-size range, as were the settlements in the area during the previous Terminal Susa A period.

There is some reason to believe that the western portion of the plain, and the Abu Fanduweh area in particular, offered greater ease of irrigation, and thus of more intensive agricultural production, than other areas of the plain. Even under an aggrading river regime, such as postulated for the Uruk period on the plain, watercourses on the northern portion of the plain would have been characterized by higher gradients than those to the south. The southern portion of the plain would thus have offered the greatest potential for the formation of natural river levees above the level of the plain in general. With rivers or streams flowing on natural levees, it would have been a very simple matter to obtain irrigation water by merely cutting into a levee and letting water either spread freely over nearby fields or directing its flow with small canals. The configuration of the Dezful anticline may have differentially funneled a greater proportion of permanent streams and seasonal runoff onto the western portion of the plain, thus affording the Susa and Abu

Fanduweh area a larger and more reliable basic water supply. These factors may in some measure account for the differential development of Central Place systems on the plain.

Irrespective of the particular causes involved, the eastern portion of the plain lacked a major settlement in Early Uruk. The presence of two Central Places in the western area indicates that the administrative capacity of these systems was spatially limited, and that the eastern plain was probably something of an administrative vacuum. If the settlement system on the plain as a whole were to expand, one would predict the emergence of a dominant settlement in the eastern area.

Several kinds of data point to significant Early Uruk political and economic developments. Given my assumptions, increase in settlement area indicates increase in population; increase in average settlement type size indicates population agglomeration; and increase in the settlement hierarchy indicates increasing functional differentiation and organizational complexity. Emergence of Central Place type settlement distribution suggests administered redistribution and control of production.

Evidence has been presented for centralization of craft production and distribution of craft items. Such distribution implies complementary inputs to the producing centers or a basic redistributive system. An earlier discussion of administrative artifacts suggested an overall increase in information processing capacity in Early Uruk. Locational data suggested the scale of surplus production extracted from agricultural residents of central places, while environmental data at least partially accounted for the differential distribution of Central Place developments.

An important question remains. Was a state level of organization present in Early Uruk on the Susiana plain? Frankly this is a question that cannot be answered with the Early Uruk data alone. It will be demonstrated in the following pages, however, that state organization was certainly operative on the plain in Middle Uruk and that the differences between these periods were quantitative rather than qualitative.

MIDDLE URUK

There was an additional expansion of settlement from Early to Middle Uruk on the Susiana. The number of settlements increased to 52 while the total occupied settlement area increased from 95 hectares in Early to 126.69 (127) hectares in Middle Uruk. The total Middle Uruk settlement represents perhaps 25,000 people.

More importantly the settlement hierarchy expanded from three to four levels with the differentiation of villages and large villages (see Fig. 19).

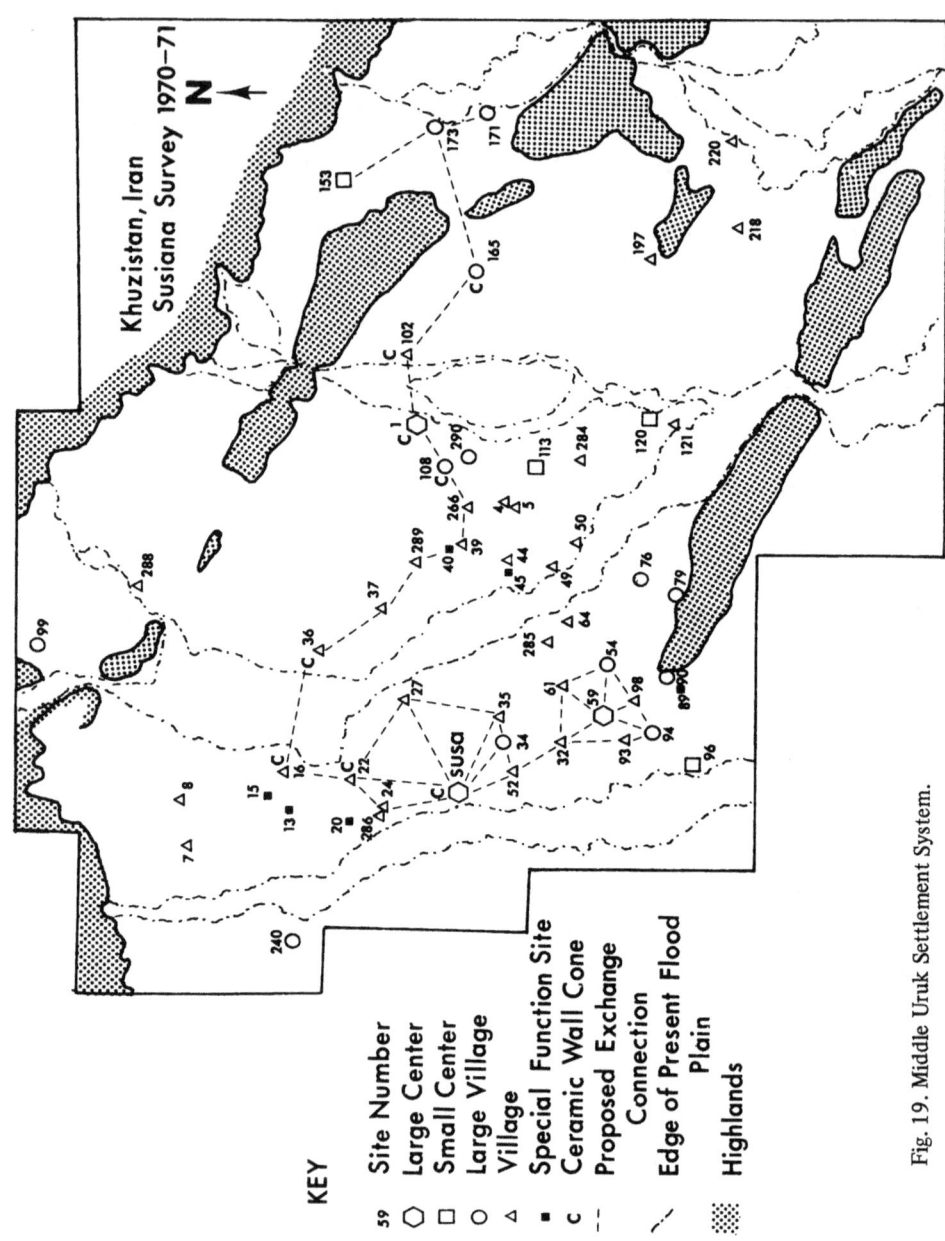

Fig. 19. Middle Uruk Settlement System.

The four-level hierarchy consisted of villages with a mean size of .94 hectares; large villages with a mean size of 2.30 hectares; small centers with a mean size of 5.31 hectares; and large centers with a mean size of 14.85 hectares.

Increase in the number and size of large centers accounted for 81 percent of the total settlement area growth (31.51 hectares). Initial Uruk settlement of Chogha Mish (KS-1) contributed an estimated 10 hectares to this figure. Susa increased from 12 to 25 hectares while Abu Fanduweh (KS-59) increased slightly from 6.92 to 9.56 (7 to 9.5) hectares. Major center growth on this scale would in itself indicate significant elaboration of Central Place functions including administrative organization.

The possible relationship between settlement area and functional size was discussed earlier in this study. The emergence of a fourth level in the settlement size hierarchy indicates an additional level of a settlement functional size hierarchy. Given our operational definition of a state, the presence of this four-level hierarchy would suggest the presence of a state level of organization.

In one sense settlements belonging to each level of this hierarchy constitute settlement types. Any typology of Middle Uruk settlements must, however, be more complex than this simple fourfold division would indicate.

Large Centers

Large Middle Uruk centers appear to have been morphologically very similar (refer to site maps for Susa, Fig. 8; Chogha Mish, Fig. 9; and Abu Fanduweh, Pl. XV). All three settlements were comprised of higher and lower areas which were apparently architecturally, as well as topographically, distinct.

Known Uruk architecture on the Acropole of Susa is fairly massive, probably indicating public buildings (Steve and Gasche, 1971) and/or minor official residences (Le Brun, 1971). Monumental architecture is present and perhaps concentrated on the high end of Chogha Mish (Delougaz, 1966:36). Extensive architectural plans of Uruk private housing have been recovered from the lower portion of the site (Delougaz and Kantor, 1969:24). Although we have no architectural plans from Abu Fanduweh, it is likely that the Middle Uruk settlement was similarly differentiated.

Early Uruk settlements of Susa and Abu Fanduweh were largely restricted to the high area of each site. The topographic differentiation of sites would seem to have been the result of Middle Uruk growth of these centers beyond the limits of the tells upon which they were originally built. The higher portions of these settlements were favored locations for monumental buildings and probably represented the locus of administration and high status residence. The lower portions of these centers accommodated an expanding population and, based on the example of Abu Fanduweh to be discussed below, were the locus of considerable Central Place craft production.

Small Centers

Small centers were a less homogeneous settlement type. Three of the four Middle Uruk small centers were probably roughly similar to one another. Middle Uruk areas of KS-96, KS-120, and KS-113 were all relatively high. KS-153, however, was morphologically and possibly functionally quite different from these settlements. The settlement was low, reaching a maximum elevation of five meters only over a small portion of the southern end of the site. Although the settlement covered over six hectares, the sherd cover on the site is very sparse, indicating an extensive low density occupation. If KS-153 represents a distinctive settlement type, it was the only example of this type in the survey area.

Villages and Large Villages

Villages and large villages were fairly distinct in terms of settlement size, although they show considerable internal variation. At least one feature crosscuts this size dimension. Ceramic cones have been collected from a number of sites in the survey area. During the Uruk and following Jemdet Nasr period these cones were used as wall decorations on elaborate or monumental buildings. A cone from the survey collections is illustrated in Plate XX. Usually various pigments were applied to the heads of cones. They were then stuck into the plaster covering building walls in a sort of geometric mosaic.

Intact cone mosaics are known primarily from Warka, where they are restricted to major temples or other public buildings. Adams and Nissen (1972:211) report cones on the surface of 18 sites in the Warka area. Many of these sites were classified as small villages. They conclude that cone mosaics were used to decorate private houses as well as temples or other public buildings.

Wall cones are abundant at Susa (Le Brun, 1971: Fig. 69; Steve and Gasche, 1971: Pl. 89) and Chogha Mish (Delougaz and Kantor, 1971, personal communication). They are not reported from Abu Fanduweh, but are almost certainly present. Cones are also known from a number of small settlements, as was the case in the Warka area. Cones were found at four sites during the 1970-71 survey. We have one cone each from the following sites: KS-16, KS-108 and KS-102. Ten cones were collected during a more intensive preexcavation survey of Tepe Sharafabad. Harvey Weiss of the University of Pennsylvania (personal communication) reports one cone from KS-165. The collections of the French Mission at Susa contain one cone from KS-22.

ANALYSIS OF THE SETTLEMENT PATTERNS

Of the six small sites from which cones have been collected, four are classified as villages (KS-16, KS-22, KS-36, and KS-102), and two are classified as large villages (KS-108 and KS-165). We hoped that excavation at KS-36 would reveal the architectural context of the cones at this site. Unfortunately the appropriate Middle Uruk levels had been largely destroyed.

The presence of cones on small sites indicates a level of architectural elaboration not expected for villages. They probably indicate the presence of a public building(s), although on a very small scale. Further these buildings were probably administrative outposts of large centers. This last proposition will be tested below after a presentation of the Middle Uruk settlement pattern. Let us assume that cones do indicate the presence of administrative specialists on the sites where they occur.

The settlement typology becomes more complex with the addition of rural administrators. Village and large village types are divided into groups with and without evidence of the presence of administrators. KS-284 adds additional complexity to the picture of villages. As will be discussed below, it was the site of a lithic workshop. This workshop was active during Early and/or Middle Uruk and indicates village-level productive specialization. To recapitulate, the proposed settlement typology includes: large centers, small centers, specialized small centers, unspecialized large villages, administratively specialized large villages, unspecialized villages, and administratively specialized villages. The three dimensions of variability considered are: settlement size hierarchy, functional specialization, and settlement administration. The relationship of these dimensions is illustrated in Figure 20.

The site typology, as distinct from the settlement typology, contains at least one additional type, the special functional site. Several Uruk sites were either found by the survey or identified in previous reports, where the Uruk ceramic material was either too specialized, or too spatially restricted to indicate the presence of a settlement. For example, only bevel rim bowls were found on two sites, KS-40 and KS-89. KS-40 has a good surface exposure and was collected under good conditions. An hour was spent on this small site (.92 hectares) and bevel rim bowls were the only Uruk ceramic type found. Elizabeth Carter of the University of Chicago collected two bevel rim bowl rims from KS-89 (Carter, 1971, personal communication). The site was revisited, mapped, and intensively collected during the 1970-71 survey. No additional Uruk material was found. It has been leveled since our survey. The presence of only bevel rim bowls on these sites must represent some special and intermittent activity.

The second type of special functional site is characterized by a very restricted spatial distribution of a variety of Uruk ceramic types. Sites in this category include: KS-13, KS-15, KS-20, and KS-45. De Mecquenem (1943) illustrates a typical droop spout from the French excavations at Tepe

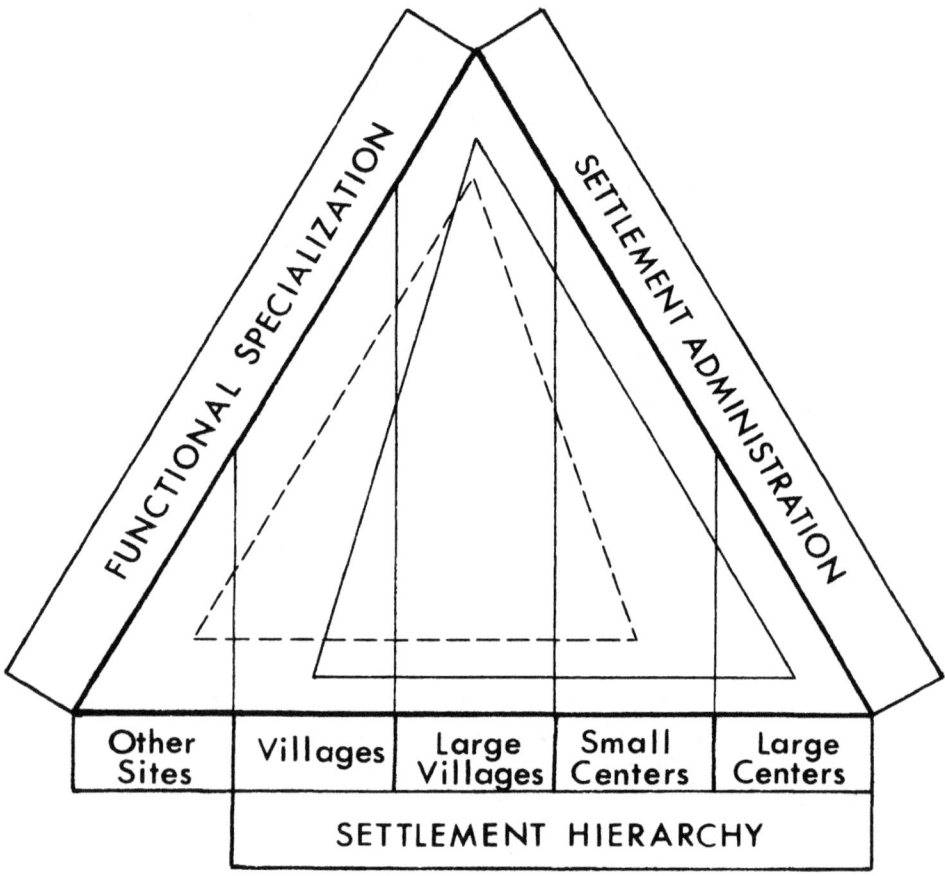

Fig. 20. Dimensions of the Middle Uruk Site Typology.

Band-i-bal (KS-13). The site was visited during the survey and no additional Uruk material could be found. A small number of Uruk sherds were collected from KS-15 during the survey. They were, however, concentrated in an area of about .02 hectares. The site has a heavy overburden of later materials which may mask a wider distribution of Uruk ceramics. The present distribution is too small for the site to be reasonably called a village.

Dollfus (personal communication) recovered a small amount of Uruk pottery from the surface of KS-20, Tepe Jaffarabad. Typical Middle Uruk types collected included bevel rim bowl rims, reserve slip, cross hatch bands, and droop spouts. Excavations on the site have revealed no further Uruk material. The survey collection from KS-45 similarly contains a number of Middle Uruk types (See Appendix I). The material was concentrated in an

ANALYSIS OF THE SETTLEMENT PATTERNS

area of about .08 hectares. Several revisits to the site failed to reveal a wider distribution of material. Again this distribution is too small to represent a village. The activities represented by this group of sites are unknown. Ephemeral single house occupations or burials are possibilities.

Though the cultural significance of both types of special function sites is unknown, they do provide some reassurance about the reliability of the survey data. Detection of sites of this type suggests that very few actual settlements were missed. These non-settlement sites will be excluded from the remainder of this discussion of the Middle Uruk settlement system.

The emergence of the large center was emphasized as an important Early Uruk development. Emergence of this type was associated with centralization of craft production in major settlement workshops. The evidence for these workshops is presented in the following pages.

Workshops

Evidence of Uruk ceramic workshops is known from three sites in the survey area. Ceramic kilns are mentioned without further comment from Middle Uruk levels of the Acropole of Susa (de Mecquenem, 1938:140). Middle and probably Late Uruk kilns have been excavated at Chogha Mish (Kantor, 1972, personal communication). Surface evidence of a Uruk ceramic workshop was collected on the 1970-71 survey from Abu Fanduweh.

Workshop remains were found on the surface, slightly off the northern edge of KS-59 (see Pl. XV for a more precise location). The remains of eight ovens were located. Each contained small sherds of overfired Uruk pottery and small pieces of slag. Nearby concentrations of slag and similarly overfired sherds are identified as waster dumps. A plan of these features is presented in Figure 21. Collections were made from the two larger dumps, (a) and (b).

The collection from dump (a) contains 52 standard bevel rim bowl rims; 2 strap handle fragments; 1 heavy round rim; 1 spout fragment; 1 flared round rim; 8 grit temper body sherds; and 7 pieces of vitrified clay or slag. The collection from dump (b) contains 34 standard bevel rim bowl rims; 1 spout fragment; 1 flat base; 5 wheel turned body sherds; and 5 pieces of slag.

The kilns and associated dumps may be securely dated to Middle Uruk. It is not known if all kilns and dumps were in use simultaneously. A few preliminary observations are in order. The kiln area is apparently located just outside the occupied area of the settlement. Both bevel rim bowls and standard ceramic types were fired in these kilns although their pre-firing fabrication involved quite different techniques. The distribution of kilns and waster dumps suggests the possibility of two work teams within the same workshop. This is a possible complicating factor in the study of spatial variability of ceramics.

108   LOCAL EXCHANGE AND EARLY STATE DEVELOPMENT

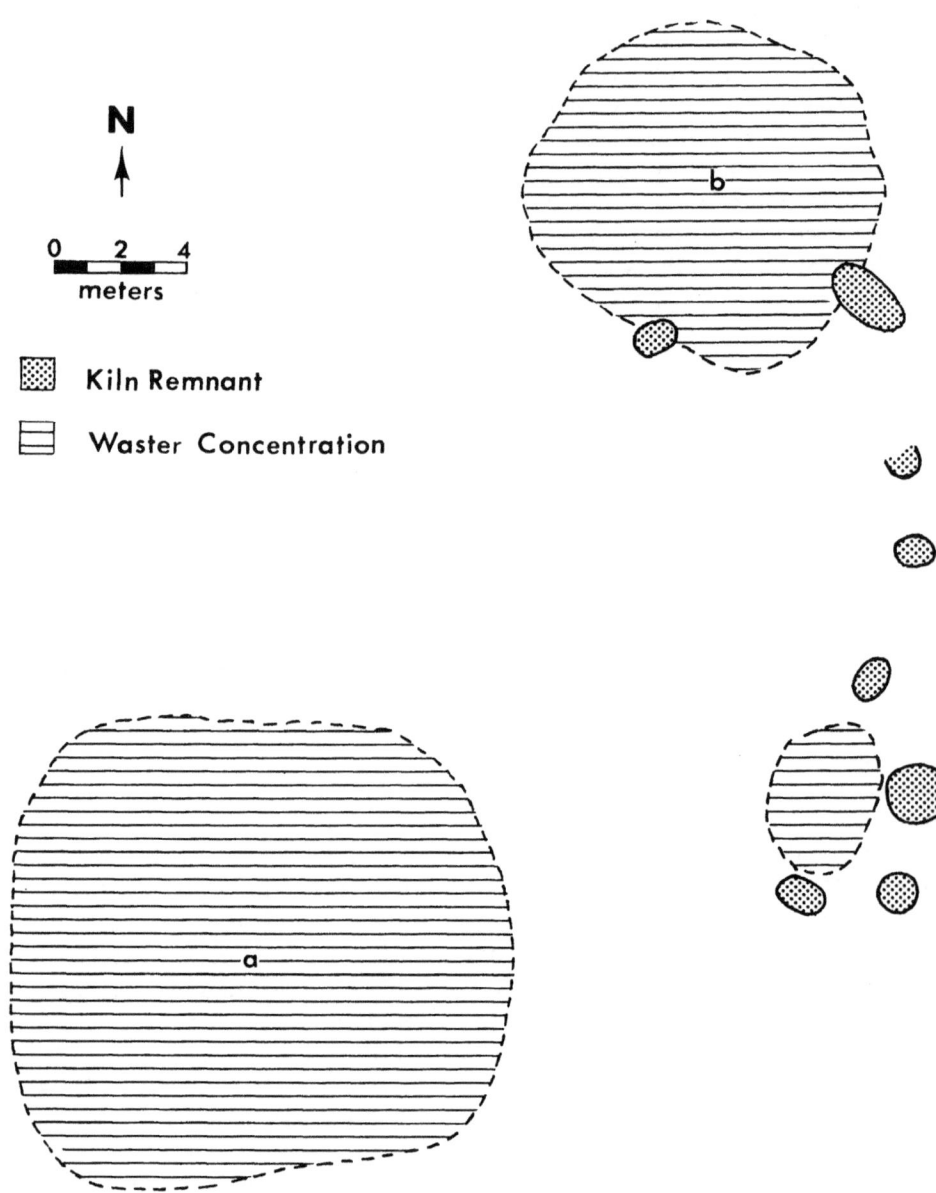

Fig. 21. Surface Evidence of an Uruk Ceramic Workshop (Abu Fanduweh – KS-59): Pace Ma

As mentioned above, there is no clear evidence for Uruk ceramic production on the Susiana plain at sites other than Susa, Chogha Mish, and Abu Fanduweh. Excavations at Tepe Sharafabad (KS-36) revealed a few pieces of slag, though no wasters. Some limited ceramic production probably did occur on smaller settlements. The bulk of Uruk pottery would appear, however, to have been produced in large centers as one of a large number of Central Place functions.

There is also some available evidence of Uruk lithic workshops. De Morgan encountered a large amount of lithic material in Middle Uruk deposits of Gallery D on the Acropole of Susa. He felt that the amount of material encountered was sufficient to postulate the presence of a workshop in the area (de Morgan, 1900:84-85). The amount of lithic material on Chogha Mish suggests that lithic workshops were present on the site, although one has yet to be excavated (James Phillips, 1971, personal communication). One lithic workshop was located by the survey.

The evidence for this workshop comes from KS-284 located on the eastern side of the plain roughly half way between Chogha Mish and KS-120. The site is small (.84 hectares) and otherwise undistinguished, except for a remarkable surface concentration of lithic material. The surface of most sites in the area will yield one or two blade cores and several blades. The following lithic materials were collected from KS-284: 35 prepared blade cores (see Pl. IX); 3 core fragments; 4 platform preparation flakes; 3 decortation flakes; 65 blades and blade fragments; 2 flakes with heat spalling; 2 naturally backed utilized blades; 1 drill on a blade; and 2 hammer stones.

The blade cores are particularly interesting in that most were fully prepared but unused. Apparently this workshop specialized in the preparation of blade cores to be distributed to other settlements where the actual blades were struck off. There is some question about the date of this material. The site had a small Terminal Susa A occupation. Both Early and Middle Uruk ceramic materials are present. The Early Uruk material dominates the collection, although a significant amount of Middle Uruk material is present. The lithic material can be securely called Uruk. Whether it is Early Uruk, Middle Uruk, or both cannot be said.

Direct evidence of Uruk workshops is thus very scanty indeed. Detailed study of such workshops directed at analysis of workshop organization, variability of craft items produced, differential raw material sources, areas of item distribution, and so on, would be a valuable part of future research. Let us now proceed to a consideration of locational aspects of the Middle Uruk settlement of the Susiana plain.

The Location of Chogha Mish (KS-1)

In Middle Uruk a newly established center appears on the eastern portion of the plain. At first glance, the location of Chogha Mish would appear to be something of a locational anomaly. The site appeared as a large center in Middle Uruk and, as will be shown below, functioned as the Central Place of the eastern portion of the plain. Its location, however, was not very central.

A partial resolution of this problem may lie in agricultural sustaining area requirements of a major settlement. Examination of the Early Uruk settlement pattern led to the proposition that a large center required a minimum of about two hectares of immediate agricultural sustaining area per settlement resident.

The areal size of Chogha Mish is estimated at 10 hectares in Middle Uruk. Application of the 200 person per hectare estimate results in a possible settlement population of 2,000 persons. The two hectare subsistence area per person estimate results in a total sustaining area requirement of 4,000 hectares. A circular area of 4,000 hectares would have a radius of 3.57 kilometers.

The Early Uruk settlement of the eastern portion of the plain was largely concentrated in a relatively small area. A large center would be expected to have appeared somewhere in or near this area for reasons of transport and administrative efficiency.

One might also expect that one of the Early Uruk settlements in the area would have developed into a large center by virtue of its strategic location. Given these assumptions the most probable Early Uruk candidates for growth were KS-4 and KS-6, because of their central location in the area of high density settlement (see the Early Uruk settlement map, Fig. 12). Other possible sites in this "core" area included: KS-39, KS-44, KS-50, KS-112, KS-113, KS-266, KS-284, KS-289, and KS-290. The remaining settlements in the area were probably too far removed from the area of high density occupation to be considered.

I would suggest that none of the sites listed above developed into a major center for at least one critical reason: none had access to a potential sustaining area sufficiently large to support the population and central functions of a large center. Remember that all of these Early Uruk sites were classified as villages, of which none appeared to be dominant over another.

The estimated radius of the sustaining area of Middle Uruk Chogha Mish is 3.57 kilometers, calculated on a two hectare per person basis. Table 21 presents first nearest neighbor distances for the Early Uruk settlements cited above as potential Middle Uruk centers. None of the distances listed in this table is equal to or greater than the estimated 3.57 kilometer requirement. Only KS-44 and KS-284 approach this requirement. It could be argued that both of these settlements were located too close to the Susa-Abu Fanduweh area to be administratively efficient.

ANALYSIS OF THE SETTLEMENT PATTERNS

TABLE 21
FIRST ORDER NEAREST NEIGHBOR DISTANCES FOR
POTENTIAL MIDDLE URUK LARGE CENTERS

Settlement	First Nearest Neighbor	Distance (kms)
KS-4	KS-6	1.36
KS-6	KS-4	1.36
KS-39	KS-289	2.19
KS-289	KS-39	2.19
KS-44	KS-49	3.47
KS-49	KS-50	2.59
KS-50	KS-49	2.59
KS-108	KS-290	1.68
KS-290	KS-108	1.68
KS-112	KS-4	2.05
KS-113	KS-6	2.47
KS-266	KS-112	2.18
KS-284	KS-113	3.35

The large center which did appear in the eastern area was immediate-adjacent to the area of major settlement concentration. It was also sufficiently removed from this concentration to allow a sustaining area large enough for development of the settlement. The estimated sustaining area radius of Chogha Mish was 3.57 kilometers. The settlement closest to Chogha Mish in Middle Uruk was KS-108 at a distance of 3.80 kilometers. The difference between these estimates is 230 meters, which can be accounted for as lying within the sustaining area of KS-108.

The sustaining area model developed can precisely account for the apparent outlying location of Chogha Mish. It would also imply that the site was intentionally founded as an administrative center. The development of such a center was predicted from analysis of the Early Uruk settlement system. It will become clear in the following pages that Chogha Mish in fact became the administrative center of the eastern portion of the Susiana plain.

The Middle Uruk Local Exchange System

Analysis of the Early Uruk settlement pattern on the Susiana produced two major predictions about subsequent developments, assuming continued growth of the settlement system. The emergence of a large center on the eastern portion of the plain was predicted. This prediction has been confirmed.

The second prediction stated that continued growth of Early Uruk large centers would require increasing large center involvement with, and control of, rural settlements. Large centers continued to grow in Middle Uruk, thus increasing control of outlying settlements should also be detectable.

The hypothesis can be indirectly tested through examination of the Middle Uruk local exchange system. Early Uruk data indicated a flow of craft items from large center workshops to outlying settlements. This must have been complemented by a flow of rural products and probably labor into the large centers.

It is not possible at present to document flow of materials or labor from villages up the settlement and administrative hierarchy to centers. I would argue however that demonstration of increasing administrative control of movement of materials from centers down the settlement hierarchy to villages would imply increasing administered movement of material in the other direction. Demonstration of such increasing control of the local exchange system would then constitute indirect demonstration of increasing control of rural production.

The proposed Middle Uruk settlement system is illustrated in Figure 19. Some expansion into the northwest and southeast corners of the plain is evident. Our primary interest here is focused on developments in the central or core area.

The western portion of the plain exhibited few changes in settlement location. The Susa system remained locationally unchanged. An additional settlement (KS-98) was added to the Abu Fanduweh system. The location of this new settlement was completely consistent with the model of the Abu Fanduweh area as a Central Place system. The site appeared 3.68 kilometers from Abu Fanduweh at a location virtually equidistant between KS-54 and KS-94. The distances from KS-98 to KS-54 and KS-94 were 3.26 and 3.20 kilometers respectively. The distance between KS-54 and KS-94 was 6.46 kilometers. This was the largest adjacent village-to-village distance in the Early Uruk system. Addition of KS-98 to the Middle Uruk system reduced the variance of center-to-village distance from 2.37 to 1.90 kilometers indicating increased coherence of the system. Mean center-to-village distance remained nearly unchanged: 3.78 kilometers in Early Uruk and 3.80 kilometers in Middle Uruk. The major locational change on the plain was the emergence of Chogha Mish discussed above.

The spatial distribution of small settlements having ceramic cones among their surface material is of major importance. It was suggested above that these settlements functioned as small administrative centers for the mediation of local exchange and control of rural production.

The location of these settlements supports this proposition. They were distributed in a roughly linear fashion from Susa in the west to Chogha Mish in the east, and KS-165 in the far eastern portion of the area. Their distribution suggests a major exchange route between Susa and Chogha Mish.

ANALYSIS OF THE SETTLEMENT PATTERNS   113

Similar sites have not been identified on the southern portion of the plain. Recall that in Early Uruk, Abu Fanduweh appeared to be the center of major influence in the eastern area. If the small sites with cones functioned as suggested, their distribution may indicate a Middle Uruk attenuation of contact or influence between Abu Fanduweh and the eastern area.

The small increase in the size of Middle Uruk Abu Fanduweh, when contrasted to the considerable expansion of Susa and the foundation of Chogha Mish, may indicate that major Central Place functions, including administrative decision making, were concentrated in these latter two centers. In this event Abu Fanduweh would probably have become a major subsidiary administrative center for Susa.

In the following pages ceramic evidence for local exchange will be examined in an attempt to test some of the hypotheses presented above. Fortunately the Middle Uruk ceramic data is far superior to that for the other periods discussed in this study.

Ceramic Evidence of Local Exchange

Cross Hatch Bands

Uruk incised cross hatch bands on jar shoulders appear as early as Early Uruk and continue through Late Uruk. In the seriation of ceramic types collected during the 1970-71 survey, cross hatch bands appear in the Middle Uruk ceramic assemblage. Cross hatch triangles, with or without bands, are primarily associated with Late Uruk material.

Cross hatching as a purely stylistic phenomenon provides an unusual opportunity to utilize spatial variability in the study of local exchange. First, however, temporal variability must be eliminated from the sample.

A description and list of cross hatch band measurements are provided in Appendix III. Sherds collected on the survey and an excavated sample from Chogha Mish are included in the analysis.[4]

The distributions of measurements on two attributes, horizontal line thickness and diagonal intersection angle, are at least bimodal (see Fig. 22). A scatter plot of these two variables is presented in Figure 23. Circles designate sherds collected from sites west of the Dez river; squares indicate sherds collected from sites east of the river; and triangles indicate the plot position of sherds from the sample excavated at Chogha Mish. Modal divisions on horizontal line thickness and diagonal intersection angle are indicated on the plot, dividing the sample into four sub-groups.

The letter "t" located next to several plot symbols indicates the association of these bands with cross hatch triangles. As discussed above, such triangles are typical of Late Uruk assemblages. Inspection of the plot reveals

---

[4]The sherds from Chogha Mish were measured with the kind permission of Dr. Helene Kantor of the Oriental Institute of the University of Chicago.

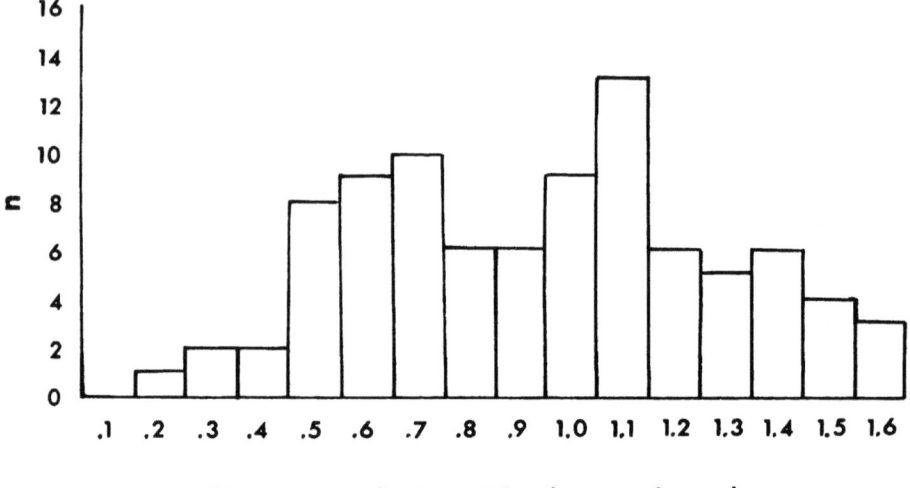

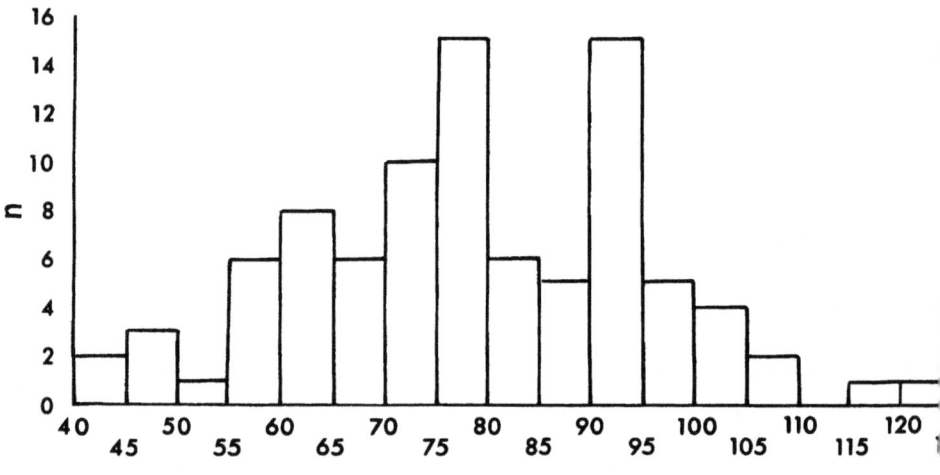

Fig. 22. Uruk Cross Hatch Bands — Histograms.

ANALYSIS OF THE SETTLEMENT PATTERNS

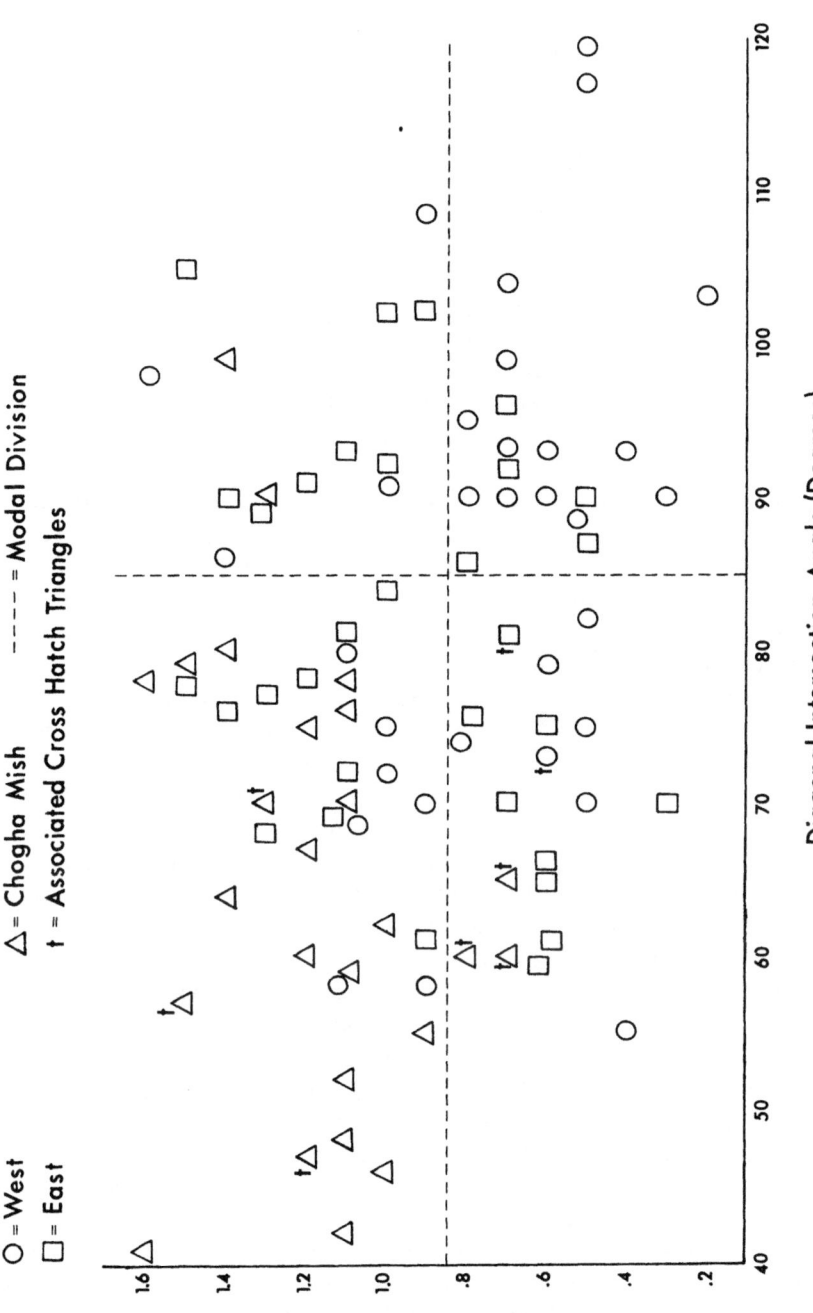

Fig. 23. Uruk Cross Hatch Bands – Scatter Plot.

that these known late sherds all fall to the left of the modal division on diagonal intersection angle. This indicates that the division is chronologically significant.

Two groups of cross hatch bands are defined. The first, presumably earlier, group is characterized by a high diagonal intersection angle having a modal value of 92 degrees. The second, presumably later, group, is characterized by a low intersection angle having a modal value of 77 degrees. It is unlikely that the 15 degree difference between these modes is due to measurement error.

The remaining modal division on horizontal line thickness may be attributed to workshop variability. Horizontal line thickness is greater for sherds from sites east of the Dez, than for sherds from sites west of the Dez. Table 22 presents student's t statistics on mean horizontal line width between eastern and western areas for all cross hatch bands, early bands, and late bands.

Table 23 is a chi square table presenting the distribution of early and late bands by area. The resulting chi square of 18.97 is significant at greater than .001. The proposed differential distribution of early and late cross hatch bands by workshop type and area is confirmed by both student's t and chi square tests.

The chronological position of the two temporally distinct groups of cross hatch bands defined above is somewhat vague. Early bands occur on the following sites: Susa, Chogha Mish, KS-7, KS-16, KS-22, KS-24, KS-32, KS-34, KS-49, KS-54, KS-59, KS-61, KS-96, KS-108, KS-113, KS-165, KS-171, KS-173, and KS-197. As discussed above, cross hatch bands appear in the Middle Uruk assemblage in the seriation of ceramic types in the survey collection. All sites on which early bands were found have Middle Uruk occupations. Further, Middle Uruk was the only period considered here during which all of these sites were simultaneously occupied. Early cross hatch bands are then a basically Middle Uruk type.

Late cross hatch bands pose a more difficult chronological problem. Examples were found on the following sites: Susa, KS-1, KS-7, KS-32, KS-34, KS-52, KS-59, KS-76, KS-96, KS-108, KS-113, KS-153, KS-171, KS-173, and KS-197. The relative chronological positions of early and late bands are defined by the association of some examples of late bands with cross hatch triangles, a known late type. Of the above mentioned sites, however, only Susa, KS-1, KS-32, KS-34, KS-59, KS-96, KS-108, KS-113, and KS-171 are known to have Late Uruk occupations.

It would appear then that the chronological distribution of "late" cross hatch bands cross-cuts the basic survey chronology, covering the latter portion of Middle and the whole of Late Uruk. This fortunate circumstance will allow some examination of the local exchange system in the Middle-Late Uruk transition.

TABLE 22
CROSS HATCH BANDS: STUDENT'S t TESTS

	Mean	t	df	p	at	adf	p	Variable
All Bands								
East	1.0431	4.283	88	0.000	4.301	66.752	0.000	Horizontal Line
West	.7469							Thickness (mm)
Early Bands								
East	1.0188	2.618	32	0.013	2.633	33.985	0.013	Horizontal Line
West	.7167							Thickness (mm)
Late Bands								
East	1.0524	2.834	54	0.006	3.137	29.025	0.004	Horizontal Line
West	.7857							Thickness (mm)

TABLE 23
CROSS HATCH BANDS: CHI SQUARE ON TYPE AND AREA

	Eastern Area	Western Area	Totals
Late Heavy Line	31	6	37
Late Fine Line	12	7	19
Early Heavy Line	11	4	15
Early Fine Line	5	14	19
Totals	59	31	90

Calculation of chi square:

Observed Frequency	Expected Frequency	(Ob.-Ex.)^2/Ex.		
31	24.26	1.87		
12	12.46	.02	chi square	= 18.97
11	9.83	.14		
5	12.46	4.47	df	= 3.00
6	12.74	3.67		
7	6.54	.03	p	= .001-
4	5.17	.26		.0001
14	6.54	8.51		

Figure 24 presents the spatial distribution of early bands among the Middle Uruk settlements in the survey area. In this illustration the two workshop varieties defined above are distinguished and exchange connections suggested by this distribution are indicated. These connections will be utilized with others suggested by the distribution of additional ceramic types to sketch the basic outline of the Middle Uruk local exchange system.

Strap Handles

The available ceramic chronology poses a major problem for the use of strap handles in the study of local exchange. These handles are known to occur as early as Susa A and throughout the Uruk sequence. Little is known about their stylistic development. The problem is then in differentiating synchronic from diachronic differences between possible types or styles. This problem will be dealt with below as each of two proposed handle types is presented.

All available handles were measured in the field. A description and list of handle measurements is presented in Appendix III. Two broad categories of strap handles are proposed: wide straps and other straps.

Wide strap handles are initially defined by bimodality in the distribution of width for 149 handles in the survey collections (see Fig. 25). All handles have a width range of 1.83 cm to 6.31 cm. The proposed wide group ranges from 4.14 to 6.31 cm.

This division is supported by a significant student's t statistic on cross section between these two groups (see Table 24). The cross sectional index was computed by division of the mean of two edge thickness measurements by a center or groove thickness measurement. Wide strap handles either lack or have a less pronounced central groove than do other strap handles.

Strap handles in general are characteristic of Middle Uruk assemblages as defined by the seriation of ceramic types from the surface collections. Wide strap handles appear to be restricted to Middle Uruk. They do not occur on sites or site areas with exclusively Early or Late Uruk occupations. The six examples from KS-108 were collected from areas C and F which appear to be relatively pure Middle Uruk areas.

TABLE 24
WIDE STRAP HANDLES VS. OTHER STRAP HANDLES:
STUDENT'S t TEST

	Mean	t	df	p	at	adf	p	Variable
Wide Handles	1.145	3.477	147	0.001	3.934	115.623	0.000	Cross Section
Other Handles	1.035							Index

ANALYSIS OF THE SETTLEMENT PATTERNS

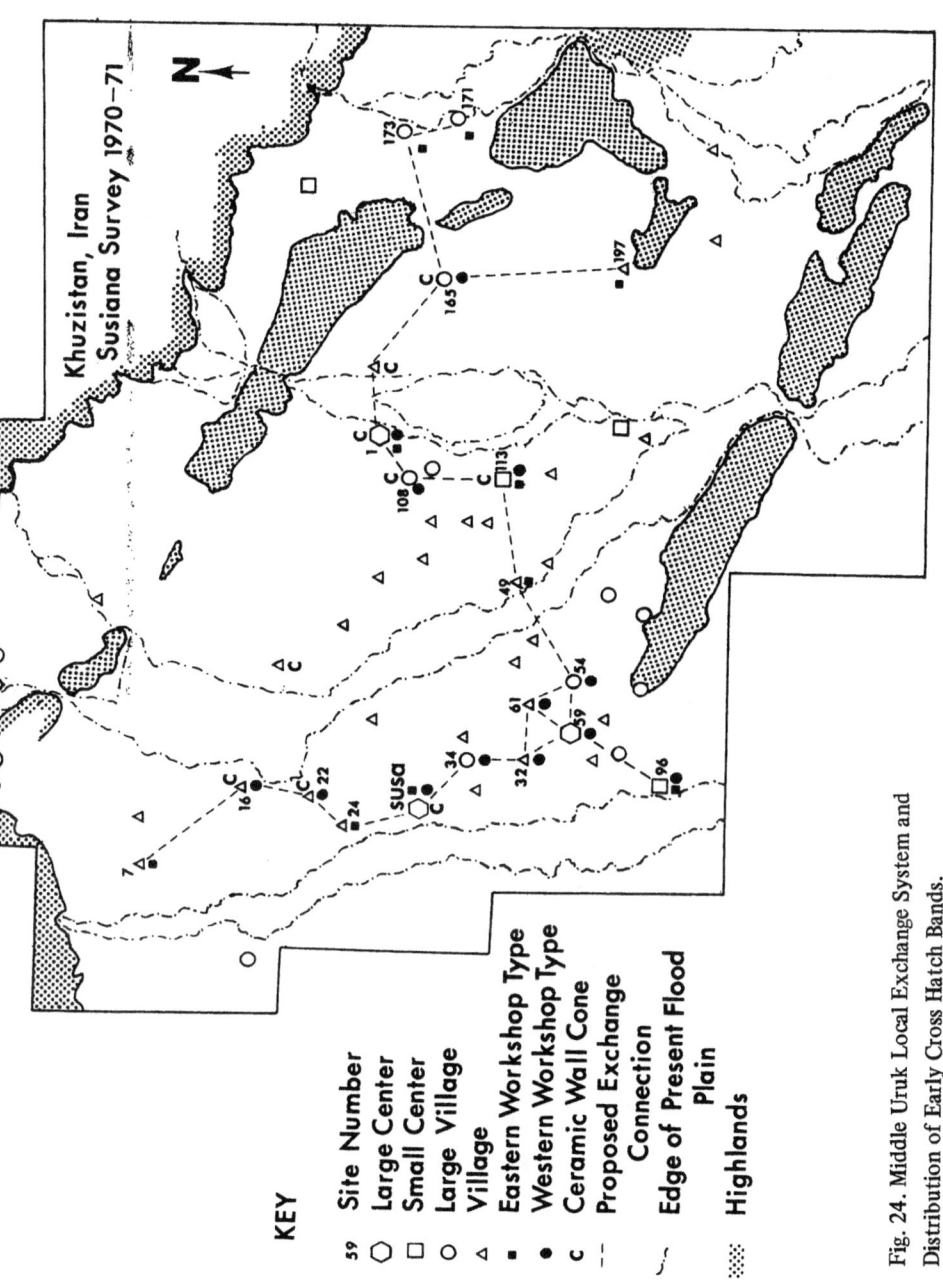

Fig. 24. Middle Uruk Local Exchange System and Distribution of Early Cross Hatch Bands.

120 LOCAL EXCHANGE AND EARLY STATE DEVELOPMENT

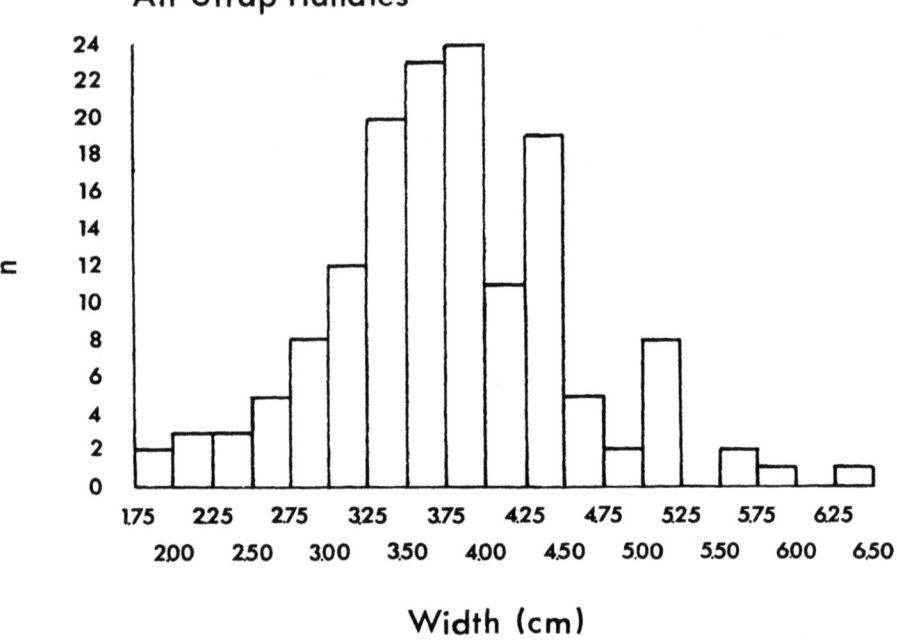

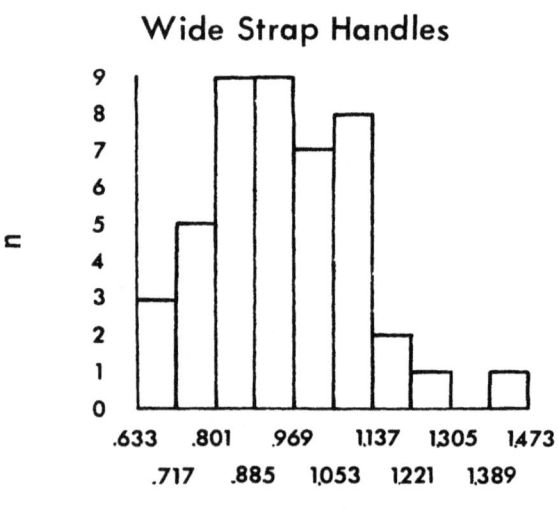

Fig. 25. Uruk Strap Handles — Histograms.

As in the case of cross hatch bands, there appears to be significant spatial variability in the distribution of wide strap handles. A histogram of handle average thickness (Fig. 25) suggests a modal division at about 1.01 cm. (Average thickness is equal to the mean of the three thickness measurements taken on each handle.)

A student's t test indicates that the 25 wide strap handles from sites east of the present course of the Dez river are significantly thicker than the 20 handles from the area west of the river (see Table 25).

TABLE 25
WIDE STRAP HANDLES: STUDENT'S t TEST

	Mean	t	df	p	at	adf	p	Variable
Western Area	.8846	-2.491	43	0.017	-2.593	44.020	0.013	Average Thickness (cm)
Eastern Area	1.0014							

A chi square statistic between area and thickness also indicates that thin, wide strap handles are primarily associated with western sites while thick, wide strap handles are primarily associated with sites in the eastern area. (See Table 26).

TABLE 26
WIDE STRAP HANDLES: CHI SQUARE ON TYPE AND AREA

	Western Area	Eastern Area	Totals
Thin Handles	17	13	30
Thick Handles	3	12	15
Totals	20	25	45

Calculation of chi square:

Observed	Expected	(Ob.-Ex.)^2/Ex.		
17	13.33	1.01	chi square	= 5.46
13	16.67	.81	df	= 1
3	6.67	2.02	p	= .02-.01
12	8.33	1.62		

The spatial distribution of the two types of wide strap handles defined above is illustrated in Figure 26. Possible local exchange connections based on these data are indicated.

122   LOCAL EXCHANGE AND EARLY STATE DEVELOPMENT

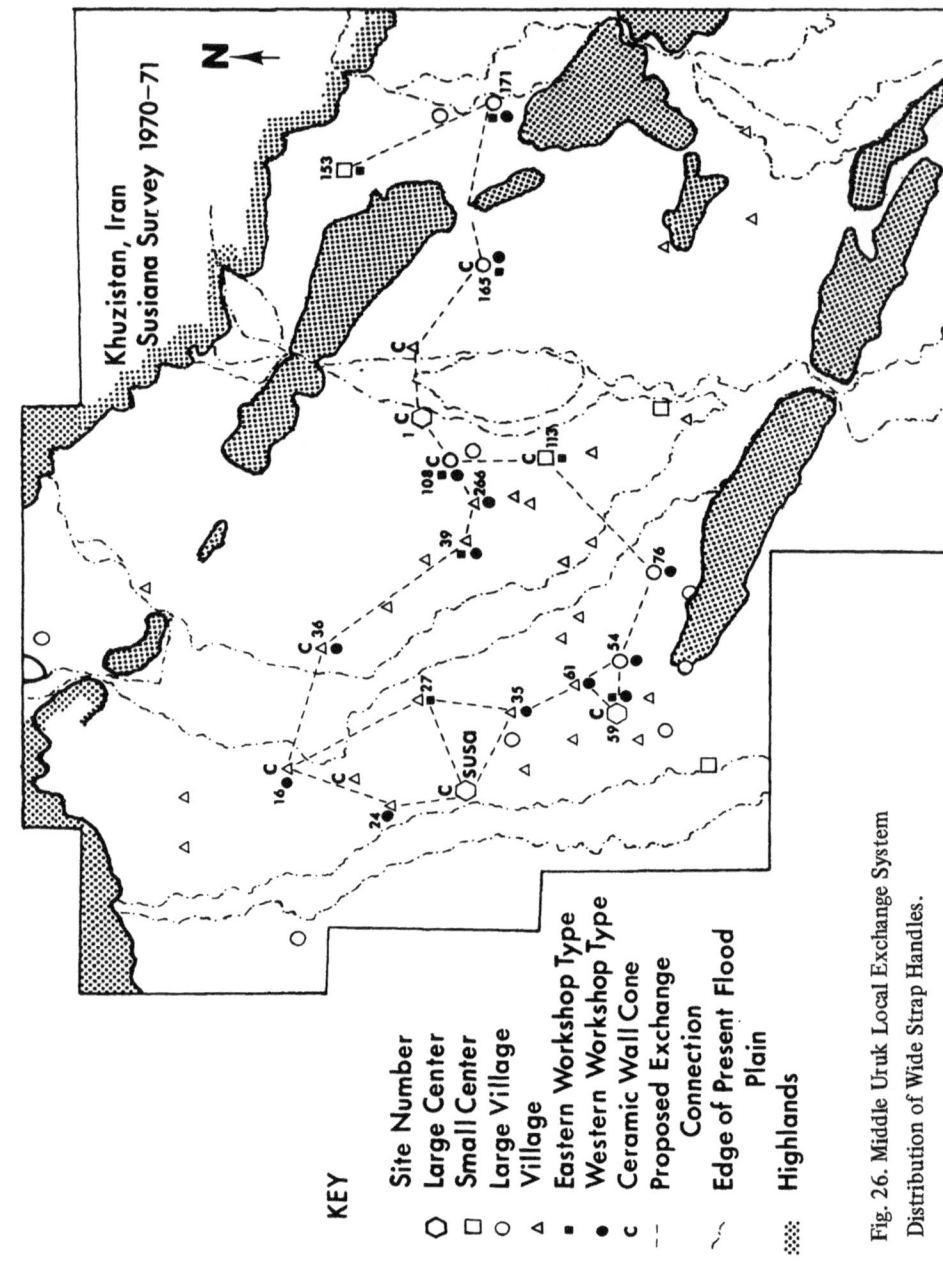

Fig. 26. Middle Uruk Local Exchange System Distribution of Wide Strap Handles.

ANALYSIS OF THE SETTLEMENT PATTERNS

The proposed exchange connections have several interesting features. The close association between the known distribution of wide strap handles and that of ceramic wall cones is particularly important. Sites with these cones were predicted above to have functioned as low level administrative centers for the mediation of local exchange.

If sites with cones performed this function, they should be associated with exchange items. Vessels having wide strap handles have been demonstrated to be an exchange item produced in at least two workshops. Their association with cone sites would then support the proposed administrative interpretation of these settlements. A Yates' corrected chi square between presence-absence of wide strap handles and ceramic cones is significant at the .05 level (see Table 27). The hypothesis that cone sites were administrative centers is supported.

TABLE 27
WIDE STRAP HANDLES AND CERAMIC WALL CONES:
YATES' CORRECTED CHI SQUARE

	Cones Present	Cones Absent	Totals
Wide Strap Handles Present	5	11	16
Wide Strap Handles Absent	2	37	39
Totals	7	48	55

Calculation of chi square:

Observed	Observed Corrected	Expected	$(Ob._c - Ex.)^2 / Ex.$
5	4.5	2.04	2.97
11	11.5	13.96	1.22
2	2.5	4.96	.43
37	36.5	34.04	.18

chi square = 4.50   df = 1   p = .05-.02

Other Strap Handles

Although it was possible to define wide strap handles as a ceramic type associated with Middle Uruk assemblages, the remaining 104 strap handles from the surface collections could not be divided into temporally restricted

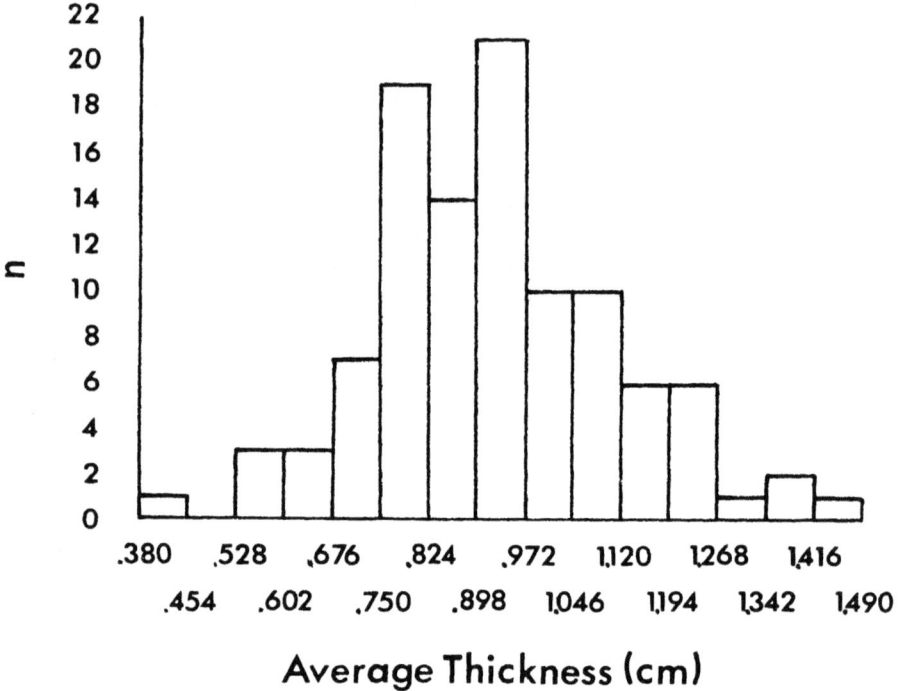

Fig. 27. Uruk Mid Width Strap Handles – Histogram.

types. This material was analyzed as a single unit, recognizing that it probably contained significant chronological variability.

Within this residual category, all variables are essentially unimodally distributed with the exception of average thickness (see Fig. 27). Average thickness appears to be bimodally distributed, with a modal break at about .86 cm. The sample was divided on this value into thin and thick categories. Student's t statistics on means of handle width and cross section between these thickness categories are both significant (see Table 28). The analysis

TABLE 28
MID WIDTH STRAP HANDLES: STUDENT'S t TESTS

	Mean	t	df	p	at	adf	p	Variable
Thin Handles	3.129	-4.248	102	0.000	-3.837	59.378	0.000	Width (cm)
Thick Handles	3.531							
Thin Handles	1.098	-2.095	102	0.038	-2.270	103.728	0.025	Cross Section
Thick Handles	1.773							Index

includes 42 thin and 62 thick handles. The results of this analysis support division of the handle sample on average thickness. Thick handles tend to be wider and to have a more pronounced cross section than do thin handles.

Figure 28 presents a three dimensional plot of handle width against cross section for thin and thick types. While thin and thick handles are generally mixed in the plot, two peripheral clusters are indicated. One cluster contains all thin handles, while the other contains all thick handles. As would be predicted from the results of the t tests, handles in the thin cluster are narrower and have a less pronounced cross section than do the handles of the thick cluster. These clusters would seem to represent the tails of two overlapping distributions. This may indicate handle production in two workshops.

Site numbers next to the plot points of these clusters indicate the location where each sherd was collected. All handles in the thick cluster were collected from sites west of the present course of the Dez. Of the nine handles in the thin cluster, three are from sites west of the Dez, while the remaining six handles are from sites east of the Dez.

This distribution would seem to indicate that again at least two workshops were involved in the production of strap handled vessels. One or more workshops, apparently east of the Dez, produced handles that were in general thinner, narrower, and less pronounced in cross section than the handles produced by at least one workshop west of the Dez. While the difference in means of width and average thickness is not significant for handles collected from sites in the western, as opposed to the eastern, area of the plain, the difference in mean cross sectional index is significant (see Table 29). The sample consists of 55 handles collected from sites in the western area, and 49 handles collected from sites in the eastern area.

TABLE 29
MID WIDTH STRAP HANDLES, PARTIONED BY AREA
COLLECTED: STUDENT'S t TEST

	Mean	t	df	p	at	adf	p	Variable
Western Area	1.182	2.091	102	0.039	2.160	85.35	0.034	Cross Section
Eastern Area	1.104							Index

Due to the chronological problems discussed above, great confidence cannot be placed in the results of this analysis. It is possible that the differences demonstrated are the result of diachronic rather than synchronic variation. At the present time there is no way to evaluate this possibility. Differential distribution of the types suggested by general geographic area does however suggest that spatial differences are a major component of the variability observed in these ceramics.

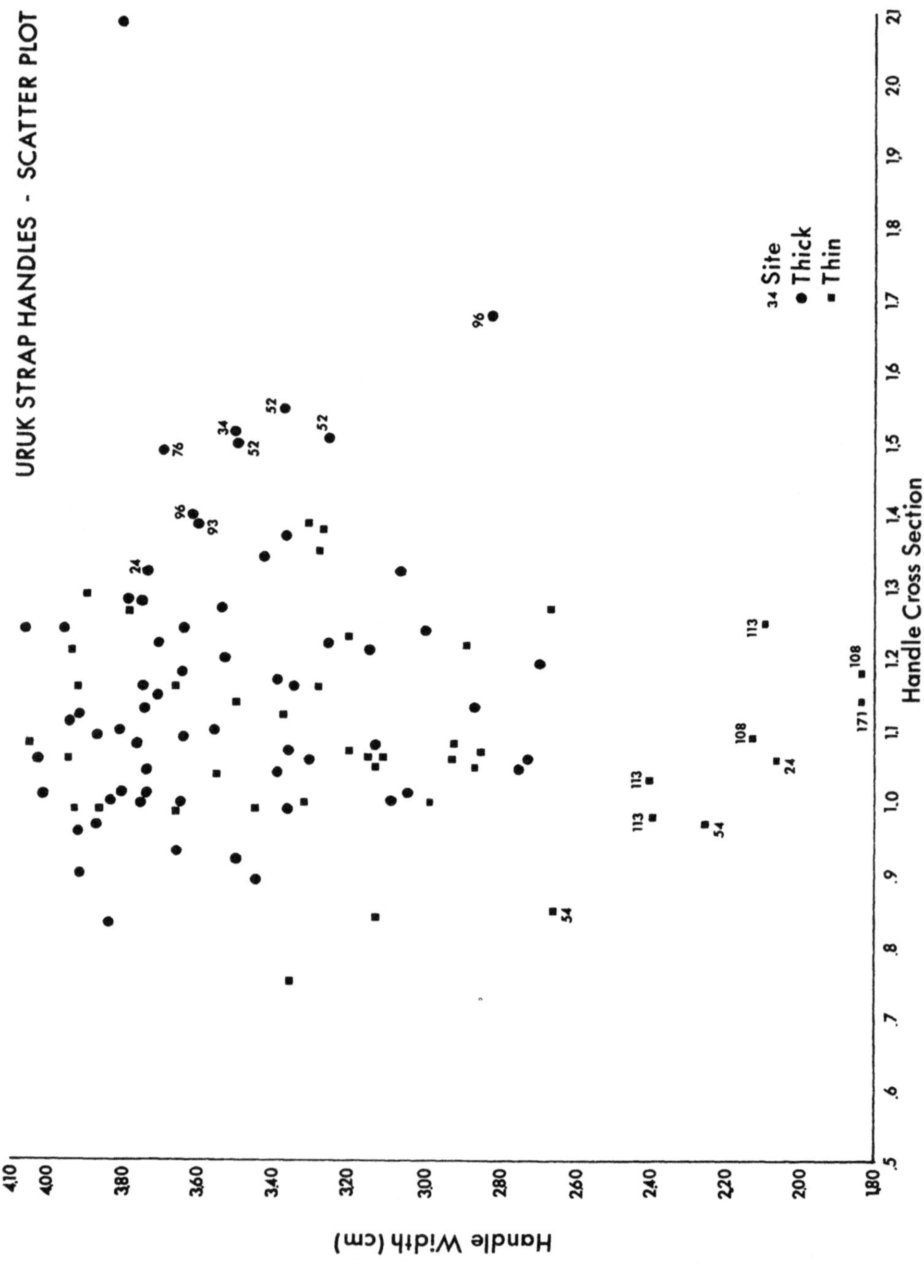
URUK STRAP HANDLES - SCATTER PLOT
Handle Width (cm)
Handle Cross Section
34 Site
Thick
Thin
4.10
4.00
3.80
3.60
3.40
3.20
3.00
2.80
2.60
2.40
2.20
2.00
1.80
.5
.6
.7
.8
.9
1.0
1.1
1.2
1.3
1.4
1.5
1.6
1.7
1.8
1.9
2.0
2.1

Fortunately the cross hatch bands and wide strap handles provided more convincing evidence of the organization of local exchange. The distributions of these types may be combined into a composite distribution map of the known local exchange evidence (see Fig. 29). Compare the exchange connections evidenced by ceramic distributions with the exchange connections predicted on the basis of locational considerations (Fig. 19). The comparison is remarkably close. The Susa and Abu Fanduweh systems are indicated. The proposed major exchange route across the plain from Susa to Chogha Mish is confirmed, and extended to the far eastern portion of the survey area. Certain additional features of the system are indicated. Direct connection is evidenced between the Abu Fanduweh and Chogha Mish areas, as well as are extensions to such marginal settlements as KS-7, KS-96, and KS-197.

The present analysis also provides confirmation of a number of other propositions. The proposition that small sites associated with ceramic wall cones were rural administrative centers is supported. The ceramic distribution conforms to the distribution predicted assuming that these settlements functioned in the mediation of local exchange.

The major hypothesis suggested for Middle Uruk remains to be discussed. It was predicted that increased growth of the system would require increased large center involvement with, and control of, village production. Increasing administrative control of local exchange was predicted as a factor of increasing control of local production. This prediction has been confirmed. Administrative specialists probably were resident in even village level sites on the plain. If this was the case, excavation of these sites should reveal artifactual evidence of administrative activity.

One small Middle Uruk settlement has been excavated in the area. Excavations were carried out on KS-36 (Tepe Sharafabad) as part of the 1970-71 Southwest Iran Project. Clear Middle Uruk deposits yielded a series of explicitly administrative artifacts. These consisted primarily of jar sealings carrying seal impressions and bale sealings (Wright, 1971, personal communication). Thus in at least this one case there was an association between the presence of ceramic cones indicating public architecture and administrative artifacts indicating the presence of administrators. I contend that the hypothesis of administrative control of village production is confirmed, though the precise operation of administration remains to be elucidated by future excavation of small sites.

Earlier in this discussion of Middle Uruk it was predicted that increasing administrative control of rural production would have at least two inputs to the major settlements themselves: village agricultural produce and village labor. Flow of agricultural products from rural areas to centers was indirectly evidenced in previous pages. Provision of evidence for labor inputs to the large centers is another matter entirely.

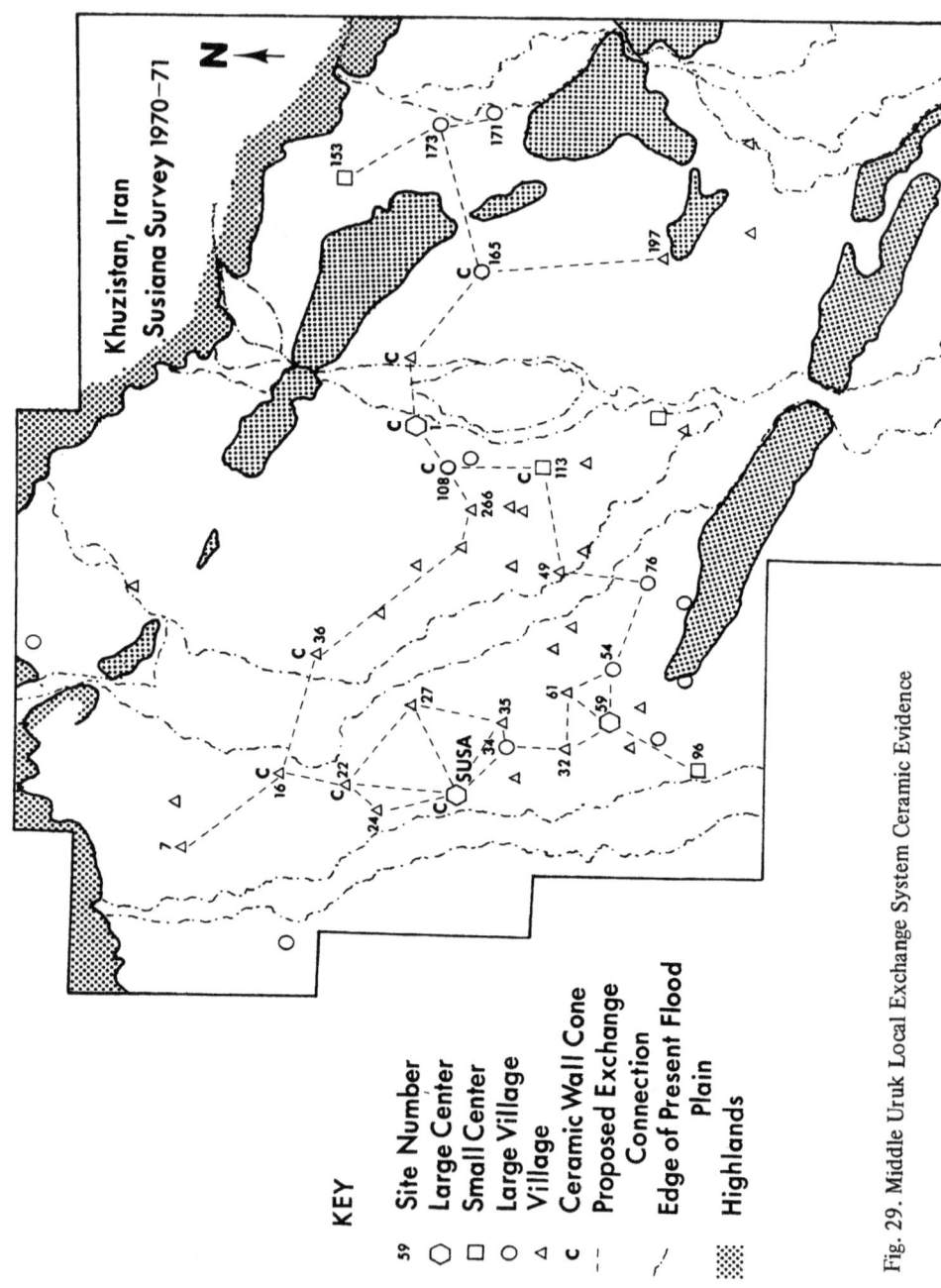

Fig. 29. Middle Uruk Local Exchange System Ceramic Evidence

This problem can however be approached with available data. Ethnographic evidence presented early in this study indicates that labor inputs in simple states are generally handled through some sort of corvée system in which groups of workers are recruited from the general population for public labor projects. These individuals may be supported by the state for the period in which their labor is required. There is some evidence for the presence of such a corvée system in Middle Uruk. This evidence is derived from analysis of a particular ceramic type: the bevel rim bowl.

Bevel Rim Bowls and Middle Uruk Ration Systems

The standard bevel rim bowl is the most common ceramic type in Middle and Late Uruk. Several functional interpretations have been suggested for this type, including use as votive objects in religious ceremonies and as implements in yogurt processing (Delougaz, 1952:128). Recently Nissen has identified them as ration bowls functioning in an administered redistribution system (1970:137). Let us consider Nissen's hypothesis.

An elaborate ration system is perhaps the most characteristic feature of the available data on later Mesopotamian economies. This is undoubtedly due in part to the fact that administrative texts are the source of most of our data on these economies. They probably constitute a highly biased sample.

Gelb (1965:230-242) has provided a composite outline of the complex ration systems in use in Mesopotamia in the Early Dynastic IIIA through Ur III periods of 2500 to 2000 B.C. which is summarized below. Differential rations were issued to individuals by various institutions according to age, sex, occupation, and social status. Three commodities were most important among the many issued at different times to different persons for different purposes—barley, oil, and wool—of which barley, the staple food of the population, was most important. These standard rations were primarily issued to individuals of the "guruš" class, a numerous group of semi-free workers. Gelb provides the following composite standard ration table derived from a sample of several hundred individual texts (236):

TABLE 30
STATE REDISTRIBUTION TO GURUŠ WORKERS

Kind	Time	Men	Women	Children	Measure
Barley	monthly	60	30	25,20,15,10	quarts
Oil	yearly	4	4	2,1.5,1	quarts
Wool	yearly	4	3	2,1.5,1	pounds

A second group of commodities was issued on occasion as replacement for standard barley, oil and wool rations. These most commonly included emmer, flour, bread, and cloth. A third group of commodities was issued irregularly, either on special occasions or as replacements for standard rations. These included meat (of sheep or cattle), milk, cheese, butter, and other dairy products; onions, legumes, cucumbers, and other vegetables; dates, figs, apples, and other fruit; condiments; beer and wine.

The complexity of the ration system present in developed states in Mesopotamia suggests that such systems had a long developmental history, perhaps appearing in rudimentary form with the primary states of the Uruk period. The presence of ration systems during the Uruk period in Khuzistan, and the related proposition that bevel rim bowls functioned as ration containers may be tested in a preliminary fashion with presently available data.

The following requirements may be suggested for containers used in an administered redistribution (ration) system assuming ration issue to individuals:

I. Cost efficiency (high ratio of container output/resource input)
   A. Low materials cost/container
   B. Low labor cost/container
II. Production efficiency
   A. Organization of production
      1. Localization of materials, labor, and facilities
      2. Production task specialization
III. Distributional efficiency
   A. Location of production close to location of distribution
   B. Standardization of container size relative to ration size

Production "costs" may be viewed in terms of depletion of institutional resources incurred in production. Materials required would include clay and temper for the containers and kilns, in addition to kiln fuel. Labor "costs" would consist of maintenance of workers engaged in materials collection and processing.

Bevel rim bowls were fabricated of readily available materials. The paste of these bowls is very coarse, occasionally including small pebbles and sherds. Such material could be obtained by superficial excavation virtually anywhere on an occupation site. The tempering material used contains a high proportion of straw, presumably another readily available material. The coarseness of the paste used suggests relatively little processing and thus low labor costs.

Actual bowl production was also a simple process. These vessels were apparently made in earthen molds. Such molds could be constructed as follows. A small hole was excavated in the ground roughly equal to the size of a bevel rim bowl. This rough mold was then shaped to the desired proportions using a previously made bevel rim bowl. A new bowl was constructed by lining this mold with a previously prepared paste and temper mixture. Finger and knuckle marks resulting from this process are usually observable on bowl interiors. The characteristic beveled rim was produced by trimming off excess material around the edge of the mold with a finger. Left in the sun, the bowl became leather hard and could easily be removed from the mold and fired. This process has been suggested from bowl characteristics (Nissen, 1970:137) and tested experimentally (Wright, 1971, personal communication). New bevel rim bowls, indistinguishable from those of the Uruk period, can be produced in this fashion. This process can be carried out quite quickly. Actual forming of each bowl in a prepared mold requires about 60 seconds (Wright, 1970, personal communication). After removal from their molds the bowls were apparently fired at relatively low temperatures in small simple kilns. It can be concluded that bevel rim bowls were produced at low materials and labor costs and thus conform to the first requirement predicted for ration bowls.

Production efficiency may be attained through appropriate organization of production. Scale economics is one aspect of such organization of production. The term refers to gains in efficiency obtained by concentrating productive activities at common locations (Garner, 1967:305). In this case, the term would refer to the spatial concentration of activities involved in container production, and such concentration was described above.

Production task specialization is the second predicted aspect of productive efficiency. Task specialization in container production would involve assigning specific productive operations to specific individuals or groups of individuals. A broad specialization breakdown for container production might include: collection of raw materials; production of unfired containers; firing of containers. Each of these broad activities might further be divided into individual tasks.

The predicted combination of spatial localization of productive activities and task specialization may be summarized as workshop production. Uruk ceramic workshops have already been discussed. Recall that there is evidence of ceramic production at three Middle Uruk sites on the Susiana plain; Susa, Chogha Mish, and Abu Fanduweh. Kilns containing bevel rim bowls occur in the Abu Fanduweh workshop described above and at Chogha Mish (Delougaz, 1971, personal communication). Although no complete bevel rim bowl workshop has been reported, firing of the bowls must have been the most complex operation in their production. There is no evidence to support, or reason to suggest, that tasks in bowl production executed before firing took place at locations far removed from kiln areas.

The frequency of bevel rim bowls in surface and excavation collections also suggests workshop production. Bevel rim bowls are the most common ceramic type in the 1970-71 survey collections. In recent excavations at Warka, bevel rim bowls constituted 60 to 70 percent of the sherd sample recovered from Uruk levels (Nissen, 1970:136). Workshop organization would appear to be the only productive mode capable of yielding the quantity of bowls found, given the restricted number of known production loci. Bevel rim bowls would then appear to conform to the predictions of productive efficiency required for ration containers.

Distributional efficiency for ration containers has at least two components. First, due to costs of transport it would be most efficient to produce ration containers as close as possible to their point of intended distribution. If distribution points are dispersed, it would be most efficient to locate production near the point of maximum intended distribution. As seen above, there is evidence for bevel rim bowl production at Chogha Mish and Abu Fanduweh. Production also undoubtedly occurred at Susa, where ceramic kilns have also been found (de Mecquenem, 1938:140). These were the major Middle Uruk centers in the survey area. As major population centers they would also be points of maximum ration distribution. The prediction of production location is confirmed.

The second predicted component of distributional efficiency is standardization of container volume according to ration size. Production of containers significantly smaller than ration size would necessitate the use of multiple containers per ration and result in inefficient distribution. Production of containers significantly larger than ration size would result in unnecessary use of materials and labor. Differential ration sizes could be handled through use of differential container sizes, multiple containers, or both.

There is some evidence that bevel rim bowls were produced with volumes proportional to a standard volume measure. The material available for analysis consisted of 278 bevel rim bowl rim-to-base profiles from the 1970-71 survey collections, and the current French excavations on the Acropole of Susa.[5] Actual volume measurement was not possible with this material. Estimated volumes were calculated using a geometric model and the three most reliable relevant measurements made on each sherd: interior base diameter, interior side height, and base angle. A diagram of these measurements and formulas for the estimation of bowl volume is presented in Figure 30. A description and list of bevel rim bowl measurements is presented in Appendix III.

For sample collection and volume estimation, only the larger site samples were used. The samples were as follows: KS-36, n=21; KS-39, n=32; KS-59, n=57; KS-108, n=43; Susa, n=36. Histograms of estimated volumes for these samples are presented in Tables 31 and 32. Modal values were defined for each sample distribution.

---

[5]The material from the Acropole of Susa was measured with the kind permission of Jean Perrot, Director of the French Mission.

TABLE 31
ESTIMATED VOLUMES OF URUK BEVEL RIM BOWLS: HISTOGRAMS

Liters		Liters		Liters	
0.318		0.472		0.388	
0.425	XXXX(4)	0.562	XXXXXX(6)	0.478	X(1)
0.532	XXXXXXXX(8)	0.582	X(1)	0.568	XXX(3)
0.638	XXXXXXXXXXXXXXXXXX(18)	0.638	X(1)	0.658	XXXXXXX(7)
0.745	XXXXXXXXXXXXXXXX(16)	0.694	XXXX(4)	0.748	XXXXX(5)
0.852	XXXXXXXX(8)	0.750	XXXXX(5)	0.838	XX(2)
0.959	XX(2)	0.806	XX(2)	0.928	XX(2)
1.066		0.862	XXX(3)	1.018	
1.172		0.918	XXX(3)	1.108	
1.279		0.974	XXX(3)	1.198	
1.386		1.030	XXX(3)	1.288	
1.493	X(1)	1.087	XXX(3)	1.378	X(1)
1.599		1.143	X(1)	1.468	
KS-59, n=57		KS-39, n=32		KS-36, n=21	
Survey Sample		Survey Sample		Survey Sample	

TABLE 32
ESTIMATED VOLUMES OF URUK BEVEL RIM BOWLS: HISTOGRAMS

Liters		Liters		Liters	
0.420		0.474		0.383	
0.465	XX(2)	0.600	XXXXX(5)	0.443	XXXXX(5)
0.510	XXXXXXX(7)	0.727	XXXXXXX(7)	0.503	XXXX(4)
0.555	XXXXXX(6)	0.853	XXXXX(5)	0.563	XXXXXX(6)
0.600	XXXXXXXXXXXXX(13)	0.980	XXXXXXXX(8)	0.623	XXXXXXXX(6)
0.645	XXXXXXXXXXXXXXXXX(17)	1.106	XXXX(4)	0.683	XXXXXXXXX(9)
0.690	XXXXXXXXX(9)	1.233	XXX(3)	0.743	XXXXXX(6)
0.735	XX(2)	1.359	XXX(3)	0.803	XXX(3)
0.780	X(1)	1.486		0.863	
0.825	X(1)	1.613		0.923	XX(2)
0.870	X(1)	1.739		0.983	X(1)
0.915		1.866	X(1)	1.042	X(1)
0.960	X(1)	1.992		1.102	X(1)
KS-36, n=60		Susa, n=36		KS-108, n=43	
Excavation Sample		Excavation Sample		Survey Sample	
Actual Volumes of Complete Bowls					

ANALYSIS OF THE SETTLEMENT PATTERNS

Measured Attributes:
A = Interior Side Height
B = Interior Base Diameter
a = Base Angle

Volume estimation:
1. c = 180 − (a + b)
2. h = $\frac{A}{\cos c}$
3. C = $h^2 - A^2$
4. r = $\frac{B}{2}$
5. R = r + C
6. Estimated volume (cm^3) = $\frac{\pi}{3}$ A (R^2 + Rr + r^2)
7. Estimated volume (ml) = .99997 Estimated volume (cm^3)
8. Estimated volume (liters) = $\frac{\text{Estimated volume (ml)}}{1000}$

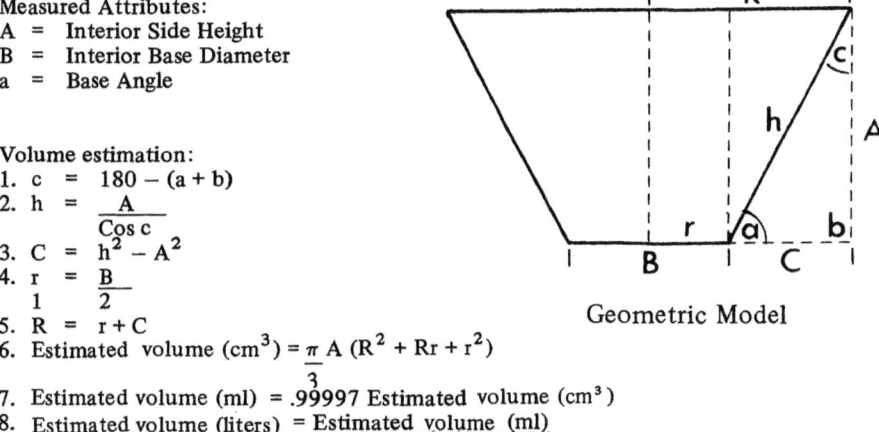

Geometric Model

Fig. 30. Estimation of Uruk Bevel Rim Bowl Volume.

Some support is available for these estimates. A sample of measured volumes for 60 complete bevel rim bowls is available from an excavated sample at KS-36 (data provided by Henry T. Wright, University of Michigan Museum of Anthropology). Two modes are evident in a histogram of the distribution of these measured volumes presented in Table 32. The first mode is at .488 liters and the second is at .623 liters. The single mode defined from the surface collection of bevel rim bowls from this site was .613 liters. This compares favorably with the value of .623 liters from actual measured volumes in the excavated sample.

The distribution of modal values calculated from the survey and Susa collections are presented in Table 33. This distribution suggests three volume categories. Modal values within each category were averaged to obtain an estimated mean volume for each. The resulting means were: .922 liters, .647 liters, and .465 liters. Probable sampling and measurement error suggests that these figures be adjusted to the nearest .05 liter or .90 liters, .65 liters, and .45 liters.

Taking .90 liters as a standard unit equal to 1.00, the remaining category averages of .65 liters and .45 liters become .72 and .50 units respectively. The apparent existence of these three volume categories and the proportional relationships of their means may indicate the existence of a standard volume measure, and the production of bevel rim bowls with volumes proportionate to this standard measure.

No standard volume measure used in the Uruk period has previously been defined. Our data indicate, however, the presence of a standard on the order of .90 liters. The standard volume unit of the later Akkadian period, the

TABLE 33
DISTRIBUTION OF URUK BEVEL RIM BOWL
MODAL VOLUMES

Bowl Volume (liters)	KS-36	KS-39	KS-59	KS-108	Susa	Possible Size Class (average volumes)
1.00						
.95		ca .95				
.90				ca .90	ca .916	.922
.85						
.80						
.75		.722				
.70						
.65				.653	.663	.647
.60	.613					
.55			.585			
.50		.517				
.45						.465
.40				.413		
.35						
.30						

sila, has been estimated from textual sources at .842 liters (Labat, 1963:66). The remarkably close values of the Akkadian sila and the Uruk volume unit suggested here can only be called provocative.

The remaining variability in bowl volumes might be accounted for by one or more additional factors consistent with their use as ration containers. Use of a container of standard volume to fill bevel rim bowls would only require that the latter be sufficiently large to hold the ration rather than having the same volume as the ration. Change in ration size over time, relative to a standard volume unit might be associated with a change in bowl size relative to that unit. Finally, some variability in the sample is probably due to errors in the method used to estimate bowl volumes.

This analysis provides supporting evidence for two hypotheses: that bevel rim bowls were primarily functional as ration containers and that rations were issued in rough proportion to a standard volume unit. The presence of a social category of individuals receiving rations and of a specialized administration supporting the ration system is implied by these propositions.

If the evidence presented for an Uruk ration system in Khuzistan is accepted, additional hypotheses about this system may be suggested. Barley is assumed, on the basis of its known later importance, to have been the primary rationed commodity in the Uruk period. For purposes of the following analysis, wheat could be substituted for barley without substantially changing the conclusions offered.

Given this initial assumption a few simplistic nutritional calculations can be made. As in the case of an earlier discussion of agricultural sustaining areas, these estimates are rough indeed. We will be concerned with caloric intake only. Additional nutritional factors could be included if better data were available.

As discussed earlier, contemporary Khuzistan villagers have an average of about 3,000 calories available from their diet per person per day: 1,976 of these calories are obtained from consumption of an average of 760 grams of bread. This represents an average of 260 calories per 100 grams of bread consumed (Gremliza, 1962:92). The daily caloric requirement for adults engaged in physical labor is about 3,000 calories (Taylor and Orrea, 1966:52). Caloric input and output would appear to be roughly equal for these modern villagers.

The caloric value of the presumed Uruk barley rations described above may be calculated as follows. One liter of barley is equal to approximately 829 grams. This value was obtained by weighing one liter of barley. Barley has a caloric value of about 350 calories per 100 grams (Watt and Merrill, 1963:9). The caloric content of one liter of barley would then equal about 2,900 calories. This assumes barley processing without caloric loss.

The Khuzistan data suggests that processing cereal into bread involves some caloric loss. The grain or combination of grains used in this bread is not specified, but caloric values for wheat and barley are approximately equal (Watt and Merrill, 1963:9,66). For present purposes, a unit volume of grain is considered equal in weight to the same unit of grain when ground into flour and baked into bread. (The water in a bread dough largely evaporates during baking.) As mentioned above, the bread consumed by villagers in Khuzistan today contains about 260 calories per 100 grams, while unprocessed barley contains about 350 calories per 100 grams. Caloric loss in processing is thus on the order of 25 percent.

Based on these estimates, Table 34 presents caloric values of unprocessed barley and equal amounts of bread for one liter of barley and each of the proposed Uruk ration sizes discussed above.

TABLE 34
CALORIC VALUE OF POSSIBLE URUK BARLEY RATIONS
ON THE SUSIANA PLAIN

	Volume (liters)	Weight (grams)	Calorie Content Barley	Calorie Content Bread
	1.00	829	2,900	2,175
Uruk Ration	.90	746	2,611	1,958
Uruk Ration	.65	539	1,887	1,415
Uruk Ration	.45	373	1,305	979

The largest estimated Uruk ration unit of barley would contain about 2,600 calories. This would probably be sufficient for one adult for one day assuming no caloric intake from other sources. Processing this barley into bread would yield an estimated 1,958 calories. This compares favorably with the figure of 1,976 calories per day obtained from bread consumption in contemporary Khuzistan villages.

Bevel rim bowls with volumes in the .90 liter range are rare. Most bowls and presumably most rations fell in the .65 liter range. Bread produced from this volume of barley would yield an estimated 1,415 calories. This is equal to about one half of the average caloric intake per person per day for contemporary villages in the area.

While reasoning of this sort is prone to error, the following statements seem justified. First, a ration system was in use during the Middle Uruk on the Susiana plain. Second, the size of the presumed average Uruk ration suggests daily ration issue. Third, the size of the presumed average Uruk ration suggests that individuals receiving this ration had access to additional food sources.

Later textual sources indicate ration issue primarily to workers of various sorts, and by analogy workers were probably the primary recipients of rations during the Uruk period. Individual workers were probably issued rations for each day of labor devoted to institutionally organized labor projects. Supplemental food sources may have derived from family owned gardens or plots of agricultural land allocated to individual workers or workers' families.

Bevel rim bowls used in this analysis were recovered from sites ranging in size from large centers to villages. This distribution would indicate operation of the ration system and corvée labor affecting all levels of the settlement hierarchy. The prediction of administrative control of labor is tentatively confirmed.

This picture of the Uruk ration system in Khuzistan is admittedly tenuous. Preliminary demonstration of characteristics of an Uruk ration system does indicate the importance of such seemingly minor data as bevel rim bowl measurements. It also indicates something of the complexity involved in analysis of even a small portion of the economic system of a state.

Administrative Technology

Given our assumptions, the complexity of Middle Uruk administered local exchange and corvée labor systems indicates an increase in the amount of information being processed by the decision making hierarchy. There should be a corresponding increase in the information storage capacity of administrative technology.

Early Uruk stamp seals and seal impressions were discussed above. Cylinder seals appear in sites on the Susiana plain in Middle Uruk. Dyson reports the first such seal from his 1965 sondage on the Acropole of Susa in Level 14 (1966:290), a late Middle Uruk deposit (1966:366). Le Brun reports the first cylinder seal from the current French Acropole sondage in Level 21 (1971:209) which, as discussed above, can be dated to the Middle Uruk period. H. T. Wright (personal communication) reports cylinder seal impressions from a Middle Uruk context at Tepe Sharafabad (KS-36) where the ratio of cylinder to stamp seal impressions is on the order of 1:5.

The use of cylinder seals permits considerable increases in design complexity relative to seal size. For example, the surface available to carry a design on a stamp seal 2 cm in diameter is 3.14 square cm, while the available area on a cylinder seal 2 cm high and 1 cm in diameter is 6.28 cm. As a cylinder seal was rolled over a wet clay seal to produce the seal impression, impressions of indefinite length could be made.

Geometric designs were largely replaced in these new seals by naturalistic representations of objects, animals, and men. Apparently standardized scenes appear in some number in Late Uruk and possibly by Middle Uruk.

A second type of administrative artifact, the bulla, makes its appearance in Middle Uruk. Bullae are hollow clay balls, often containing a number of small pebbles or specially prepared spheroid or cuboid clay objects, and carrying a seal impression on their surface. The objects contained within these balls appear to have been counters. The number of items contained in a particular goods shipment could be recorded by these counters. The seal impression could then guarantee the accuracy of the count as well as perform the other functions of seals discussed above.

The first known appearance of bullae in Khuzistan is in Middle Uruk. A single example was recovered from a secure Middle Uruk context at Tepe Farukhabad by Wright (1972:104). Numerous examples probably of the same period are reported from Chogha Mish (Delougaz, 1966:38).

The bulla recovered by Wright carried a numerical notation in addition to the counters it contained. Bullae provide direct evidence of a developing technology of information storage and transfer and indirect evidence of increasing amounts of information processing by administrative organization. Our prediction is confirmed.

Locationally this discussion has dealt primarily with the core area of the Susiana plain. A few comments on marginal sites are in order. Marginal settlement and boundary phenomena are particularly thorny problems. Settlement of the Susiana plain was not a closed system even though it is occasionally convenient to treat it as one. Boundary settlements are those locationally most likely to be influenced by factors external to the area under consideration. This seems to have been the case for marginal Middle Uruk settlements on the Susiana plain.

Inspection of the map of the Middle Uruk settlement system (Fig. 19) reveals a remarkable concentration of relatively large settlements on the margins of the system. The following settlements are defined as marginal: KS-240, KS-7, KS-8, KS-99, KS-288, KS-153, KS-173, KS-171, KS-220, KS-218, KS-120, KS-121, KS-79, KS-90, and KS-96. Six of these settlements are classified as villages, six as large villages, and three as small centers. Average marginal settlement size was 2.50 hectares, a figure in the large village range.

One possible explanation for this distribution would involve contact of these marginal settlements with actually or potentially hostile groups from outside the plain. The possibility of boundary hostilities would select for relatively large marginal settlements for defensive reasons. In a later section of this study it will be suggested that contact between specialized transhumant herding groups and the resident agriculturalists of the plain played an important role in political and economic developments on the Susiana during

ANALYSIS OF THE SETTLEMENT PATTERNS 141

the Uruk period. Real or potential conflict might be a factor in such contact, resulting in the observed size distribution of marginal settlements.

The foregoing discussion has provided evidence for a complex Middle Uruk administrative organization which exerted control on members of the society from residents of large centers to those of the smallest villages. Administrative organization was highly differentiated. A minimally four-level administrative hierarchy is indicated. Administrative specialists were located in at least a portion of the settlements at each level. Middle Uruk decision making organization was well above the minimal requirements for a state discussed at the outset of this study.

I would argue, however, that Middle Uruk organization was not qualitatively different from that operative during the Early Uruk period. For example, Early Uruk locational data indicated the presence of an administered local exchange system. Limited ceramic evidence supported this proposition. The introduction of the proto bevel rim bowl in Early Uruk would seem to have marked the development of a corvée labor system which differed from that of Middle Uruk only in scale.

The presence of a three-level settlement hierarchy in Early Uruk can be interpreted as indicating the presence of a three-level decision making hierarchy in light of Middle Uruk organization. It can now be said that the state developed during the Early Uruk period on the Susiana plain. It is likely that this assertion can be tested with data provided by future excavations of administrative buildings, a study of administrative technology, and so on.

The Middle-Late Uruk Transition

Analysis of Middle Uruk survey and excavation data resulted in a preliminary outline of various aspects of the Middle Uruk state on the Susiana plain. It also clarified some of the problems encountered in discussion of the Early Uruk settlement of the area. Hypotheses derived from the Early Uruk analysis were tested and confirmed. Hypotheses about subsequent Late Uruk developments can be generated in much the same manner. Analysis of Middle Uruk ceramics provided information about the Middle Uruk local exchange system for the plain as a whole. The cross hatch band was one ceramic type used in this analysis. Two chronologically distinct groups were defined of which the first was associated with Middle Uruk and the second with Middle-Late Uruk.

The chronologically transitional type allows detection of change in the local exchange system during the Middle-Late Uruk transition. Figure 31 presents the mapped distribution of late cross hatch bands, the transitional type. Compare this distribution with that of early (Middle Uruk) cross hatch

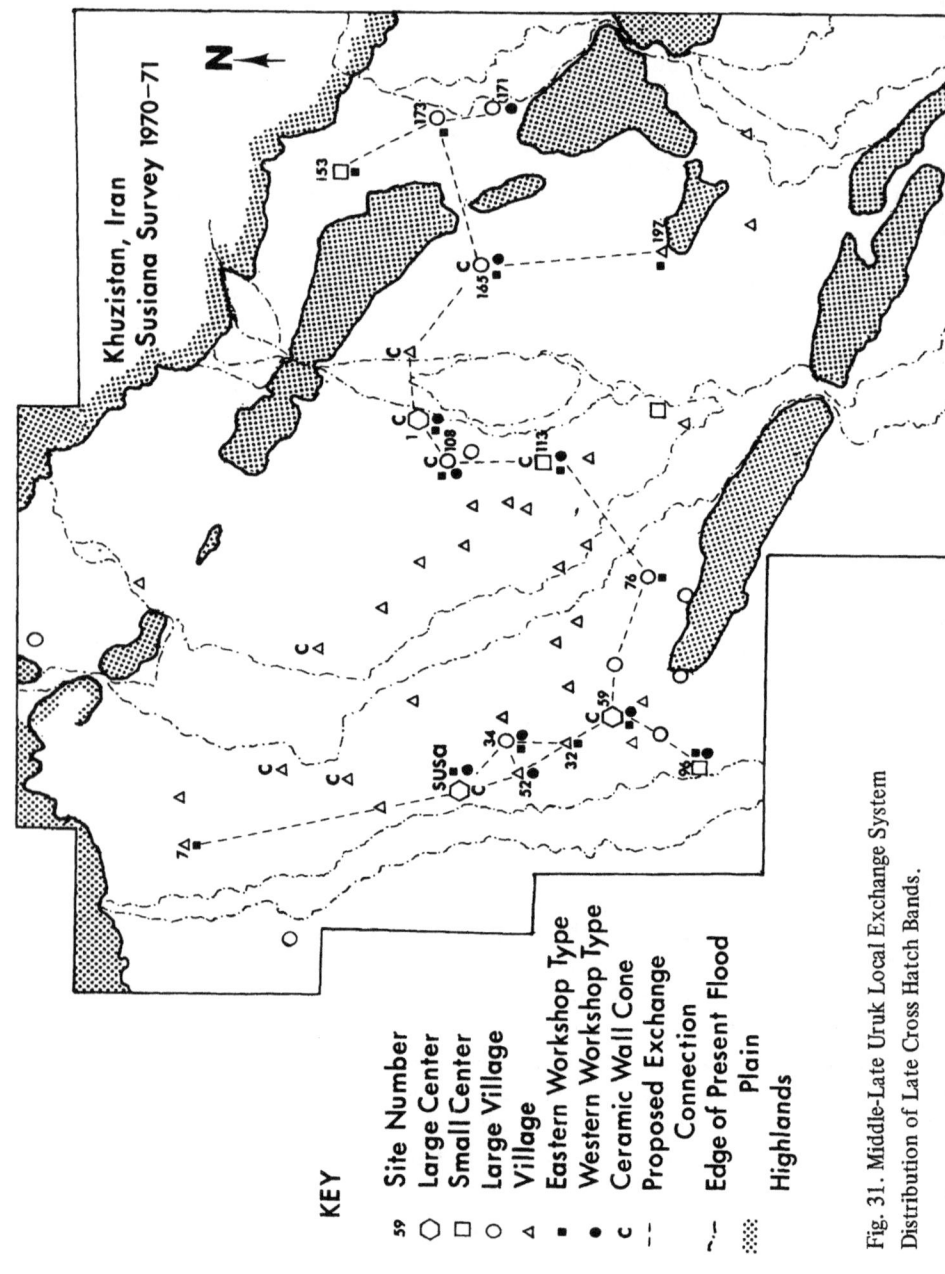

Fig. 31. Middle-Late Uruk Local Exchange System Distribution of Late Cross Hatch Bands.

ANALYSIS OF THE SETTLEMENT PATTERNS 143

bands in Figure 24. Several interesting differences between these distributions are evident.

These differences are primarily seen in the western portion of the plain, in the Susa and Abu Fanduweh areas. Briefly, there appears to have been a marked contraction of the local exchange system. North of Susa, late bands occur only at KS-7. Early bands were recovered from KS-7 as well as from KS-16, KS-22, and KS-24. In the southern area the distribution was also reduced. Further, no late bands were recovered from the western portion of the Chogha Mish area where early bands had been present.

Although these differences could be due to sampling error, they do seem to indicate a consistent pattern. The late band distribution reveals at least a partial collapse of the Middle Uruk local exchange system, possibly due to settlement abandonment. Examination of the Late Uruk settlement pattern resolves this problem.

LATE URUK

The apparent breakdown of the Middle Uruk local exchange system in fact occurred. The extent of this contraction is revealed in the Late Uruk settlement pattern (see Fig. 32). All settlements above Susa on the western portion of the plain were abandoned. These sites included: KS-7, KS-8, KS-22, KS-24, KS-27, KS-99, KS-240, and KS-286. The dense settlement below Susa became considerably attenuated. KS-35, KS-52, KS-64, KS-76, KS-90, KS-93, KS-98, and KS-285 were abandoned. This amounts to a total abandonment of some 22.5 hectares of settlement area, possibly representing some 4,500 people.

Changes on the eastern side of the plain were equally drastic. Only KS-36 remained above Chogha Mish. KS-37, KS-288, and KS-289 were abandoned. South of Chogha Mish, KS-4, KS-5, KS-44, KS-49, KS-50, KS-120, KS-121, KS-284, and KS-290 were abandoned along with KS-102, KS-153, KS-165, KS-173, KS-197, KS-218, and KS-220 east and southeast of Chogha Mish. This amounts to a total abandonment of some 33 hectares of settlement area and represents perhaps 6,600 people.

An initial hypothesis might be proposed that this does not represent actual population decrease but rather population agglomeration into the remaining settlements. Predictably the situation is not this simple. Susa decreases in areal size from a maximum of 25 hectares to an estimated nine hectares in Late Uruk. Abu Fanduweh (KS-59) decreases from 9.56 to 8.16 hectares. At KS-96 the estimated 5.2 hectares occupied during Middle Uruk were abandoned and the settlement moved several hundred meters to a new location (Area H) of four hectares. KS-34 decreases from 1.88 to .92 hectares. KS-61 decreases from 1.28 to .68 hectares. KS-79 decreases from 2.32 to 1.84

144 LOCAL EXCHANGE AND EARLY STATE DEVELOPMENT

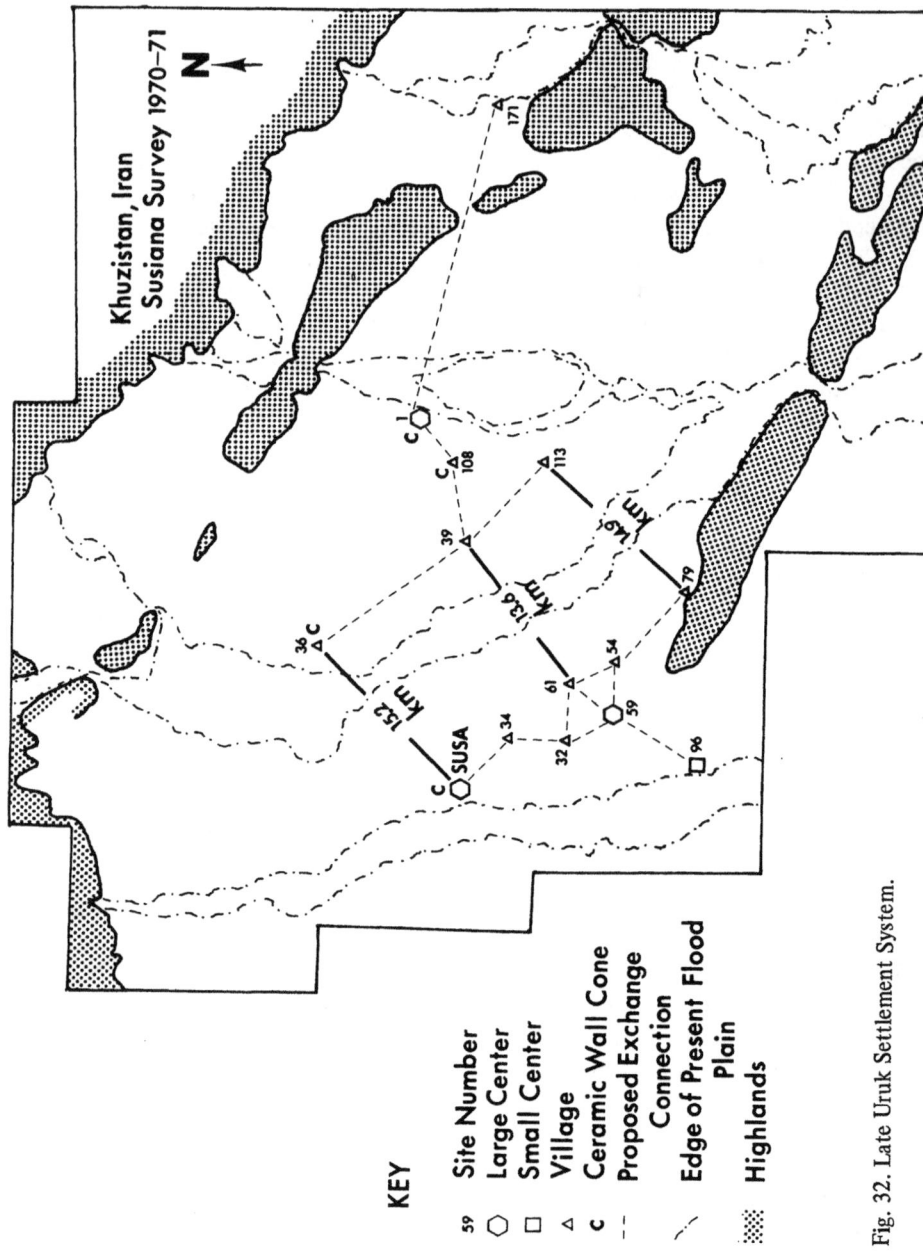

Fig. 32. Late Uruk Settlement System.

hectares. On the western side of the plain only KS-32 and KS-54 maintain their Middle Uruk sizes.

Thus on the western side of the plain, even the sites occupied during Late Uruk were generally smaller than they had been during Middle Uruk. The total areal reduction of these sites amounts to an additional 18.64 hectares. The total areal abandonment on the western portion of the plain was thus some 40 hectares. The total settlement area apparently occupied during Late Uruk for this area is calculated as 28.58 (29) hectares. It would be difficult to account for this apparent population decrease by agglomeration alone. Population densities at the remaining sites would have to average in excess of 400 persons per hectare, an unreasonable figure.

The situation on the eastern side of the plain was somewhat different. Of the six sites remaining in this area, three were smaller than in Middle Uruk: KS-36 decreased from 1.04 to .31 hectares; KS-39 decreased from 1.50 to 1.38 hectares; and KS-108 decreased from 2.80 to .56 hectares. KS-171 appears to have retained its Middle Uruk size of 2.80 hectares. The total areal abandonment for the eastern area was thus some 36 hectares.

In contrast to the Susa area however, one settlement probably saw considerable growth during the Late Uruk period. Chogha Mish occupied at least 18 hectares in Late Uruk, a possible eight-hectare increase over its Middle Uruk size. The total loss of settlement area is thus reduced to 28 hectares, with a total occupied area of 32.86 (33) hectares. Again, it is difficult to account for this apparent population decrease by a process of agglomeration alone.

To review the situation, the transition from Middle to Late Uruk saw a decrease in total settlement area of about 68 hectares and an estimated growth of Chogha Mish by eight hectares, resulting in an overall occupied area of 53 hectares. This amounts to 41 percent of the Middle Uruk occupation.

Though the number of Late Uruk settlements was greatly reduced over Middle Uruk levels, the settlement pattern is particularly intersting. It is important to note that the settlement hierarchy was reduced from four levels in Middle Uruk to three levels in Late Uruk (see Fig. 10). This would suggest a decrease in overall administrative complexity for reasons discussed earlier.

The most striking characteristic of the settlement pattern is the spatial separation of the Susa and Chogha Mish areas (see Fig. 32). While in Middle Uruk there was a virtually continuous distribution of settlements between these areas, in Late Uruk settlement was contracted toward Susa and Chogha Mish. A zone between these areas, some 14 kilometers in width, was free of permanent settlement. The impressive uniformity and width of this zone suggests that it was a textbook example of the operation of Christaller's administrative separation principle. According to Christaller, the operation of this principle results in a settlement distribution such that ". . . a spatial community has the nucleus as the capital (a central place of higher rank), around it, a wreath of satellite places of lesser importance, and toward the edge of the region a thinning population density—and even uninhabited areas" (1966:52). Such a distribution insures explicit on-the-ground definition of administrative boundaries.

Security may be a second factor influencing such distributions in addition to administrative boundary definition. Uninhabited or sparsely inhabited areas may serve as buffer zones in the event of real or threatened hostilities. "It may be desired to keep a certain distance from the settlements of enemies and be as near as possible to the settlements of potential or actual friends and allies" (Rowlands, 1972:445).

Two hypotheses are suggested: first, that Late Uruk was a period of state fission on the plain with the emergence of Chogha Mish as an autonomous administrative center; and second, that Late Uruk was a period of major hostility or threat of hostility on the plain.

Further features of the settlement pattern are of interest. The settlements on the western side of the plain in the vicinity of Susa and Abu Fanduweh conformed quite well to a central place distribution during the Middle Uruk period. This suggested that the organization of local exchange played a major role in the determination of settlement locations. This pattern collapsed in Late Uruk. The settlements abandoned were discussed above and included most of the sites in the immediate area of Susa, as well as a large proportion of those in the area of Abu Fanduweh.

Near Abu Fanduweh the settlements abandoned were those roughly west of the site, while those between Abu Fanduweh and the Chogha Mish area were maintained. These sites included KS-32, KS-61, and KS-54.

Similarly on the eastern portion of the plain, most settlements east of Chogha Mish were abandoned, while the surviving sites were located between Chogha Mish and the Susa-Abu Fanduweh area. The single exception was KS-171.

This pattern of abandonment and survival supports the hypothesis of major hostilities on the plain. The smaller settlements occupied during Late Uruk were in a position to insulate the remaining major settlements from the boundary zone discussed above, and ultimately from one another.

These additional locational considerations suggest that the organization of local exchange was no longer a major factor in the determination of settlement location. Considerations of administrative security and maintenance of two autonomous decision making organizations from external influence appear to have been more important factors.

Data are not presently available to directly demonstrate the existence of two Late Uruk states or to test possible explanations of their development. The locational data indicated a decline in the importance of local exchange in

Late Uruk. Differential distributions of exchange items might be expected to indicate an attenuation of exchange contact between the Susa-Abu Fanduweh and Chogha Mish areas, if these areas did indeed represent autonomous political systems. Unfortunately the local exchange data for Late Uruk is not very satisfactory.

The Local Exchange System: Ceramic Evidence

The small number of diagnostic Late Uruk ceramic types coupled with the small number of Late Uruk sites make the study of local exchange in this period difficult indeed. A sufficiently large sample of any one sherd type is not available.

Some indication of exchange, however, may be suggested. This is based on a small sample (31) of measurable Late Uruk twisted handles from the surface collections. A description and list of twisted handle measurements appear in Appendix III.

Full twist handles were distinguished from flat twist handles in the field typology. Full twist handles are roughly circular in cross section. The grooves in the handle occur uniformly around its circumference. Flat twist handles are more ovoid in cross section. Handle grooves are smoothed over on the underside of the handle.

This initial distinction is borne out by analysis of the handle measurements. A cross sectional index was calculated for each example by division of handle width by handle thickness. Handles with a roughly circular cross section thus have an index approximating 1.0. The more ovoid (flat) a handle is, the greater will be the value of its index.

A histogram of the distribution of these indices is presented in Figure 33. The field typology would predict a bimodal distribution, however a trimodal distribution is indicated by the histogram. Handle width and thickness, the components of the index are plotted against one another in Figure 34. Full twist handles are indicated by circular plot points. Their distinctiveness is relatively clear.

Measurements of handles represented by the remaining two modes are indicated by triangular and square plot points. These are less clearly distinctive. Flat twist handles as a group appeared to be somewhat later than full twist handles in the seriation of ceramic types from the surface collections. I suspect, but cannot demonstrate, that full twist handles are in reality generally later than flat twist handles, and that this relationship is obscured in the seriation by the size and especially the diversity of Late Uruk materials recovered from Area H of KS-96. This has possibly resulted in full twist handles showing higher correlations with a greater range of other Late Uruk types than do the flat twist variety.

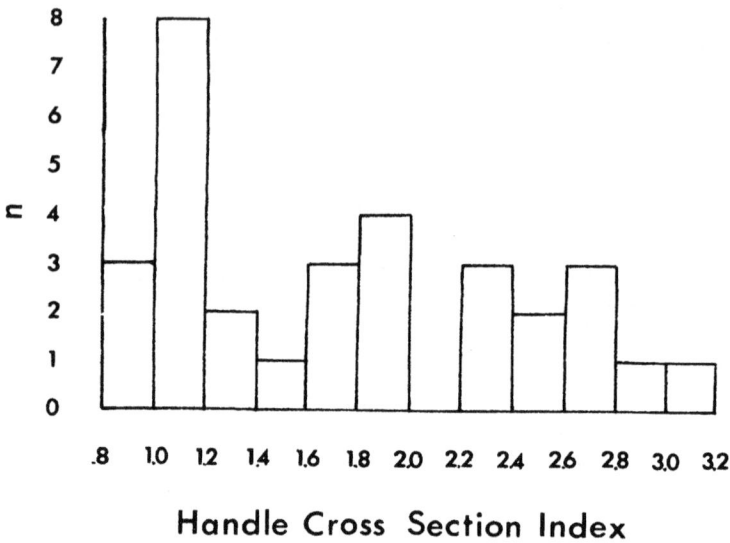

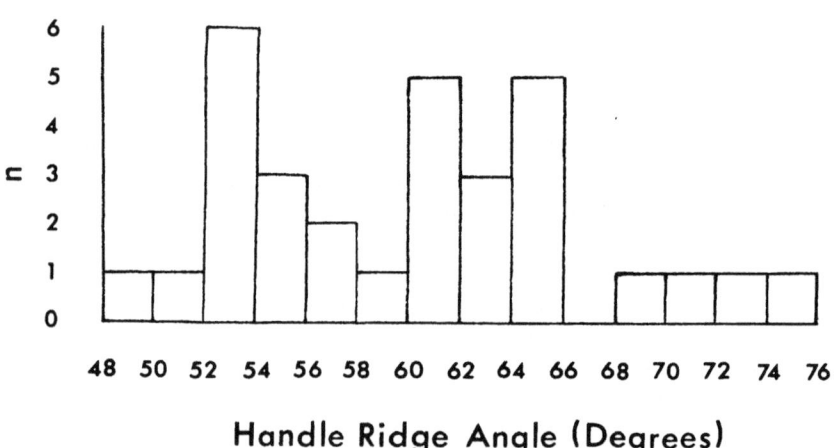

Fig. 33. Uruk Twisted Handles — Histograms.

ANALYSIS OF THE SETTLEMENT PATTERNS 149

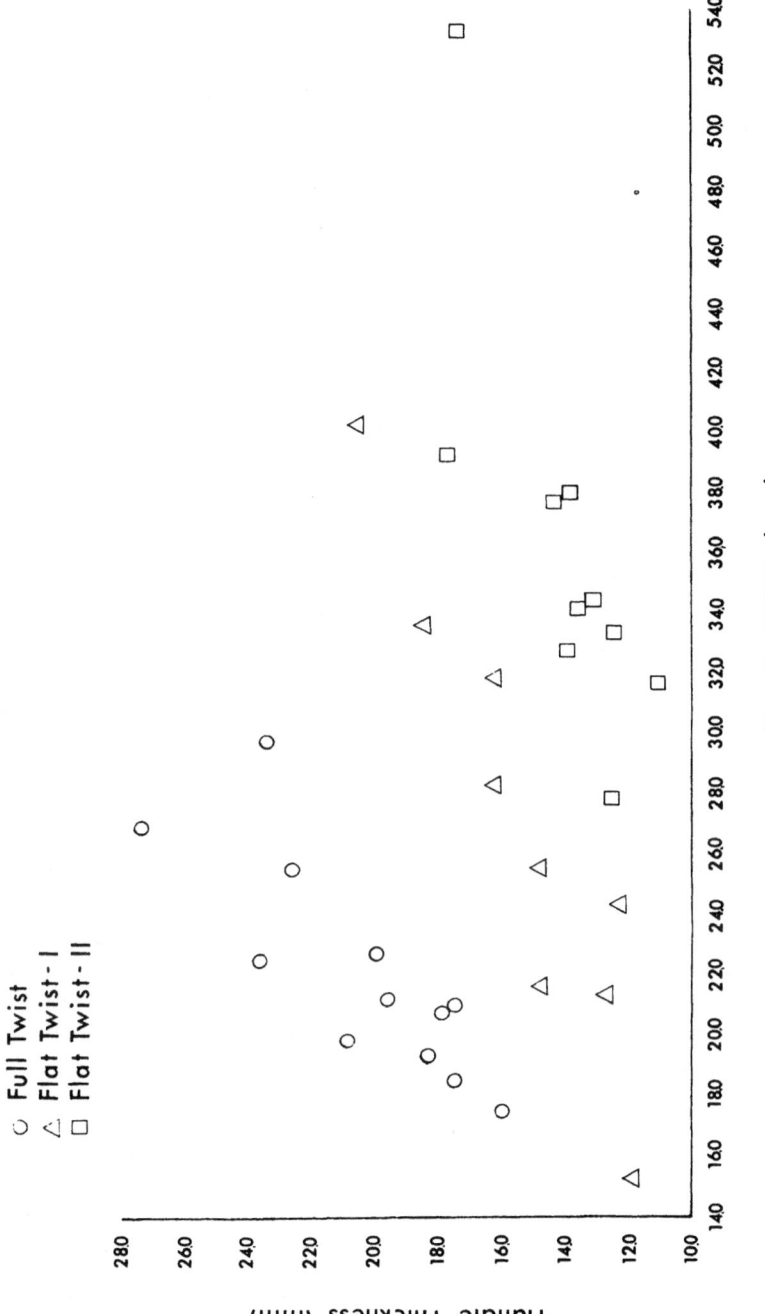

Fig. 34. Uruk Twisted Handles – Scatter Plot.

If the nature of temporal variation in twisted handles is not entirely clear, spatial variation within the type is even less obvious. Figure 33 presents a histogram of the distribution of ridge angle measurements for the available sample. A minimally trimodal distribution is indicated. Ridge angle does not show a significant correlation with cross section index ($r = -0.27$). A coefficient of at least -0.335 would be required for significance at the .05 level.

Figure 35 presents a scatter plot of ridge angle on cross section index for the 31 available handles. The shape types suggested above are indicated by the same plot symbols used above. Modal divisions on ridge angle are indicated by dashed lines. By analogy with the analyses of strap handles and cross hatch bands, the modal divisions on ridge angle probably represent workshop variability. Quite conveniently, three known workshop sites are available for Late Uruk: Susa, Chogha Mish, and Abu Fanduweh. The concentration of twisted handles in the surface collection from KS-96 precludes study of differential spatial distributions of these types.

The meager data available on Late Uruk twisted handles indicates the presence of significant temporal variability within the group, and suggests that three workshops were engaged in the production of vessels with these handles. Additional data from Susa and Chogha Mish can be expected to clarify these problems.

The local exchange data do not provide a satisfactory test of hypotheses derived from the locational data. Certain of these hypotheses can however be tested with excavation data. The locational analysis suggested the emergence of major hostilities or threat of hostilities on the plain in Late Uruk. Such hostilities would not be expected to emerge within the context of a single functioning state system unless induced from outside the system. Independent evidence of the emergence of hostilities would then support the hypothesis of state fission. Such evidence is available and is primarily to be found in cylinder seals and seal impressions.

As discussed above, cylinder seals first appeared in Middle Uruk and by Late Uruk became the dominant sealing implement. The wide range of known seal designs and the degree of design complexity probably indicate increasing information processing and administrative complexity. The fact that apparently military scenes appear for the first time in Late Uruk is of interest here:

> A major class of glyptic at Chogha Mish has military activities as its subject matter. Sealings showing conflict on the battlefield have parallels from other sites. One impression is noteworthy for a large figure of an archer with his equipment rendered in detail. So far unparalleled at other sites is a scene which shows a group of men marching in close formation, suggesting a well-trained and disciplined army unit (Delougaz and Kantor, 1969:25).

Another scene is interpreted as a siege of a fortified city, although the scene might well be interpreted as the construction of a major building. The avail-

ANALYSIS OF THE SETTLEMENT PATTERNS 151

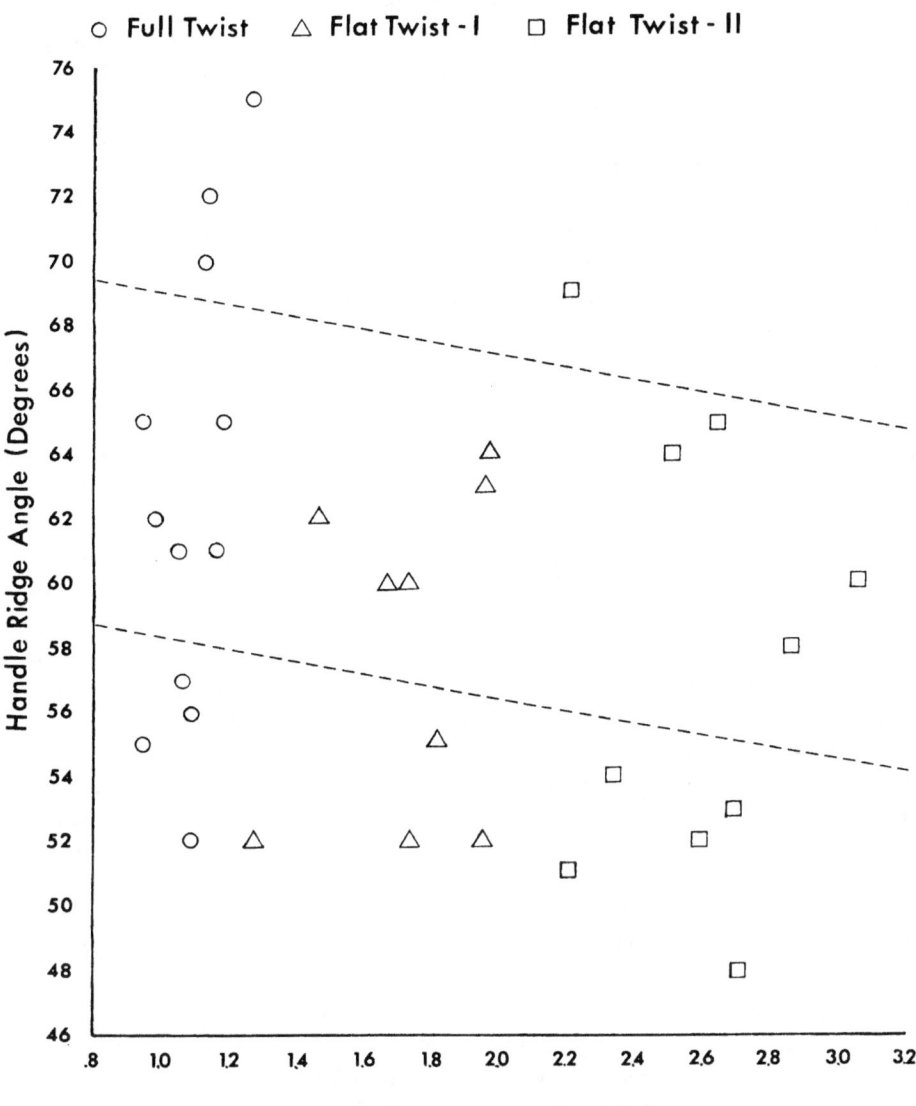

Fig. 35. Uruk Twisted Handles – Scatter Plot.

able corpus of scenes of this type from Chogha Mish will be published in a forthcoming preliminary report (H. Kantor, 1972, personal communication).

Similar cylinder seal designs are known from Susa. One example shows a line of men whose hands are apparently bound behind their backs. These men are interpreted as captives (Amiet, 1961:251). A second example shows a bearded figure armed with a bow and arrow. In front of this individual are three men with arrows protruding from their bodies. A building interpreted as a temple forms a third element in the design, although its intended location, behind the archer or behind his targets is unclear (Amiet, 1961:312).

Other evidence for hostilities is scanty indeed. The first mace head from the current French excavations on the Acropole of Susa appears in a Late Uruk context (Level 17A) (Le Brun, 1971:Fig. 55:2), along with a bone projectile point (Le Brun, 1971:Fig. 57:8).

The artifactual evidence is thus not very impressive. Representation of conflict situations on cylinder seals is assumed to indicate actual occurrence of at least analogous situations. Little can be made of one mace head and one projectile point.

There are no architectural remains that could be interpreted as overt fortifications. Given the current excavated sample of major centers, however, fortifications may still have been present. Furthermore, architecture can have defensive functions without being overt fortifications. An outer ring of shared wall, domestic housing with defensible entry points might be a functional analog of a fortified settlement wall. There is no way to evaluate this possibility in Khuzistan with presently available data.

In sum, the settlement pattern data provides the best evidence for major political divisions, competition, and probably hostility on the plain during the Late Uruk period. Independent supportive evidence is provided by conflict scenes on cylinder seals and seal impressions. It is difficult to estimate the scale of this conflict. Actual and/or threatened hostilities seem to have had a major effect on the settlement pattern. Warfare may have existed on the plain in the Late Uruk.

The Late Uruk settlement of the area presents a number of major explanatory problems including an apparently marked population drop; extensive abandonment of areas of the plain; fission of the Middle Uruk state; and the emergence of major hostilities in the area. These are not isolated, but undoubtedly interrelated, processes. None of the mutual causal relationships between and among these processes can be satisfactorily described at the present. A few working hypotheses can, however, be suggested.

Previously the suggestion of the fission of a state during the Uruk period would have sounded strange indeed. It may still sound so to some readers. Remember that in an ethnographic perspective the approximate 400 years of Middle and Late Uruk is a long period, even though it seems quite short from an archaeological point of view.

ANALYSIS OF THE SETTLEMENT PATTERNS

The problem may be approached at a very general level via an information processing model. The final advance in Uruk information storage is recorded by the appearance of numerical tablets during the Late Uruk. The earliest reported and securely datable numerical tablets in Khuzistan appear in Level 17 of the current French Acropole sondage at Susa (Le Brun, 1971:179). Similar tablets appear during the same period at Warka in southern Sumer (Falkenstein, 1936:3). The conflict between this indication of increasing information processing and increasing complexity of administrative organization, and other suggestions of decreasing complexity derived from the settlement pattern will be discussed below.

Despite increasing information processing capability, the demands on the Middle Uruk administrative hierarchy seem to have exceeded its processing capacity, leading to partial breakdown of the administrative system and fission of the state. Examples of systemic breakdown are rare in the ethnographic literature. The Bulamogi discussed early in this study may, however, provide an instructive example. The changing fortunes of princes over time may reflect systemic adjustments to an overloaded administrative organization. Fallers relates control of princes and princely areas to an individual ruler's "personal administrative ability and force of character " (1965:134). During the reign of some rulers the entire Bulamogi territory was controlled by a single administrative hierarchy, while during the reign of others, princely areas became effectively autonomous states.

I would suggest that at some points in time, perhaps periodically, information processing and decision making requirements exceeded the capacity of the administrative hierarchy. Bulamogi political organization was structured to allow systemic adjustment to this situation by fission of the state into two or more effectively autonomous units, thus reducing the overall information input and required decision output.

As in the case of specific processes leading to primary state formation, the processes resulting in fission of states probably varied from case to case. A number of environmental and/or social factors could operate, increasing information processing and decision making requirements beyond the capacity of a given administrative hierarchy. Just what these might have been in the case of the Late Uruk period on the Susiana plain is open to question.

Emergence of Major Hostilities

The emergence of major hostilities on the plain in the Late Uruk period was probably a function of the process of state fission—of the emergence of Chogha Mish as an independent administrative center. There is, of course, no direct evidence to support this suggestion. Once Chogha Mish had been established as a major administrative center it seems possible that a gradual erosion of the direct influence of officials at Susa might ensue. Efforts on the part of officials at Susa to maintain administrative control might well have led to conflict. By the time that the administrative hierarchy at Chogha Mish became independent of higher authority at Susa, the process of fission was complete and two states occupied the plain. Each would then be concerned with maintaining its administrative integrity—by force if necessary.

Population Decline

Intermittently throughout this discussion an "apparent" Late Uruk population decline has been discussed. The qualification was intentional. It was shown above that this apparent decline cannot be resolved by a process of population agglomeration into the remaining Late Uruk settlements. The only evidence of possible agglomeration comes from Chogha Mish with a poorly estimated increase in settlement size from 10 to 18 hectares in Late Uruk. Such an increase could only account for a very small proportion of the "missing" population.

There are other possibilities. Settled population may have become highly dispersed rather than agglomerated. A large movement from former nucleated settlements to dispersed hamlets and farmsteads could account for a large number of people. Such sites, if sufficiently small and occupied for a sufficiently short period, might well have been missed by the survey. This alternative would seem highly unlikely. Not a single Late Uruk site fitting this description has been found. Furthermore, evidence for major hostilities in Late Uruk would argue for agglomeration rather than dispersal on grounds of security.

A third possibility might have involved a large scale shift from settled agriculture to transhumant herding such that a large proportion of the population was resident on the plain only during the winter rainy season. Such transitory occupations would be difficult to identify archaeologically. This alternative is attractive in that there is no evidence to cast doubt upon it. There is no evidence to support it either.

The decline in settled population as opposed to total population would appear to have involved some 16,000 people as an order of magnitude estimate. It is difficult to visualize this number of people deciding to give up agriculture and take up herding within a relatively short span of time, say 100 years. Further we have very little knowledge about Late Uruk occupation of highland summer pasture areas or highland agricultural valleys. Until data of this sort are available, the herding hypothesis will have to be set aside.

It would appear that a major population decline on the Susiana in Late Uruk will have to be accepted. Several processes might account for this decline. One alternative might involve some sort of environmental catastrophe. Extended severe drouth with low temperatures and other adverse conditions such as prevailed on the plain during the winter cropping season of A.D. 1963-64 might account for a population decline through repeated crop failure and large scale starvation and/or emigration. "Acts of God" do not make very satisfactory explanations especially when supported by no evidence whatsoever. They do remain theoretically possible contributing factors.

Acts of man which contribute to environmental deterioration are more intrinsically pleasing. Soil salinization and resulting decreased agricultural yields all due to excessive zeal in irrigation might be proposed. The first recorded incidence of extensive salinization in the Near East affected the area of southern Iraq beginning about 2400 B.C., but did not seriously affect the settlement pattern until about 1700 B.C., a span of 700 years (Jacobsen and Adams, 1958:1252). This was a period of major state-sponsored hydraulic works on a scale far greater than anything probably undertaken during the Uruk period.

Helbaek (1969:415) attributes changes in crop selection in Deh Luran to salinization at a period as early as 6000 B.C. He notes gradual replacement of wheats by barleys, a more salt resistant cereal. The settlement pattern does not, however, seem to have been affected. The only highly salinized portion of the Susiana today is in the area of Deh Now (KS-120). This salinization may date to the Sassanian period. In sum, salinization would not seem to be a viable explanation for Late Uruk population decrease and areal abandonment.

Population decrease through development of "urban" diseases is another theoretically possible, though uninteresting and unsupported, explanation. None of the alternative processes presented thus far have been able to account for the Late Uruk population drop. On the other hand it has not been possible to demonstrate that one or more of these processes were not operative to some extent.

Whatever the specific causes, population decline was probably related to political instability and eventual hostilities on the plain. Security appears to have been a major administrative concern in Late Uruk. Presumably it was a problem before it affected the settlement pattern and was reflected in seal designs. Development of hostilities may have made agriculture an uncertain pursuit over large portions of the plain. Administrative conflict between Susa and Chogha Mish could have produced conflicts in corvée labor demands, irregularities in the local exchange system, and other administrative aberrations. Factors such as these could potentially have been more important in producing agricultural uncertainty than actual hostilities.

This discussion of the Late Uruk occupation of the Susiana survey area has been highly speculative and beset by many interpretive problems. The difficulty may well reside not only in insufficient data but also in an insufficient scale of analysis. Quite possibly a satisfactory explanation of processes operative on the Susiana during the Late Uruk period cannot be sought at even the regional level.

It is informative to consider events in the areas of Warka and Nippur during the Late Uruk period. The Uruk occupational history in the Nippur area was apparently very similar to that of Khuzistan. Population increased throughout Early and Middle Uruk (Adams' Early Uruk). Late Uruk saw a sharp population decline and extensive areal abandonment (Adams, 1971; personal communication).

While population dropped markedly in both the Nippur and Susa areas, it underwent a considerable expansion in the Warka area. The number of occupied settlements grew from 18 in Early Uruk to 108 in Late Uruk, an increase of 600 percent in perhaps 400 years (Adams and Nissen, 1972). Adams proposes three processes to account for this increase: one, natural population growth; two, conversion of semi-sedentary fishing, hunting and herding groups to sedentary pursuits; and three, immigration into the Warka area. He feels that the last possibility is "perhaps more likely" to account for the magnitude of the apparent population growth.

Warka is about 280 kilometers from Susa, a journey of perhaps a week or ten days. A significant proportion of the Late Uruk population decline around Susa and Nippur may be accounted for by the corresponding population increase around Warka.

Developing connections between the Susiana area and Mesopotamia proper might account for some of the contradictory evidence of information processing in Late Uruk. On the Susiana, decreasing population and apparent deterioration of the local exchange system implied decreasing information inputs to administrative organization. Artifactual indicators of information processing, cylinder seals and numerical tablets, implied an increased level of information processing. Militarism, if it existed on the plain, might account for increased information inputs. An additional emphasis on production for export might account for significant additional information processing requirements. Wright (1972) has demonstrated a resurgence in long range trade at Farukhabad in Deh Luran during the Jemdet Nasr period immediately subsequent to Late Uruk. Such a hypothesis remains to be tested for the Susiana.

To conclude this section, I would suggest that at least by Late Uruk times it is no longer sufficient to speak of the occupation of the Susiana plain or even of southwest Iran. Instead, the scale of analysis must be increased to that of Greater Mesopotamia as a whole. This will be a formidable project, but one which should be very rewarding.

IV

SUMMARY AND CONCLUSIONS

DEVELOPMENTS of the Late Uruk period on the Susiana plain constitute the chronological limit of this study. We are now in a position to evaluate both the operation of reputed prime movers of state origins and the broader theoretical position advocated here, in light of the appearance of the state on the Susiana. The state as defined here appeared on the Susiana plain of Khuzistan in the Early Uruk period. The first indication of potential external conflict appears in Middle Uruk with a concentration of large settlements on the margins of the settlement system. The first indications of internal conflict do not appear until Late Uruk, well after the development of state level organization.

Internal and external conflict cannot then be adduced as primary or even contributing factors in primary state development in this area. Internal and perhaps external conflict did, however, appear shortly after state formation. Minimally, internal conflict, though of a different sort than the class struggle proposed by Diakonov, was a major factor during the Late Uruk period.

Of the overtly managerial theories, administrative requirements of major irrigation may be eliminated as a prime mover. Irrigation agriculture was certainly present, probably long prior to the Uruk period (Hole, Flannery, and Neeley, 1969:361). We have no evidence, however, of major Uruk irrigation works and have argued for the presence of an efficient, though simply constructed and maintained, irrigation system. Adams has presented evidence of canals up to 15 kilometers in length constructed near Warka during the succeeding Jemdet Nasr period. He has also argued that canals of this seemingly impressive size can be constructed, operated, and maintained within the context of corporate kin groups and without state initiation or coordination (1970:115).

Elimination of irrigation as a prime mover of state formation does not preclude its consideration, where present, as a contributing factor. We will return to this point below.

Long range trade was presented as another possible prime cause of state development. The present study has not dealt directly with this aspect. Long range trade in Khuzistan during the late Susiana, Uruk, and Jemdet Nasr periods has been studied by Wright, who demonstrates a decrease in long range trade in the Early Uruk period during which the state appeared on the Susiana. Such trade did not increase until it underwent apparently marked reorganization in the final phases of Late Uruk and particularly in the Jemdet Nasr period (Wright:1972). Long range trade may thus be eliminated as a possible cause of primary state origins in Khuzistan. It was, however, probably important in the development of secondary states of the Jemdet Nasr period.

Population increase may also be eliminated as the cause of state origins on the Susiana. As discussed above, population densities equivalent to, or in excess of, those of the Early Uruk period were probably reached at least once previously on the plain. If population increase were the sole cause of state development, such development should have occurred much earlier than it actually did.

It should be pointed out however that even given our poor understanding of Susa A developments on the plain, there was an undeniable increase in population from Terminal Susa A to Early Uruk. Demographic changes may then have been a contributing factor to state development in the area.

The presence of two factors thought to be prime movers of state development has been identified—irrigation and population increase—neither of which taken individually or in combination is sufficient to explain state development on the Susiana.

This study has identified the operation of an additional factor, local exchange, in conjunction with state development. The organization of local exchange in Early and Middle Uruk has been shown to have involved centralization of craft production and the emergence of a centrally controlled local exchange system.

Reorganization of local exchange involved a major increment in information processing and decision making requirements. These requirements were met by increasing vertical specialization of the administrative hierarchy and by increasing information storage capacity of administrative technology.

Emergence of the state was clearly a "combination of ingredients product." Operation of a single causal factor, such as increase in local exchange, population, or irrigation, cannot be adduced as an explanation. This comes as no great surprise. Adams was perhaps the first anthropological archaeologist to emphasize the importance of multiple causality of state origins in *The Evolution of Urban Society* (1966). This approach has received considerable recent discussion (Adams, 1970; Wright, 1970; Flannery, 1972).

We have identified a series of processes operative in one case of state development. If changes in demography and the organization of local

ANALYSIS OF THE SETTLEMENT PATTERNS 159

exchange were among the immediate processes leading to the state, it is reasonable to ask why the population increased and why local exchange was reorganized. Increasingly fine chronological control and detailed areal surveys are gradually changing our picture of demographic trends in the ancient Near East. A picture of steady, if gradual, population increase is being replaced by a picture of marked demographic oscillations. Such oscillations were undoubtedly the result of the operation of a number of diverse factors for any given case. Tentative hypotheses about processes leading to the Middle-Late Uruk oscillation on the Susiana plain were outlined above. The Terminal Susa A-Early Uruk oscillation remains a mystery. Whatever the final resolution of these demographic problems, the sources of population change cannot be sought in strictly demographic processes.

Similarly, reorganization of local exchange is probably not to be explained in the context of a previously operative exchange system. Adams, among others, has suggested an additional factor for consideration in discussion of state origins in the Near East. He suggests that, "... urbanization in this case involved the concomitant appearance of new symbiotic relationships with nomads or semi-nomadic groups" (1970:119). The plain today provides extensive winter pasture for transhumant herders who retire to highland pastures during the intense heat of lowland Khuzistan summers. Emergence of large scale specialized animal husbandry in the Susa A-Early Uruk time range might well have provided pressure for the reorganization of local production on the plain to meet sharply increased seasonal demands for craft items and agricultural produce. Coordination of local production and seasonal exchange with herders may thus, in conjunction with other processes discussed above, have increased decision making requirements to the point that an expanded decision making organization was necessary.

Archaeologically there is virtually no data with which to test such a hypothesis. We know that by Early Uruk there was significant Uruk occupation of highland valleys (Goff, 1971:139-145). By Middle Uruk the presence of bevel rim bowls in highland cave sites (J. Speth, 1971, personal communication) may indicate camps of herders with lowland exchange connections. Their presence need not imply ration issue to specialized herders, but rather secondary use of ration bowls. Further, it is possible that these bowls did not have a lowland source, but were obtained from highland Uruk centers such as those found in Luristan by Goff (1971:139 ff.). Thus far no sites which can be identified as herding camps have been discovered on the Susiana plain itself.

The settlement pattern data are equally tenuous. The appearance of large Early Uruk settlements in the Vale of Andimeshk on the far eastern portion of the plain may be important in this regard. This area was on a major migration route of the Baktiari in the recent past (Pierre, 1917). During discussion of the Middle Uruk settlement pattern the apparently anomalous status of KS-153 as a small center was mentioned. Appearance of this settlement with KS-171 and KS-173 in Early Uruk may then have been coterminous with early major movements of herders through the area. Middle Uruk articulation of these settlements with the core of the Susiana may then have been effected through a small administrative center at KS-165 (see Fig. 19).

Nomad-agriculturalist symbiosis remains an untested hypothesis in the Uruk period. Plans are currently being made for resolution of this problem in the near future. Assuming that emergence of large scale specialized animal husbandry does prove to have been an important factor in the emergence of the Early Uruk state, we are still left with major theoretical problems.

The first problem is where to terminate a chain of causal factors. An "explanation" of the origin of the state could be carried back to the paleolithic and beyond. I would argue as follows. We have defined the state in terms of a certain level of complexity of decision making organization. For any *particular* case, demonstration of the immediate processes leading to differentiation of a three-level administrative hierarchy constitutes explanation of the development of a state. This has been done for the development of the state on the Susiana plain.

The second problem involves the necessity of building a general theory of state origins. Presumably anthropological archaeologists are concerned with the elucidation of processes of culture change which have general applicability. We are interested in primary state development as a general phenomenon. In this regard I would argue that even if it were possible, precise determination of the operation and interrelation of specific processes resulting in a single primary state, or any number of primary states is only a step in research rather than an end in itself.

This study has been addressed to many particularistic problems, but it has also dealt with generalized concepts of information processing in their relation to problems of primary state development. I have argued on an abstract level that organization of information processing and decision making is a useful criterion for cross cultural comparison, and a useful framework for process explanation. Specifically, use of this framework provides a new perspective and new set of problems in the investigation of state origins. What, for example, is the processing capacity of a given type of decision making organization? Under what conditions will increasing information inputs lead to increases in organizational complexity, and under what conditions will they lead to systemic breakdown or collapse?

I would suggest, for example, that primary state development involves overloading the decision making organization of a chiefdom. Since no single factor such as increasing irrigation, population, warfare, local exchange, or whatever can be shown to have led to state development, it would appear that

SUMMARY AND CONCLUSIONS

multiple sources of information input are required to force basic organizational changes at this level. The decision making organization of a chiefdom seems to be able to accommodate information increments from one or perhaps two sources, but not from a number of sources. In conclusion, I would like to suggest that diversity of information input is perhaps equally important as amount of input in primary state development. This is, however, a matter for future research.

It is difficult to conclude a study such as this with something more than a dull thud and a soft whimper. I am impressed with our lack of knowledge about virtually all of the topics which have been discussed here. There is evidence that we are making some progress in the study of state formation in general and of the Uruk of Khuzistan in particular.

Nearly 50 years ago Frankfort discussed the transition from what we now call Susa A to Uruk at Susa:

> We may then, without trusting ourselves to hazardous hypotheses conclude that through the incipient drought, by thinning the woods, made connexions with the North and hence an influx of new ideas and perhaps new people possible, its continuation ruined the prosperity of the first civilization. It went downhill, figuratively—and literally, as we shall see in dealing with Mesopotamia. Perhaps part of the population followed the retreating game into the mountains; others certainly descended into the plain of the Two Rivers, where the marshes in the now deposited alluvium were drying up, but water was still plentiful. "Musyan," westward of Susa, shows us a station on their route. The life of those who remained was encompassed with ever increasing difficulties. We have seen that the burial ritual had already been very scanty in their most flourishing period of which we know. But now the poverty of their life led them to give up even those remnants, and with them the manufacture of the thin-walled unserviceable pottery, which we admire so much. They made rough ware for their bare needs.
>
> It seems that subsequently life even for this small remainder of the population became impossible; the site was deserted, the houses crumbled to ruins, wind, sun, and desert dust completed the work, thus producing the effect which M. Jéquier took for wholesale leveling" (1924:39).

The present rate of research insures that this study will have a similar ring in far less than 50 years. May it quickly be so.

APPENDIX I

TYPE COUNTS: 1970-71 SURVEY

Explanatory note:

The following table contains the basic Uruk ceramic type counts from the 1970-71 survey surface collections. Individual ceramic types are identified by index numbers 1 to 54. These are the column numbers in the Count Table. A list of ceramic types included in the table and their associated index numbers is provided.

Row identification codes in the Count Table refer to sites and site collection areas. The code "108D" would indicate collection area "D" of site "KS-108." Site locations are indicated on Figure 5. Collection areas are indicated on the site maps, Plates X through XX. The ceramics themselves are illustrated in Plates I through IX.

The arrangement of the Count Table is as follows. Counts for types 1 through 18 are listed for all sites in the first three pages of the table. Counts for types 19 through 36 and 37 through 54 are listed for all sites in the second and third three-page sets.

Ceramic Type Index Numbers for the 1970-71 Survey Surface Collections
 1. Bevel Rim Bowl—Rim to Base Section
 2. Bevel Rim Bowl—Rim
 3. Bevel Rim Bowl—Base
 4. Proto Bevel Rim Bowl—Rim to Base Section
 5. Proto Bevel Rim Bowl—Rim
 6. Chaff Tempered Tray
 7. Band Rim Bottle
 8. Ledge Rim Bottle
 9. Sinuous Sided Cup—Rim
10. Sinous Sided Cup—Base
11. Lip Spout
12. Round Rim Bowl

13. Flat Rim Bowl
14. Bevel Lip Bowl
15. Ledge Expanded Rim Bowl
16. Ledge Rim Bowl
17. Beaded Rim Bowl
18. Impressed Strip Bowl
19. Straight Round Rim Jar
20. Heavy Round Rim Jar
21. Grooved Round Rim Jar
22. Straight Flared Rim Jar
23. Straight Expanded Rim Jar
24. Flared Expanded Rim Jar
25. Out-turned Expanded Rim Jar
26. High Expanded Band Rim Jar
27. Low Expanded Band Rim Jar
28. Ledge Rim Jar
29. Ledge Expanded Rim Jar
30. Neckless Ledge Rim Jar
31. Impressed Strip Jar Shoulder
32. Hatched Strip Jar Shoulder
33. Punctate Jar Shoulder
34. Reserve Slip Jar Shoulder
35. Punctate + Reserve Slip Jar Shoulder
36. Incised Cross Hatch Band Jar Shoulder
37. Incised Cross Hatch Triangle Jar Shoulder
38. Incised Oblique Band Jar Shoulder
39. Grooved Jar Shoulder
40. Groove and Oblique Jar Shoulder
41. Rocker Stamp Jar Shoulder
42. Surface Combing
43. Nose Lug
44. Heavy Lug
45. Straight Spout
46. Droop Spout
47. Conical Spout
48. Truncated Straight Spout
49. Other Spout
50. Strap Handle
51. Flat Twisted Handle
52. Full Twisted Handle
53. Rim Lug
54. Clay Sickle

APPENDIX I

TABLE 35
TYPE COUNTS: 1970-71 SURVEY SURFACE COLLECTIONS

									TYPES									
SITE	1	2	3	4	5	6	7	8	9	10	11	12	13	14	15	16	17	18
004A	0	0	0	0	0	0	0	0	0	0	0	0	0	0	0	0	0	1
004C	0	0	1	0	0	0	0	0	0	0	0	0	5	2	0	0	0	0
004E	0	1	9	2	8	0	0	0	0	0	0	0	1	1	0	0	0	0
005	0	6	0	0	0	0	0	0	0	0	0	0	0	0	0	1	0	0
006S	0	6	3	0	2	0	0	0	0	0	0	0	1	0	0	0	0	0
007O	0	15	1	0	0	0	0	0	0	0	0	0	0	0	0	0	0	0
008A	0	10	6	0	0	1	0	0	0	0	0	0	0	0	0	0	0	0
008B	0	3	0	0	1	1	0	0	0	0	0	1	0	0	0	0	0	2
008C	0	0	0	0	0	0	0	0	0	0	0	0	0	0	0	0	0	0
015	0	4	1	0	0	0	0	0	0	0	0	0	0	0	0	0	0	0
016	5	43	3	0	8	0	0	0	3	0	0	0	8	0	0	0	2	1
022A	0	0	0	0	1	0	0	0	2	0	0	0	0	0	0	1	0	1
022B	5	7	0	0	0	0	0	0	0	0	0	0	1	0	0	4	0	0
022C	5	0	0	0	0	0	0	0	0	0	0	0	0	0	0	0	0	2
024	7	18	8	0	4	0	0	0	1	0	0	0	1	1	0	0	0	0
027	2	16	1	0	4	0	1	0	1	0	0	0	1	0	0	0	0	1
032	2	62	6	0	4	0	2	0	0	0	0	0	0	0	0	0	0	0
033	0	0	1	0	0	0	0	0	0	0	0	0	1	0	0	0	0	1
034A	0	13	0	0	0	0	0	0	0	0	0	0	0	0	0	0	0	0
034B	0	4	0	0	0	0	0	0	0	0	0	0	0	0	0	0	0	0
034C	0	7	0	0	0	0	0	0	0	0	0	0	1	0	0	0	0	0
035A	4	18	3	0	0	0	0	0	2	0	0	0	2	0	0	0	0	0
035B	0	5	1	0	2	0	0	0	0	0	0	0	1	0	0	0	0	0
036A	2	15	1	0	0	0	0	0	0	0	0	0	0	0	0	0	0	0
036B	0	5	0	0	0	0	0	0	0	0	0	0	1	0	0	0	0	1
036BP	5	3	0	0	0	0	0	0	0	0	0	0	0	0	0	1	0	0
036C	0	2	2	0	0	0	0	0	0	0	0	0	0	0	0	1	0	0
036D	0	1	0	0	0	0	0	0	0	0	0	0	0	0	0	0	0	0
036E	1	8	0	0	0	0	0	0	0	0	0	0	0	0	0	0	0	0
036F	0	3	0	0	0	2	0	0	0	0	0	0	0	0	0	1	0	0
036G	12	8	0	0	0	0	0	0	0	0	0	0	1	0	0	0	0	0
037	0	1	0	0	0	0	0	0	0	0	0	0	0	0	0	0	0	0
039A	26	4	0	0	0	1	0	0	1	0	0	0	0	0	0	0	0	0
039B	0	0	0	0	0	0	0	0	0	0	0	0	0	0	0	0	0	0
039C	2	5	0	0	0	0	0	0	1	0	0	0	0	0	2	0	0	0
039E	9	0	0	0	0	0	0	0	2	0	0	0	0	0	0	0	0	0
039F	0	0	0	0	0	0	0	0	0	0	0	0	0	0	0	0	0	0
039G	1	7	0	0	0	1	0	0	0	0	0	0	0	0	0	0	0	0
039H	0	6	1	0	0	0	0	0	0	0	0	0	0	1	0	0	0	0
040A	0	4	1	0	0	0	0	0	0	0	0	0	0	0	0	0	0	0
040B	0	0	0	0	0	0	0	0	0	0	0	0	0	0	0	0	0	0
044A	1	6	1	0	0	0	0	0	0	0	0	0	0	0	0	0	0	0
044B	1	1	0	0	0	0	0	0	0	0	0	0	0	0	0	0	0	1
044C	0	0	0	0	0	0	0	0	0	0	0	0	0	0	0	0	0	1
045	1	5	3	0	0	0	0	0	0	0	0	0	0	0	0	0	0	0
049A	1	19	5	1	2	3	0	0	0	0	0	0	0	0	0	0	0	1

166 LOCAL EXCHANGE AND EARLY STATE DEVELOPMENT

TABLE 35
TYPE COUNTS: 1970-71 SURVEY SURFACE COLLECTIONS

	TYPES																	
SITE	1	2	3	4	5	6	7	8	9	10	11	12	13	14	15	16	17	18
049B	0	0	0	0	0	1	0	0	0	0	0	0	0	0	0	0	1	0
049C	0	6	2	0	1	0	0	0	0	0	0	0	0	0	0	0	1	0
050	0	1	0	0	0	0	0	0	0	0	0	0	0	1	0	0	0	0
052A	0	4	5	0	3	0	0	0	0	0	0	0	6	0	0	1	0	2
052B	0	1	0	0	1	0	0	0	0	0	0	0	1	0	0	0	0	0
052C	0	1	0	0	1	0	0	0	0	0	0	0	0	0	0	0	0	0
054	14	17	0	0	0	1	1	1	7	0	0	4	3	1	1	0	0	0
059A	0	3	0	0	0	0	0	0	0	0	0	0	0	0	0	0	0	0
059B	4	11	0	0	2	0	1	0	0	0	0	0	2	0	0	1	0	0
059C	3	5	0	0	0	1	0	0	0	0	0	0	1	0	0	0	0	1
059D	5	7	0	0	0	0	0	0	0	0	0	0	1	0	0	0	0	0
059E	0	3	0	0	1	0	1	0	0	0	0	0	0	0	0	0	0	0
059F	18	6	1	0	0	0	0	0	0	0	0	0	0	0	0	0	0	0
059G	26	10	0	0	0	1	2	0	2	0	1	0	1	1	1	2	0	0
059H	1	3	0	0	0	0	0	0	1	0	0	0	0	0	0	0	0	0
059I	5	3	0	0	1	0	0	0	0	0	0	0	0	0	0	0	0	2
061A	5	14	2	0	1	0	0	0	0	0	0	1	2	0	0	1	0	0
061B	0	4	0	0	0	0	0	0	0	0	0	0	0	0	0	3	0	0
064A	0	1	1	0	1	0	0	0	0	0	0	1	3	0	0	0	0	0
064B	0	3	0	0	3	0	0	0	0	0	0	0	0	1	0	0	0	1
064C	0	2	3	0	0	0	0	0	0	0	0	0	0	0	0	0	0	0
067	0	0	0	0	0	0	0	0	0	0	0	0	13	0	0	0	0	0
076	3	7	1	0	1	0	0	0	0	0	0	1	1	0	0	0	0	0
079A	0	19	2	0	0	0	0	0	0	0	0	0	0	0	0	0	0	0
079B	0	5	1	0	0	0	0	0	0	0	0	0	0	0	0	0	0	0
079C	0	3	0	0	0	0	0	0	0	0	0	0	0	0	0	0	0	0
079D	0	1	0	0	0	0	0	0	0	0	0	0	0	0	0	0	0	0
090A	0	4	0	0	2	0	0	0	0	0	0	0	0	0	0	0	0	0
090B	0	6	3	0	1	0	0	0	0	0	0	0	0	0	0	0	0	0
090C	0	2	0	0	0	0	0	0	0	0	0	1	0	0	0	1	0	1
093	2	9	1	0	3	0	0	0	0	0	0	0	1	0	0	0	0	0
094	0	4	0	0	0	0	0	0	0	0	0	0	3	1	0	0	1	3
096B	3	5	3	2	10	0	0	0	0	0	0	0	3	0	0	0	0	5
096C	0	4	1	0	0	0	0	0	0	0	0	0	0	0	0	0	0	0
096F	0	1	0	0	0	0	0	0	0	0	0	0	0	0	0	0	0	0
096H	10	9	0	0	0	0	5	0	0	1	0	0	0	1	0	0	0	0
096I	0	14	0	0	0	0	0	0	0	0	0	0	0	0	0	0	0	0
098	0	36	2	0	0	1	0	0	0	0	0	1	0	0	0	0	0	0
099	0	5	3	0	0	0	0	0	0	0	0	0	0	1	0	0	0	1
101	0	0	0	0	0	0	0	0	0	0	0	0	0	0	0	0	0	0
102	0	1	0	0	0	0	0	1	0	0	0	0	0	0	0	0	0	0
108A	0	1	2	0	1	0	0	0	0	0	0	4	5	0	0	0	0	0
108B	0	7	29	1	21	1	0	0	0	0	0	2	4	0	0	8	0	1
108C	16	20	2	0	0	0	0	0	0	0	0	2	0	0	1	1	0	0
108D	5	0	0	0	0	0	0	0	0	0	0	0	0	0	0	1	0	0

APPENDIX I

TABLE 35
TYPE COUNTS: 1970-71 SURVEY SURFACE COLLECTIONS

	TYPES																	
SITE	1	2	3	4	5	6	7	8	9	10	11	12	13	14	15	16	17	18
108E	0	2	0	0	0	0	0	0	0	0	0	0	0	0	0	0	0	0
108F	29	5	1	0	0	0	0	0	0	0	0	0	0	0	0	0	0	0
112	0	0	0	0	0	0	0	0	0	0	0	0	0	0	0	0	0	1
113A	5	5	2	0	0	0	0	0	2	0	0	1	0	0	0	0	0	0
113B	0	3	0	0	0	0	0	0	0	0	0	0	0	0	0	0	0	0
113C	1	2	0	0	0	0	0	0	0	0	0	0	0	0	0	0	0	0
113D	0	1	0	0	0	0	0	0	0	0	0	0	0	0	0	0	0	0
113G	0	0	0	0	0	0	0	0	0	0	0	0	0	0	0	0	0	1
120	0	6	1	0	0	0	0	0	0	0	0	0	0	0	0	0	0	1
121	0	14	7	0	3	0	0	0	0	0	0	0	0	0	0	0	0	0
153A	0	15	0	0	0	5	0	0	0	0	0	0	0	0	0	8	0	4
153B	1	10	0	0	0	0	0	0	0	0	0	0	2	0	0	3	0	0
165A	0	1	1	0	2	0	0	0	0	0	0	0	0	0	0	0	0	0
165B	1	10	0	0	0	0	0	0	0	0	0	0	2	0	0	0	0	0
165C	0	3	1	0	0	1	0	0	0	0	0	1	0	1	0	0	0	0
171A	3	25	0	0	0	0	0	0	2	0	0	0	0	0	0	0	0	0
171B	1	21	3	0	0	1	0	0	0	1	0	0	0	0	1	0	0	0
173	7	4	0	0	0	0	0	0	0	0	0	0	0	0	0	1	0	0
182	0	0	0	0	0	0	0	0	0	0	0	0	0	0	0	0	0	3
190	0	1	0	0	0	0	0	0	0	0	0	0	0	0	0	0	0	5
197	0	13	5	0	0	0	0	0	0	0	0	0	0	0	0	0	0	0
218	2	19	9	0	0	0	0	0	0	0	0	0	0	0	0	0	0	0
240	0	4	0	0	1	0	0	0	0	0	0	0	2	1	0	0	0	0
266	6	39	7	5	9	0	0	0	2	0	0	4	8	0	0	2	0	0
269	0	3	0	0	0	0	0	0	0	0	0	5	15	0	0	0	0	0
284A	0	6	2	0	5	0	0	0	0	0	0	0	2	0	0	1	1	1
284B	0	0	0	0	0	0	0	0	2	0	0	0	0	0	0	1	0	0
285	0	5	2	0	2	0	0	0	0	0	0	0	0	0	0	0	0	0
286	0	4	0	0	0	0	0	0	0	0	0	0	0	0	0	0	1	0
288	0	16	1	0	0	1	0	0	0	0	0	4	0	4	4	3	4	0
289	0	15	1	0	0	0	0	0	0	0	0	0	0	0	0	0	0	0
290A	0	6	1	0	4	0	0	0	0	0	0	0	0	0	0	0	0	0
290B	0	10	2	0	0	0	0	0	0	0	0	0	0	0	0	0	1	2

TABLE 35
TYPE COUNTS: 1970-71 SURVEY SURFACE COLLECTIONS

SITE	19	20	21	22	23	24	25	26	27	28	29	30	31	32	33	34	35	36
004A	0	0	0	0	0	0	0	0	0	0	0	0	0	0	0	0	0	0
004C	1	0	1	0	0	0	1	2	2	1	1	0	0	0	0	0	0	0
004E	0	0	0	2	1	3	1	2	0	0	0	0	0	0	0	0	0	0
005	0	1	0	0	0	0	0	0	0	0	0	0	0	0	0	0	0	0
006S	0	1	0	0	0	0	0	0	0	0	0	2	0	0	0	0	0	0
007O	0	1	0	0	0	0	0	1	0	0	0	0	0	0	0	0	0	2
008A	0	3	0	3	0	2	3	2	3	1	0	0	0	0	0	0	0	0
008B	0	2	0	0	0	0	0	0	1	0	0	0	0	0	0	0	0	0
008C	0	0	0	0	0	0	0	0	1	0	0	0	0	0	0	0	0	0
015	0	0	0	0	0	0	0	0	1	0	0	0	0	0	0	0	0	0
016	0	0	4	11	5	10	1	0	1	4	2	1	0	0	5	4	1	5
022A	0	2	0	0	0	0	0	1	0	0	0	0	0	0	0	0	0	0
022B	0	4	0	2	0	4	2	0	2	0	1	1	1	3	0	4	0	0
022C	0	1	0	0	0	0	0	0	0	0	0	0	0	0	0	2	0	1
024	0	10	0	6	0	11	2	1	2	0	0	0	0	0	0	2	1	0
027	1	0	4	6	2	5	2	0	2	0	0	2	0	0	0	10	0	0
032	0	4	1	4	1	0	1	0	1	0	0	0	0	0	2	3	0	3
033	0	0	0	0	0	0	0	0	0	0	0	0	0	0	0	0	0	0
034A	1	3	0	3	0	3	0	0	2	1	2	0	0	1	1	0	0	0
034B	0	0	1	0	2	1	2	2	1	0	0	1	0	3	1	0	0	3
034C	0	0	0	4	1	0	4	0	1	1	0	0	0	0	1	1	0	2
035A	0	2	2	5	4	4	4	0	5	4	1	0	1	1	2	0	0	0
035B	0	0	0	0	2	2	0	1	1	2	0	0	0	0	0	0	0	0
036A	1	1	1	2	2	0	0	0	1	1	0	0	0	0	2	0	0	0
036B	1	4	0	2	1	0	3	4	8	1	1	0	0	3	2	2	0	3
036BP	0	3	3	4	0	1	2	0	1	0	0	0	1	0	2	1	0	1
036C	1	0	0	2	0	0	1	0	0	0	1	0	0	0	0	0	0	0
036D	0	0	0	0	0	1	0	0	0	0	0	0	0	0	0	0	0	0
036E	0	1	0	0	1	0	0	0	0	0	0	0	0	0	0	0	0	0
036F	1	2	0	2	0	0	1	0	0	0	0	0	0	0	0	0	0	0
036G	0	2	0	5	1	0	4	1	1	2	1	0	1	0	0	0	0	0
037	0	0	0	0	0	0	0	0	0	0	0	0	0	0	0	0	0	0
039A	1	3	0	1	0	0	2	0	0	0	0	0	0	0	0	0	0	0
039B	0	1	0	2	0	0	1	0	1	0	0	0	0	0	0	1	1	0
039C	0	3	0	0	1	0	1	1	2	0	0	0	0	1	0	0	1	0
039E	1	5	0	2	1	1	2	0	3	0	0	0	0	0	0	0	0	0
039F	0	0	0	0	0	0	0	1	0	0	0	0	0	0	0	0	0	0
039G	0	0	0	0	0	0	0	1	0	0	0	0	0	0	0	0	0	0
039H	0	0	0	0	0	1	1	1	0	0	0	0	0	0	0	0	0	0
040A	0	0	0	0	0	0	0	0	0	0	0	0	0	0	0	0	0	0
040B	0	0	0	0	0	0	0	0	0	0	0	0	0	0	0	0	0	0
044A	0	0	0	0	0	0	0	2	0	0	1	0	0	0	0	0	0	0
044B	1	0	2	0	1	0	0	0	1	0	1	0	0	0	0	0	0	0
044C	0	0	0	0	0	0	0	0	0	0	0	0	0	0	0	0	0	0
045	0	0	0	0	0	0	0	0	0	0	0	0	0	0	0	0	0	0
049A	0	2	0	2	1	4	0	3	0	0	0	0	0	0	0	0	0	1

APPENDIX I

TABLE 35
TYPE COUNTS: 1970-71 SURVEY SURFACE COLLECTIONS

	TYPES																	
SITE	19	20	21	22	23	24	25	26	27	28	29	30	31	32	33	34	35	36
049B	0	1	0	1	0	2	0	3	0	0	0	0	0	0	0	2	0	0
049C	0	0	2	2	0	2	0	3	0	0	0	0	0	0	0	0	0	0
050	0	0	0	0	0	2	0	0	0	0	0	0	0	0	0	1	0	0
052A	0	0	0	7	1	2	0	0	0	0	0	0	0	2	2	1	0	2
052B	0	0	0	0	0	0	0	0	0	0	0	0	0	0	0	0	0	0
052C	0	0	0	0	0	0	0	0	0	0	0	0	0	0	0	0	0	0
054	2	10	0	4	5	1	2	0	4	1	2	0	4	1	1	0	1	2
059A	0	0	0	0	1	1	0	1	0	0	0	0	0	0	0	1	0	0
059B	0	3	0	2	4	2	3	2	2	0	2	0	2	3	0	7	1	2
059C	0	0	0	2	1	0	1	3	1	1	0	0	0	0	0	6	0	2
059D	2	2	0	0	0	0	1	1	0	2	0	0	0	1	0	0	0	0
059E	0	0	0	0	0	0	0	0	1	0	0	0	1	0	0	0	0	0
059F	0	1	0	1	1	0	2	0	5	0	0	0	1	1	1	0	0	2
059G	1	5	0	3	5	5	1	2	0	5	0	0	2	0	1	1	0	2
059H	0	0	0	0	0	0	0	0	1	0	0	0	0	0	0	0	0	0
059I	0	2	0	1	1	0	1	1	0	0	1	0	0	1	1	3	1	2
061A	1	1	1	3	2	2	1	0	2	1	1	0	0	0	4	0	0	1
061B	0	1	0	0	1	0	0	0	1	0	0	0	0	0	1	0	0	0
064A	0	0	0	0	0	1	0	0	0	0	0	0	0	0	0	0	1	0
064B	0	1	0	1	0	1	0	0	0	0	0	0	1	0	0	0	0	0
064C	0	1	2	1	0	0	0	0	0	0	0	0	0	0	0	0	0	0
067	0	0	0	0	0	0	0	0	0	0	0	0	0	0	0	0	0	0
076	1	4	2	6	1	6	4	3	1	1	2	0	0	0	0	0	0	2
079A	1	2	0	0	1	0	0	0	1	0	0	0	0	0	0	0	0	0
079B	0	1	0	0	0	0	0	0	0	0	0	0	0	0	0	0	0	0
079C	0	1	0	0	1	0	0	0	0	0	0	0	0	0	0	0	0	0
079D	0	1	0	1	0	0	0	0	0	0	0	0	0	0	0	0	0	0
090A	0	0	0	1	0	0	0	0	0	0	0	0	0	1	1	0	0	0
090B	0	1	0	0	0	0	0	0	0	0	0	0	0	0	0	0	0	0
090C	0	0	0	0	0	0	0	0	0	0	0	0	0	0	0	0	0	0
093	0	3	0	1	0	1	0	0	0	0	0	0	0	1	0	1	0	0
094	1	0	0	4	1	0	0	0	0	6	3	0	0	0	0	0	0	0
096B	1	3	0	2	0	3	0	2	0	2	0	9	0	0	2	0	0	13
096C	0	0	0	0	0	0	0	0	0	0	0	0	0	0	0	0	0	0
096F	0	0	0	0	0	0	0	0	0	0	0	0	0	0	0	0	0	0
096H	4	2	0	0	2	0	0	0	4	1	1	0	0	0	1	0	0	2
096I	0	1	0	0	0	0	0	0	0	0	0	0	0	0	0	0	0	0
098	0	0	1	0	0	0	1	0	0	0	0	0	0	0	0	0	0	0
099	0	0	0	2	0	1	0	1	0	0	0	2	0	0	0	1	0	0
101	0	0	0	0	0	1	0	0	0	0	0	0	0	0	0	0	0	0
102	0	0	0	0	0	0	0	0	0	0	0	0	0	0	0	0	1	0
108A	1	0	0	1	0	2	0	0	0	1	0	0	0	0	0	0	0	0
108B	0	1	1	5	2	12	0	0	0	0	0	4	0	0	1	0	0	0
108C	1	3	2	9	0	5	10	2	4	0	3	0	2	4	4	9	0	7
108D	0	7	2	0	0	2	1	4	4	0	0	0	0	0	1	3	1	1

TABLE 35
TYPE COUNTS: 1970-71 SURVEY SURFACE COLLECTIONS

	TYPES																	
SITE	19	20	21	22	23	24	25	26	27	28	29	30	31	32	33	34	35	36
108E	0	0	0	0	0	0	0	0	0	0	0	0	0	0	0	0	0	0
108F	1	11	1	2	2	0	3	4	6	1	0	0	0	2	1	0	0	1
112	0	0	0	0	0	1	0	0	0	0	0	0	0	0	0	0	0	0
113A	0	5	0	1	4	0	0	0	2	0	0	0	0	1	2	2	0	3
113B	0	0	0	0	0	0	0	0	0	0	0	0	0	0	0	0	1	1
113C	0	0	0	0	0	0	0	1	1	0	0	0	0	0	0	0	0	0
113D	0	0	0	0	0	0	0	0	0	0	0	0	0	0	0	0	0	0
113G	0	0	0	0	0	0	0	0	0	0	0	0	0	0	0	1	1	3
120	0	0	0	0	0	1	0	0	0	0	0	0	0	0	0	0	0	0
121	0	0	0	0	0	3	0	0	0	0	0	0	0	1	0	1	0	0
153A	1	11	0	0	0	7	3	2	10	0	2	2	2	0	1	0	0	2
153B	1	3	0	1	0	1	2	2	4	0	0	1	1	0	1	0	0	0
165A	0	1	0	1	0	0	0	0	0	0	0	0	0	0	0	0	0	0
165B	0	5	2	2	4	3	0	3	2	0	1	0	2	1	3	0	1	5
165C	0	0	0	0	0	0	0	0	0	1	0	0	0	0	0	0	0	0
171A	1	7	0	0	2	2	8	6	3	0	0	0	0	2	0	0	0	4
171B	2	4	1	1	0	1	2	0	3	2	0	0	2	0	2	0	0	0
173	0	2	2	1	1	1	3	2	2	2	1	0	0	1	1	0	0	13
182	0	0	0	0	0	0	0	0	0	0	0	0	0	0	0	0	0	0
190	0	0	0	0	0	0	0	0	0	0	0	0	0	0	0	0	0	0
197	1	3	1	2	0	1	1	3	3	1	0	0	1	0	1	0	0	3
218	0	1	0	0	0	0	0	0	0	0	0	0	0	0	0	0	0	0
240	1	1	0	0	0	1	0	0	1	0	0	0	0	0	0	1	0	1
266	2	7	5	10	2	8	1	4	3	0	0	5	1	1	2	0	0	0
269	1	0	0	11	0	3	0	0	0	1	0	0	0	0	0	0	0	0
284A	0	0	0	9	0	6	2	4	0	0	0	1	0	0	0	0	0	0
284B	0	0	0	0	0	1	0	2	0	0	0	1	0	0	0	0	1	0
285	0	0	0	0	0	0	0	1	0	0	0	0	0	0	0	1	0	0
286	0	0	0	0	0	0	0	1	0	0	0	0	0	0	0	0	0	0
288	1	2	2	1	0	0	0	0	0	0	0	0	0	1	0	0	1	1
289	0	0	0	3	0	1	2	0	0	1	0	0	0	1	0	4	1	1
290A	0	1	0	1	1	0	0	0	0	0	0	0	1	0	0	0	0	0
290B	0	3	0	0	0	2	0	0	0	0	2	0	0	0	0	0	0	0

APPENDIX I

TABLE 35
TYPE COUNTS: 1970-71 SURVEY SURFACE COLLECTIONS

							TYPES										
SITE	37	38	39	40	41	42	43	44	45	46	47	48	49	50	51	52	53	54
004A	0	0	0	0	0	0	0	0	1	0	0	0	0	2	0	0	0	0
004C	0	0	0	0	0	0	1	0	0	0	0	0	0	0	0	0	0	0
004E	0	0	0	0	0	0	0	0	0	0	0	0	0	2	0	0	0	5
005	0	1	0	0	0	0	0	0	0	0	0	0	0	0	0	0	0	0
006S	0	0	0	0	0	0	0	0	1	0	0	0	0	0	0	0	0	2
007O	0	0	0	0	0	0	0	0	0	0	0	0	0	0	0	0	0	0
008A	0	0	0	0	0	0	0	0	0	0	0	0	0	4	0	0	0	0
008B	0	0	0	0	0	0	0	0	0	0	0	0	0	1	0	0	0	0
008C	0	0	0	0	0	0	0	0	0	0	0	0	0	0	0	0	0	0
015	0	0	0	0	0	0	0	0	0	0	0	0	0	0	0	0	0	0
016	0	2	2	2	1	0	3	2	3	0	1	0	0	2	0	0	0	7
022A	0	0	0	0	0	0	0	0	0	0	0	0	0	1	0	0	0	0
022B	0	0	0	0	1	0	1	0	1	0	0	0	0	1	0	0	0	2
022C	0	0	1	0	0	0	0	0	0	0	0	0	0	1	0	0	0	0
024	0	0	1	1	0	0	0	0	0	0	0	0	0	3	0	0	0	1
027	0	1	0	0	1	1	0	0	2	0	1	0	2	0	0	0	0	0
032	0	0	0	0	1	1	2	0	2	7	0	0	0	1	2	0	0	0
033	0	0	0	0	0	0	0	0	0	0	0	0	0	2	0	0	0	0
034A	1	0	3	3	0	0	1	0	1	1	0	1	0	0	3	0	1	0
034B	0	1	0	0	0	1	0	0	0	0	0	0	0	3	1	0	0	1
034C	0	2	0	0	0	0	0	0	0	0	0	0	0	3	0	0	0	2
035A	1	0	0	0	0	0	1	0	2	0	0	0	0	3	0	0	0	0
035B	0	0	0	0	0	0	0	0	0	1	0	0	0	1	0	0	0	2
036A	0	0	0	0	0	0	0	0	0	0	0	0	0	0	0	0	0	0
036B	0	0	6	1	0	1	2	0	2	1	0	0	0	4	0	0	0	0
036BP	0	0	1	0	0	0	1	0	1	0	3	0	0	1	0	0	1	0
036C	0	0	0	0	1	0	1	0	1	0	1	0	0	0	0	0	0	0
036D	0	0	0	0	0	0	0	0	0	0	0	0	0	0	0	0	0	0
036E	0	0	0	0	0	0	0	0	0	0	0	0	0	0	0	0	0	0
036F	0	0	0	0	0	0	0	0	1	0	0	0	0	0	0	0	0	0
036G	1	1	1	0	0	0	0	0	0	0	1	0	1	0	0	1	0	0
037	0	0	0	0	0	0	0	0	0	0	0	0	0	0	0	0	0	0
039A	0	0	0	1	0	0	0	0	0	0	0	0	0	0	0	0	0	0
039B	0	0	0	0	0	0	0	0	0	0	0	0	1	1	0	0	0	0
039C	0	0	0	0	0	0	0	0	0	0	0	0	1	1	0	0	0	0
039E	1	0	1	0	0	0	0	0	0	0	0	0	0	4	2	0	0	0
039F	0	0	0	0	0	0	0	0	0	0	0	0	0	0	0	0	0	0
039G	0	0	0	0	0	0	1	0	0	1	0	0	0	2	0	0	1	0
039H	0	0	0	0	0	0	0	0	0	0	0	0	0	0	0	0	0	0
040A	0	0	0	0	0	0	0	0	0	0	0	0	0	0	0	0	0	0
040B	0	0	0	0	0	0	0	0	0	0	0	0	0	0	0	0	0	0
044A	0	0	0	0	0	0	0	0	0	0	0	0	0	0	0	0	0	0
044B	0	0	0	0	0	0	0	0	0	0	0	0	0	1	0	0	0	0
044C	0	0	1	0	0	1	0	0	0	0	0	0	0	0	0	0	0	0
045	0	0	0	0	0	0	0	0	1	0	0	0	0	0	0	0	0	0
049A	0	0	0	0	0	0	0	0	0	0	0	0	1	1	0	0	0	0

TABLE 35
TYPE COUNTS: 1970-71 SURVEY SURFACE COLLECTIONS

								TYPES									
SITES	37	38	39	40	41	42	43	44	45	46	47	48	49	50	51	52	53	54
049B	0	0	0	0	0	0	0	0	0	0	0	0	0	0	0	0	0	0
049C	0	0	0	0	0	0	0	0	0	0	0	0	0	0	0	0	0	0
050	0	0	0	0	0	0	0	0	0	0	0	0	0	0	0	0	0	0
052A	0	0	0	0	0	0	0	0	2	0	0	0	1	3	0	0	0	6
052B	0	0	0	0	0	0	0	0	0	0	0	0	0	1	0	0	0	0
052C	0	0	0	0	0	0	0	0	0	0	0	0	0	0	0	0	0	0
054	0	0	2	5	0	0	1	0	0	5	4	1	0	9	3	4	0	0
059A	0	0	0	0	0	0	0	0	1	2	0	0	0	0	0	0	0	0
059B	2	1	1	0	0	1	2	0	1	3	0	0	0	4	0	0	0	0
059C	0	1	0	2	0	0	0	0	2	0	0	0	0	3	0	0	0	0
059D	0	0	0	0	0	0	0	0	2	0	0	0	0	3	0	0	0	0
059E	0	0	0	0	0	0	1	0	0	0	0	0	0	0	0	0	0	0
059F	0	0	1	0	0	0	0	0	0	1	1	1	0	1	1	0	0	3
059G	1	2	3	3	2	0	1	0	2	1	0	0	0	3	3	1	1	0
059H	0	0	1	0	1	0	0	0	0	0	0	0	0	0	3	0	0	0
059I	1	1	0	0	0	0	0	0	0	1	0	0	1	2	1	1	0	0
061A	0	0	0	0	1	0	0	0	3	0	0	1	0	2	0	0	0	0
061B	0	0	0	0	0	0	0	0	1	0	0	0	1	0	1	0	1	0
064A	0	0	0	0	0	0	0	1	1	0	0	2	0	0	0	0	0	0
064B	0	0	0	0	0	0	0	0	0	0	0	0	0	0	0	0	0	0
064C	0	0	0	0	0	0	0	0	0	0	0	0	0	0	0	0	0	0
067	0	0	0	0	0	0	2	0	0	0	0	0	0	0	0	0	0	0
076	0	0	0	0	1	0	2	0	0	0	0	0	0	0	0	0	0	0
079A	0	0	2	1	0	0	0	0	0	1	0	0	0	1	2	3	1	0
079B	0	0	0	0	0	0	0	0	0	1	0	0	0	1	0	2	0	0
079C	0	0	0	1	0	0	0	0	0	0	0	0	0	1	0	0	1	0
079D	0	0	0	0	0	0	0	0	0	0	0	0	0	0	1	0	0	0
090A	0	0	0	0	0	0	0	0	0	0	0	0	1	0	0	0	0	0
090B	0	0	0	0	0	0	0	0	0	0	0	0	0	0	0	0	0	1
090C	0	0	0	0	0	0	0	0	0	0	0	0	0	0	0	0	0	0
093	0	0	0	0	0	0	1	0	3	0	0	0	2	3	0	0	0	1
094	0	0	0	0	0	1	1	1	1	0	0	0	0	0	0	0	0	0
096B	0	0	1	1	3	1	0	1	2	2	0	0	0	3	0	0	0	0
096C	0	0	0	1	0	0	0	0	0	0	0	0	0	1	0	0	0	0
096F	0	0	0	0	0	0	0	0	0	0	0	0	0	0	0	0	0	0
096H	3	0	6	31	0	0	1	0	2	8	0	0	0	5	4	5	3	0
096I	0	0	0	0	0	0	0	0	0	1	0	0	0	0	0	0	0	0
098	0	0	0	0	0	0	0	0	0	0	0	0	0	0	0	0	0	0
099	0	0	1	0	0	0	0	0	0	0	0	0	0	0	0	0	0	0
101	0	0	0	0	0	0	0	0	0	0	0	0	0	0	0	0	0	0
102	0	0	0	0	0	0	0	0	1	0	0	0	0	0	0	0	0	0
108A	0	0	0	0	0	0	2	0	1	0	0	0	0	0	0	0	1	2
108B	0	0	1	0	0	0	1	1	3	0	0	0	0	1	0	0	0	4
108C	0	0	0	0	0	0	0	0	2	0	1	0	0	12	0	0	0	4
108D	0	0	1	0	0	0	0	0	0	0	0	1	0	3	0	0	0	0

APPENDIX I

TABLE 35
TYPE COUNTS: 1970-71 SURVEY SURFACE COLLECTIONS

								TYPES									
SITE	37	38	39	40	41	42	43	44	45	46	47	48	49	50	51	52	53	54
108E	0	0	0	0	0	0	0	0	0	0	0	0	0	0	0	0	0	0
108F	0	0	1	0	0	0	1	0	0	0	0	0	0	9	0	1	1	2
112	0	0	0	0	0	0	0	0	1	0	0	0	0	0	0	0	0	0
113A	0	1	1	0	1	1	0	0	1	0	0	0	0	5	0	0	0	0
113B	0	0	0	0	0	0	0	0	1	0	0	0	0	1	1	0	0	0
113C	0	0	0	0	0	0	0	0	0	0	0	0	0	0	0	0	0	0
113D	0	0	0	0	0	0	0	0	0	0	0	0	0	0	0	0	0	0
113G	0	0	0	0	0	0	0	0	0	0	0	0	0	0	0	0	0	0
120	0	0	0	0	0	0	0	0	0	0	0	0	0	0	0	0	0	0
121	0	1	0	0	0	0	0	1	0	0	0	0	0	2	0	0	0	0
153A	0	0	0	0	0	1	2	1	1	0	0	0	0	4	0	0	0	0
153B	0	1	1	1	0	1	1	0	1	0	0	0	1	2	0	0	0	0
165A	0	0	0	0	0	0	0	0	0	0	0	0	0	0	0	0	0	0
165B	0	0	1	0	1	3	0	0	2	0	1	0	0	8	0	0	1	1
165C	0	0	0	0	0	0	0	0	0	0	0	0	0	0	0	0	0	0
171A	0	0	5	0	0	2	4	0	0	0	0	0	1	7	0	1	0	1
171B	0	0	0	0	0	0	0	0	0	0	0	0	0	5	0	1	0	1
173	1	0	1	0	0	2	1	1	2	1	1	1	5	0	0	0	0	0
182	0	0	0	0	0	0	0	0	0	0	0	0	0	0	0	0	0	0
190	0	0	0	0	0	0	0	0	0	0	0	0	0	0	0	0	0	0
197	0	0	4	0	0	0	0	0	2	1	0	0	3	0	0	0	0	0
218	0	0	0	0	0	0	0	0	0	0	0	0	0	0	0	0	0	0
240	0	0	0	0	0	0	0	0	1	0	0	0	0	1	0	0	0	0
266	0	1	1	0	1	0	1	0	3	0	0	1	1	5	0	0	0	3
269	0	0	0	0	0	0	1	0	0	0	1	0	0	0	0	0	0	0
284A	0	0	0	0	0	0	0	0	2	0	0	0	1	5	0	0	0	3
284B	0	0	0	0	0	0	1	0	0	0	0	0	0	0	0	0	0	0
285	0	0	0	0	0	0	0	0	0	0	0	0	0	0	0	0	0	0
286	0	0	0	0	0	0	0	0	0	0	0	0	0	0	0	0	0	0
288	0	0	2	0	0	2	2	0	1	0	0	0	0	2	0	0	0	0
289	0	0	0	0	0	1	0	0	2	0	0	0	0	1	0	0	0	0
290A	0	0	0	0	0	0	1	0	0	0	0	0	0	0	0	0	0	0
290B	0	0	0	0	0	0	0	0	1	0	0	0	0	0	0	0	0	0

APPENDIX II

GRID COORDINATES FOR DETERMINATION OF SITE-TO-SITE DISTANCES

Explanatory note:

An effort has been made in this study to provide an adequate number of maps to illustrate points under discussion. Some readers may wish to rework the site distributional data with their own hypotheses in mind. The maps provided in this study would be inadequate for this purpose.

The following table of grid coordinates has been included to allow the reader to calculate reasonably accurate site-to-site distances. The coordinates were derived as follows. A 1.0 millimeter interval grid was placed over a 1:50,000 map of the survey area, oriented along a magnetic north-south line. The 0-0 origin was placed in the extreme northwest corner of the grid. The numbers entered in the table represent the distance in millimeters from each site to the east-west axis (vertical measurement) and the north-south axis (horizontal measurement). Each millimeter on the 1:50,000 map represents 50 meters or .05 kilometers. The distance from any site to any other site may be calculated in kilometers through use of the respective grid coordinates, the Pythagorean theorem, and a scale factor of .05. The survey area covers some 3,000 square kilometers for the benefit of those interested in nearest neighbor analysis.

Measurements for grid coordinates were taken to the center of each site and are theoretically accurate to within 50 meters. Such accuracy is, however, highly unlikely. General accuracy within 150 meters with occasional larger errors is more probable.

TABLE 36
GRID COORDINATES FOR DETERMINATION OF
SITE-TO-SITE DISTANCES

Site Number	Horizontal Coordinate	Vertical Coordinate	Site Number	Horizontal Coordinate	Vertical Coordinate
Susa	0250	0640	121	0814	0966
1	0818	0580	153	1195	0475
4	0700	0712	165	1055	0674
5	0693	0725	171	1297	0692
6	0708	0738	173	1278	0613
7	0173	0236	182	0991	0718
8	0243	0229	190	1051	0852
13	0230	0387	197	1077	0934
15	0251	0356	218	1121	1058
16	0286	0374	220	1260	1053
20	0214	0480	240	0026	0392
22	0270	0477	266	0694	0657
24	0230	0525	269	0499	0740
27	0395	0559	284	0766	0822
32	0326	0792	285	0480	0779
33	0329	0734	286	0226	0523
34	0328	0707	288	0567	0158
35	0363	0703	289	0616	0589
36	0417	0432	290	0766	0656
37	0533	0527			
39	0635	0644			
40	0628	0625			
44	0615	0715			
45	0596	0718			
49	0597	0782			
50	0626	0825			
52	0281	0722			
54	0447	0862			
59	0335	0875			
61	0412	0798			
64	0513	0804			
67	0450	0703			
76	0582	0913			
79	0548	0970			
89	0410	0974			
90	0440	0962			
93	0326	0888			
94	0337	0930			
96	0285	0988			
98	0394	0901			
99	0486	0018			
101	0921	0563			
102	0924	0570			
108	0756	0624			
112	0729	0683			
113	0745	0756			
120	0833	0929			

APPENDIX III

CERAMIC MEASUREMENTS

Explanatory Note:
    1. Each table of measurements for a specific ceramic type is preceded by a line drawing illustrating the measurements made. Each measurement is assigned a number: 1, 2, 3 ... n used to identify the measurements listed in the tables.

    2. Unless otherwise specified, all linear measurements in the tables are given in tenths of a millimeter. For example, the number 213 would indicate a measurement of 21.3 millimeters or 2.13 centimeters.

    3. All angular measurements in the tables are given to the nearest degree. For example the number 45 would indicate a measurement of 45 degrees.

    4. In all cases, the number "-1" in the tables indicates missing data.

    5. Each sherd for which measurements are given is identified by an alpha-numeric code. The code "93-06" would indicate sherd number 6 of the type listed in a particular table, from site KS-93. The code "108C01" would indicate sherd number 1 of the type listed in a particular table from collection area of C of site KS-108. Measurements of sherds from Susa are identified by a six character code. For example the code S18-21 would indicate sherd number 21 from Level 18 of the Acropole Sondage. Measurement of sherds from Chogha Mish are identified by a five-character code. For example the code "CM-11" would indicate sherd 11 of a particular type from Chogha Mish.

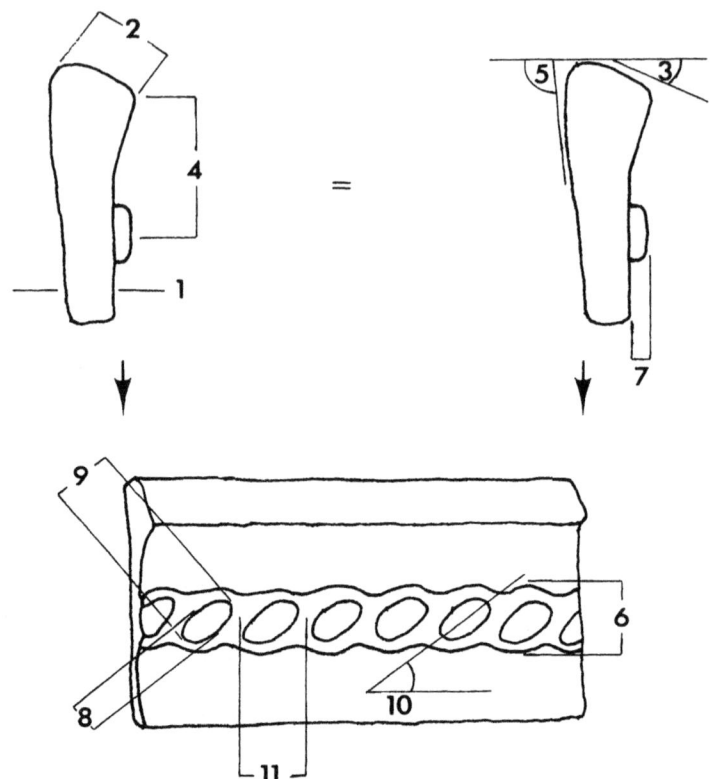

MEASUREMENT KEY

1 Side Thickness
2 Rim Thickness
3 Rim Angle
4 Rim to Strip Midpoint
5 Interior Side Angle
6 Strip Width
7 Strip Thickness
8 Impression Width
9 Impression Length
10 Impression Angle
11 Impression Interval
12 Temper Code: 1= Fine, 2= Coarse

Fig. 36. Impressed Strip Bowl Measurements.

APPENDIX III

TABLE 37
IMPRESSED STRIP BOWL MEASUREMENTS

MEASUREMENTS

ID	1	2	3	4	5	6	7	8	9	10	11	12
6S01	246	322	90	302	107	196	48	144	144	0	171	1
16-01	111	136	79	175	96	136	49	129	167	0	200	1
16-02	179	299	92	293	108	193	51	110	193	27	320	1
16-03	209	319	100	281	111	182	87	149	270	79	207	1
16-04	122	227	90	213	116	172	54	166	191	65	225	2
16-05	143	209	139	190	110	150	49	128	163	0	170	2
16-06	94	264	119	262	82	153	84	130	167	49	202	2
22B01	132	112	90	650	55	207	41	124	124	0	223	1
33-01	73	206	95	400	88	130	20	108	108	0	150	2
46A01	108	259	94	243	106	135	61	98	190	34	203	2
52A01	77	165	90	248	122	114	58	101	205	62	207	2
52A02	89	179	104	203	94	136	42	119	119	50	141	2
52A03	97	182	90	178	110	105	32	105	135	59	154	2
52A04	112	158	92	263	92	165	39	117	117	50	140	2
52A05	112	172	95	150	104	112	42	107	133	58	185	2
59B01	106	101	90	203	68	169	52	140	186	54	215	1
59B02	130	228	90	284	112	220	70	150	220	48	279	2
59B03	105	232	90	197	106	171	58	158	226	46	256	2
59C04	152	181	90	276	92	177	34	150	170	0	250	1
59G05	154	230	90	277	96	147	50	126	127	0	160	1
59I06	108	129	90	225	68	116	31	103	145	0	210	1
59I07	96	112	90	239	90	120	23	110	117	0	152	1
64A01	120	150	90	203	83	173	46	156	172	0	200	1
64A02	162	153	90	267	66	143	24	135	162	0	119	1
64A03	154	189	94	359	92	177	43	142	163	0	186	1
67-01	141	236	100	175	93	168	35	136	157	0	174	1
67-02	130	200	90	163	80	198	72	176	176	90	215	1
67-03	138	233	94	262	90	188	80	155	192	0	220	1
67-04	125	221	90	249	89	182	60	162	180	0	211	1
67-05	145	190	98	199	81	175	79	140	175	83	215	1
67-06	181	286	104	274	80	169	66	112	130	0	158	1
93-01	116	224	90	277	110	180	41	129	193	44	168	2
94-01	133	158	93	168	95	131	51	104	154	0	197	1
96B01	80	146	90	74	108	115	33	100	161	45	161	2
96B03	84	234	104	270	110	153	38	103	170	57	160	2
108A01	140	175	90	147	78	163	48	130	130	50	160	1
108A02	133	199	90	143	93	175	37	146	164	0	196	1
108B03	127	327	113	357	93	236	63	196	207	0	265	1
165B01	92	241	106	296	101	159	49	140	150	0	178	2
182-01	141	182	73	200	94	144	48	104	141	0	220	1
182-02	117	235	90	177	88	169	69	134	151	0	202	1

TABLE 37 (continued)

| | MEASUREMENTS | | | | | | | | | | | |
ID	1	2	3	4	5	6	7	8	9	10	11	12
266-01	107	232	92	281	110	207	108	153	220	48	247	2
266-02	129	116	90	238	80	152	23	139	172	6	230	1
266-03	130	195	88	322	85	204	85	179	211	40	222	2
269-01	131	261	92	275	116	151	55	125	149	65	192	1
269-02	192	289	90	435	96	226	82	152	174	0	200	1
269-03	95	112	90	153	59	117	33	108	151	33	190	1
269-05	137	216	90	423	84	161	41	126	142	0	161	1
269-06	100	92	90	277	84	140	20	123	164	33	205	1
269-07	144	365	91	340	98	165	80	159	208	0	269	1
269-09	96	119	90	273	85	156	58	131	151	0	163	1
269-10	142	151	90	177	83	135	46	124	163	0	196	1
269-12	129	166	92	312	87	146	37	130	141	1	176	1
269-13	192	262	91	371	101	184	74	174	182	2	224	1
269-14	129	129	90	168	84	121	31	106	124	3	137	1
269-15	112	171	90	213	83	168	52	135	163	1	202	1
269-16	178	237	92	504	88	150	39	129	140	0	157	1
284A01	130	305	106	378	107	185	71	137	162	0	201	2

APPENDIX III

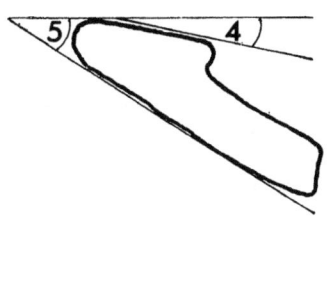

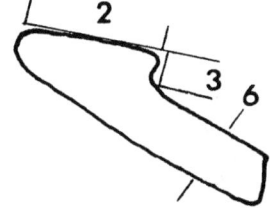

MEASUREMENT KEY

1 Rim Diameter   (Estimated to .5 cm)
2 Rim Width
3 Rim Height
4 Rim Angle
5 Interior Rim Angle
6 Side Thickness

Fig. 37. Uruk Neckless Ledge Jar Rim Measurements.

TABLE 38
URUK NECKLESS LEDGE RIM JAR MEASUREMENTS

	MEASUREMENTS					
ID	1	2	3	4	5	6
6S01	150	159	150	2	35	104
6S02	120	214	209	0	20	152
22B01	210	199	194	16	33	129
27-01	130	189	159	18	29	80
34B01	110	140	114	12	20	83
96B01	150	228	163	4	31	114
96B02	160	263	163	15	28	108
96B03	150	217	165	8	30	115
96B04	150	165	122	8	33	101
96B05	170	236	146	12	44	97
96B06	140	229	161	4	20	113
96B07	150	194	131	5	22	107
96B08	130	178	139	20	20	99
99-01	160	163	130	22	41	103
99-02	110	219	184	18	40	122
108B02	200	205	182	5	43	152
108B03	100	159	156	10	41	120
108B04	110	119	125	0	40	97
108B05	130	213	180	24	39	107
108B06	130	176	99	11	22	94
108B07	170	138	58	9	51	72
153A01	130	224	142	11	33	92
153A02	160	187	106	0	28	66
153B03	180	207	192	18	43	117
266-01	160	219	134	0	11	51
266-02	220	263	129	19	18	84
266-03	170	183	138	3	24	91
266-04	130	158	135	12	30	82
284B01	150	209	177	3	31	109

APPENDIX III

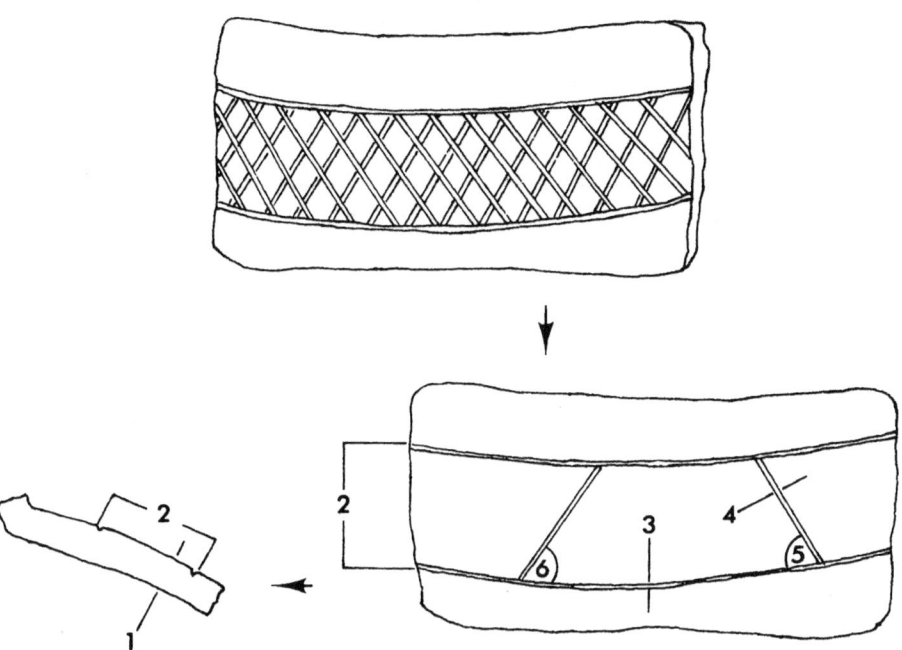

MEASUREMENT KEY

1. Sherd Thickness
2. Band Width
3. Horizontal Line Thickness
4. Diagonal Line Thickness
5. Left Diagonal Angle
6. Right Diagonal Angle
7. Associated Cross Hatch Triangles
   (0 = Absent, 1 = Present)

Fig. 38. Uruk Cross Hatch Band Measurements.

TABLE 39
URUK CROSS HATCH BAND MEASUREMENTS

	MEASUREMENTS						
ID	1	2	3	4	5	6	7
7-01	98	282	9	9	42	30	-1
7-02	104	-1	10	11	35	73	-1
16-02	64	-1	6	7	45	45	-1
16-03	88	-1	8	7	35	55	-1
16-04	59	158	3	2	50	40	-1
22C02	73	-1	2	5	37	40	-1
24B01	85	-1	16	8	32	50	-1
32-01	62	147	5	3	30	30	-1
32-02	92	-1	9	6	44	78	-1
34B01	67	188	4	6	55	70	-1
34B02	140	-1	9	9	30	80	-1
34B03	84	130	5	6	50	42	-1
34C05	86	-1	5	5	50	55	-1
34C06	95	-1	8	5	35	50	-1
49A01	92	252	12	13	39	50	0
52A01	64	-1	5	7	58	40	-1
52A02	88	-1	5	6	68	42	-1
54-01	81	102	7	4	60	30	-1
59B01	107	-1	7	5	37	50	-1
59C02	67	279	8	6	58	47	-1
59F08	81	-1	7	5	35	41	-1
59G09	94	-1	6	7	57	44	-1
59I12	65	153	4	7	45	42	-1
59I13	86	-1	11	11	50	50	-1
61A01	84	-1	6	4	32	55	-1
76-01	79	-1	11	10	58	53	-1
96B01	91	244	5	5	31	32	-1
96B02	94	314	7	5	40	41	-1
96B03	91	-1	10	7	40	49	-1
96B06	97	307	6	8	52	55	1
96H12	114	-1	14	7	32	62	-1
96H13	113	483	11	8	68	53	-1
113A01	120	-1	8	10	55	50	-1
113A02	73	-1	10	4	48	40	-1
113A03	84	460	11	8	55	55	-1
113B04	84	-1	9	8	64	50	-1
113G05	107	238	7	9	35	53	-1
113G06	70	-1	14	8	45	45	-1
113G07	77	257	10	8	35	61	-1
108C01	99	-1	7	4	42	42	-1
108C02	113	-1	13	13	48	55	-1

TABLE 39 (continued)

ID	MEASUREMENTS						
	1	2	3	4	5	6	7
108C03	92	387	5	5	58	35	-1
108C04	98	-1	6	7	60	45	-1
108C05	92	-1	7	6	58	52	-1
108C07	80	-1	6	7	80	40	-1
108D08	72	-1	14	10	65	39	-1
108F09	115	-1	8	7	35	60	-1
153A01	89	-1	11	7	58	50	-1
165B01	92	-1	6	5	65	55	-1
165B02	86	-1	15	9	50	52	-1
165B03	111	-1	6	7	50	65	-1
165B04	66	-1	12	8	55	47	-1
165B05	51	-1	5	5	43	48	-1
171B01	79	-1	13	15	48	42	-1
171B02	108	-1	3	8	52	58	-1
171B03	99	-1	6	3	66	48	-1
173-01	125	327	9	7	36	42	-1
173-02	104	288	7	6	51	48	1
173-04	138	-1	15	8	30	45	-1
173-06	79	-1	10	8	29	49	-1
173-07	106	380	13	9	62	50	-1
197-01	81	-1	11	4	40	59	-1
197-02	94	-1	11	7	47	40	-1
288-01	83	139	7	5	35	33	0
CM-01	104	593	14	15	70	46	-1
CM-02	93	520	12	7	63	50	-1
CM-03	100	-1	16	9	50	52	-1
CM-04	59	120	11	7	46	58	-1
CM-05	83	389	11	10	40	62	0
CM-06	122	-1	12	13	60	45	0
CM-07	81	484	14	7	42	39	0
CM-08	102	-1	10	7	60	58	-1
CM-09	101	-1	11	11	66	55	-1
CM-10	106	192	10	10	45	89	-1
CM-11	65	183	11	8	80	52	-1
CM-12	109	325	15	11	48	53	0
CM-13	93	555	13	12	40	50	0
CM-14	87	546	7	9	55	60	1
CM-15	84	-1	10	12	68	70	0
CM-16	90	-1	12	13	68	65	1
CM-17	64	343	11	13	78	50	-1
CM-18	92	338	9	13	65	60	-1
CM-19	95	434	11	11	50	60	-1
CM-20	105	179	8	9	60	60	1
CM-21	120	421	16	13	60	80	0
CM-22	78	327	12	9	60	60	-1
CM-23	85	416	15	14	80	43	1
CM-24	142	-1	7	9	50	70	1
CM-25	115	269	13	8	65	45	1
CM-26	113	412	14	12	48	52	-1

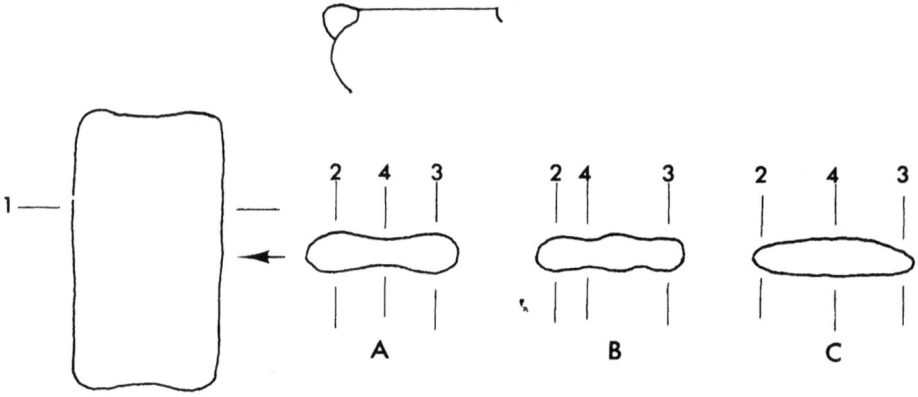

MEASUREMENT KEY

1 Handle Width
2 Edge Thickness – 1
3 Edge Thickness – 2
4 Groove or Center Thickness
5 Number of Grooves (A=1, B=2, C=0)

Fig. 39. Uruk Strap Handle Measurements.

APPENDIX III

TABLE 40
URUK STRAP HANDLE MEASUREMENTS

MEASUREMENTS

ID	1	2	3	4	5	ID	1	2	3	4	5
004C01	313	62	62	74	0	054-01	379	81	89	66	1
004E02	339	112	127	120	1	054-02	438	82	85	79	1
008A01	392	78	82	69	2	054-03	364	98	105	86	1
016-01	477	88	96	76	2	054-04	226	78	83	83	1
016-02	313	75	80	74	1	054-05	266	58	67	74	1
016-03	320	64	69	62	1	054-06	448	71	78	68	2
016-04	424	72	85	70	2	059B01	509	98	104	79	1
016-05	394	74	91	68	1	059B02	508	97	114	94	2
022A01	343	132	138	101	1	059B03	507	98	101	87	1
022B02	313	97	117	99	2	059C04	436	79	86	79	2
022B03	299	71	71	71	1	059C05	274	87	88	84	1
024-01	425	74	80	70	1	059C06	556	110	112	134	0
024-02	309	92	94	93	1	059C07	339	112	117	110	1
024-03	386	81	90	86	1	059D08	345	78	82	81	2
024-04	374	95	100	74	1	059D09	449	89	90	84	1
024-05	207	53	55	51	1	059G10	377	100	104	88	1
027-01	338	71	86	70	1	059G11	454	95	97	109	1
027-02	452	100	120	96	1	059H12	378	92	116	81	1
033-01	524	60	70	82	0	059H13	331	93	97	90	1
033-02	366	48	57	70	0	059I14	446	72	89	94	1
034B01	355	72	92	79	1	059I15	500	73	86	110	0
034B02	350	110	114	74	1	061A01	314	70	89	75	1
034B03	395	82	86	79	2	061A02	436	79	80	76	1
034C04	364	92	96	86	2	076-01	381	102	109	96	1
034C05	306	94	104	75	1	076-02	353	90	100	79	1
034C06	394	70	88	80	1	076-03	431	94	104	10	1
034C07	287	70	75	69	1	076-04	370	113	129	81	1
035A01	417	79	82	86	1	079A01	267	82	96	70	1
035A02	272	107	111	103	1	079A02	391	98	111	93	1
035A03	436	88	95	83	2	093-01	300	105	110	87	1
036B01	289	77	84	66	1	093-02	361	108	129	86	1
036B02	320	71	76	60	1	094-01	371	102	112	93	1
036B03	434	80	102	72	2	094-02	328	86	97	68	1
036F04	396	124	138	106	1	096B01	380	129	145	65	0
039B01	392	82	97	99	1	096B02	282	95	123	65	1
039E02	485	77	97	92	1	096H01	366	138	153	156	1
039E03	345	74	102	98	1	096H02	347	135	148	140	1
039E04	312	79	83	76	1	096H03	384	84	92	106	1
039E05	449	82	93	81	1	096H04	362	99	106	73	1
039E07	468	95	113	115	3	096H05	293	73	84	74	0
039E08	374	106	113	97	1	108C01	183	39	41	34	1
052A01	325	137	141	92	1	108C02	213	282	84	76	1
052A02	350	123	120	81	1	108C03	435	109	113	109	2
052A03	270	107	120	95	1	108C04	387	122	128	129	0
052A04	337	124	134	83	1	108C05	422	78	80	82	1

TABLE 40 (continued)

				MEASUREMENTS						
ID	1	2	3	4	5	ID	1	2	3	4	5
108C06	332	84	86	85	1	165B05	402	105	119	111	1
108C07	354	104	120	112	1	165B06	447	101	105	106	1
108C08	377	100	105	95	2	171A01	183	57	62	52	1
108C09	350	83	98	98	1	171A02	420	107	114	119	1
108C10	501	103	112	110	2	171A03	445	96	103	95	1
108C11	356	94	106	91	1	171A04	354	122	124	97	1
108D12	381	92	102	96	1	171A05	337	133	133	97	1
108F13	287	90	94	81	1	171A06	365	76	92	86	1
108F14	335	97	113	89	1	171A07	419	79	100	79	2
108F15	293	76	81	73	1	171A08	364	95	98	78	1
108F16	366	81	86	72	1	171B09	415	90	99	82	1
108F17	349	96	101	84	2	171B10	473	91	145	100	2
108F18	446	90	105	89	1	171B11	305	86	88	86	1
108F19	567	101	116	154	2	171B12	631	135	140	167	1
108F20	439	92	92	100	1	171B13	581	118	126	119	1
108F21	335	89	97	87	1	171B14	502	90	124	89	1
113A01	331	77	79	56	1	173-01	406	83	92	81	1
113A02	403	111	112	105	1	173-02	393	132	142	122	1
113A03	240	70	77	75	1	173-03	371	113	129	99	2
113A04	431	97	131	108	1	173-04	387	92	98	87	1
113A05	241	80	87	81	1	197-01	390	80	82	63	1
113B06	210	71	76	59	1	197-02	375	90	90	90	1
153A01	406	96	100	79	1	266-01	351	81	97	78	1
153A02	380	100	110	104	1	266-02	414	68	76	70	1
153A03	507	115	129	92	1	266-03	392	77	105	95	1
165B01	426	89	109	90	1	266-04	445	63	67	60	2
165B02	314	106	109	89	1	240-01	379	137	165	118	1
165B03	329	82	95	76	2	284A01	326	112	115	93	1
165B04	453	95	108	91	1	288-01	327	80	86	60	1
						288-02	285	69	72	66	1

APPENDIX III

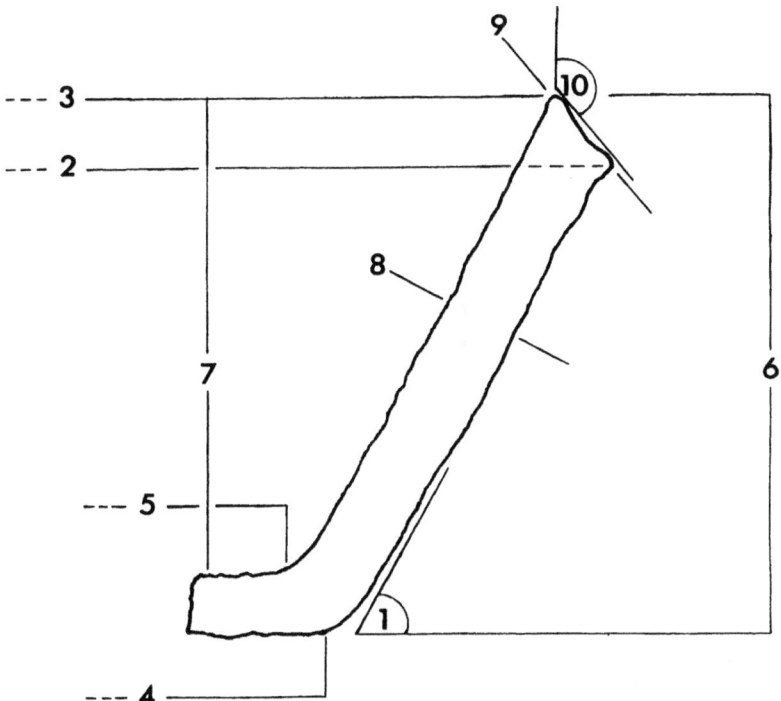

MEASUREMENT KEY

1 Base Angle
2 Rim Diameter   (Estimated to .5 cm)
3 Interior Rim Diameter   "
4 Base Diameter   "
5 Interior Base Diameter   "
6 Side Height   (Measured to .1 cm)
7 Interior Side Height   "
8 Side Thickness
9 Rim Thickness
10 Rim Angle

Fig. 40. Uruk Bevel Rim Bowl Measurements.

TABLE 41
URUK BEVEL RIM BOWL MEASUREMENTS

					MEASUREMENTS					
ID	1	2	3	4	5	6	7	8	9	10
016-01	58	160	150	80	70	73	65	108	145	128
016-02	57	140	130	70	65	67	62	94	111	137
016-03	55	175	155	70	70	71	61	107	110	137
016-04	58	180	170	70	65	84	80	106	121	154
016-05	62	195	180	80	70	86	72	108	135	150
022B01	60	165	160	70	65	85	78	111	130	159
022B02	53	180	170	80	65	85	75	120	123	148
022B03	68	130	120	60	50	71	65	108	104	150
022B04	48	150	140	70	60	70	55	133	129	165
022B05	58	200	190	80	75	96	84	159	141	147
022C06	47	210	200	85	75	79	74	114	135	163
024A01	60	160	150	80	70	87	80	110	121	136
024A02	55	180	170	80	80	88	83	109	118	160
024A03	65	190	165	80	75	91	79	132	169	150
024A04	63	190	170	75	70	89	85	137	129	155
024B05	67	220	210	80	75	118	105	145	138	170
027-01	44	170	150	80	70	58	44	103	123	154
027-02	63	185	170	75	80	80	74	117	139	148
032-01	52	160	150	60	55	75	69	109	126	148
032-02	62	215	200	90	85	97	81	138	128	133
034C01	41	175	160	65	60	70	62	110	137	151
035A01	47	190	170	75	80	69	58	120	129	148
035A02	50	185	160	70	65	94	80	126	143	152
035A03	55	195	180	70	65	85	80	130	129	151
035B04	49	195	180	70	65	77	69	124	102	148
036B02	58	140	120	65	60	66	54	113	143	130
036C03	62	170	160	65	60	90	70	94	131	137
036E04	55	135	120	70	65	73	64	109	102	136
036F05	53	170	160	70	65	78	64	123	124	135
036F08	60	175	160	70	60	83	70	112	142	155
036F09	52	140	120	70	65	73	62	116	126	145
036F10	59	150	140	75	70	88	76	101	126	135
036F11	61	140	130	70	60	92	85	116	103	152
036F12	56	145	130	65	60	72	65	125	134	136
036F13	60	175	160	75	65	93	78	111	160	130
036G14	53	165	160	70	60	74	65	111	62	160
036G15	49	165	150	80	75	75	62	129	147	154
036G16	60	160	140	70	65	78	66	114	146	143
036G19	59	170	160	70	60	91	77	138	119	146
036G20	57	165	160	80	63	77	60	91	124	170
036BP21	55	170	160	80	65	70	66	140	121	149

APPENDIX III 191

TABLE 41 (continued)

					MEASUREMENTS					
ID	1	2	3	4	5	6	7	8	9	10
036BP22	55	175	160	70	60	80	68	159	151	146
036BP23	45	170	160	65	60	69	53	111	143	152
036BP24	52	165	160	80	70	68	55	138	96	166
036BP25	49	245	230	90	80	99	79	178	233	176
036BP26	48	165	155	65	65	70	52	120	110	142
039A01	62	165	150	60	65	86	78	116	122	148
039A02	55	165	150	65	60	79	68	100	124	140
039A03	50	180	160	60	60	74	63	125	136	131
039A04	47	175	160	70	65	84	71	110	127	141
039A05	60	165	150	90	75	92	85	122	129	135
039A06	61	170	160	60	65	87	75	133	139	142
039A07	50	175	160	65	70	79	68	107	131	132
039A08	55	155	140	70	60	85	79	102	140	145
039A09	52	170	160	70	70	68	58	114	124	161
039A10	68	185	160	65	70	86	83	98	127	131
039A12	65	180	170	70	60	76	69	110	135	150
039A13	50	190	170	60	55	87	72	127	158	128
039A14	55	165	150	70	65	84	75	122	117	142
039A15	62	165	150	70	70	79	70	106	117	155
039A16	60	175	150	70	65	84	80	208	140	134
039A17	59	175	150	70	65	88	77	130	143	130
039A18	58	165	160	65	55	78	68	130	97	143
039A19	64	165	150	70	60	77	68	95	90	128
039A20	63	180	170	55	60	76	68	83	136	149
039A21	60	180	160	60	65	86	79	128	123	140
039A22	55	185	180	90	70	89	83	127	166	171
039A23	50	160	150	70	65	67	63	119	98	150
039A24	55	160	150	80	75	87	76	115	123	145
039A26	58	140	130	80	75	87	72	122	116	143
039A27	52	175	160	70	65	85	74	135	115	132
039C28	70	195	180	70	75	94	77	119	148	125
039C29	50	180	170	75	80	71	64	111	124	156
039E30	52	125	110	70	65	70	64	109	126	143
039E31	56	180	170	80	75	82	72	115	127	137
039E32	63	180	160	80	70	74	62	121	145	112
039E33	48	170	150	60	55	65	53	130	149	156
039E36	50	150	130	65	55	70	58	119	138	142
044A01	47	170	160	70	65	70	61	114	128	164
045-01	59	170	160	70	65	81	74	124	127	147
049A01	62	200	190	90	60	89	69	137	145	137
049A02	51	173	170	70	60	98	84	108	126	184
054-01	60	165	150	75	70	78	72	97	151	142
054-02	56	170	150	65	60	78	69	85	136	131
054-03	51	170	160	80	70	70	64	120	131	140
054-04	47	165	150	65	60	66	55	97	112	138
054-05	59	175	150	80	70	81	74	124	131	142
054-06	57	195	180	80	75	79	69	140	127	148

TABLE 41 (continued)

ID	\multicolumn{10}{c}{MEASUREMENTS}									
	1	2	3	4	5	6	7	8	9	10
173-07	64	160	150	70	70	95	85	129	143	148
173-08	59	165	150	80	75	74	65	121	132	138
218-01	58	170	160	70	65	90	84	125	100	156
218-02	45	160	150	70	60	72	68	108	113	155
266-01	64	165	160	80	75	94	82	84	81	169
266-02	50	160	145	90	80	65	56	91	117	138
266-04	59	175	160	65	60	75	65	118	108	128
266-05	67	165	155	70	65	88	75	121	119	143
266-07	65	155	150	80	75	107	95	108	77	175
266-08	64	145	145	80	75	99	86	106	102	167
266-09	69	165	140	70	65	90	83	103	129	124
S21-01	60	170	155	70	55	80	66	95	142	140
S21-02	57	160	150	70	75	80	62	122	138	141
S21-03	61	165	150	70	55	82	70	112	117	134
S21-04	65	170	160	60	60	85	78	109	141	132
S21-05	58	160	140	60	55	78	68	141	155	140
S21-06	54	185	180	80	75	82	70	117	171	175
S21-07	60	210	200	70	60	91	82	111	167	155
S21-08	48	170	160	70	60	59	58	116	132	160
S21-09	58	170	160	60	60	77	65	121	141	140
S21-10	55	210	200	70	55	83	75	106	132	151
S21-11	60	140	130	80	60	79	75	115	141	152
S21-12	61	155	140	70	65	82	75	127	150	138
S21-13	63	195	195	80	65	87	77	125	213	196
S21-14	53	240	240	90	75	85	75	140	212	199
S18-15	47	180	160	80	70	74	65	109	127	139
S18-16	55	210	200	80	70	99	81	121	134	139
S18-17	60	190	170	80	70	80	75	119	150	129
S18-18	57	175	160	70	60	80	70	112	129	127
S18-19	55	175	160	70	60	82	65	130	153	130
S18-20	60	175	160	80	65	87	77	120	153	135
S18-21	50	180	160	70	65	82	72	118	146	130
S18-22	59	195	180	90	75	87	78	144	115	141
S18-23	53	190	170	80	65	85	70	116	152	133
S18-24	55	190	170	75	65	84	75	119	149	138
S17-25	70	215	200	00	85	149	135	120	128	128
S17-26	70	170	150	80	70	131	111	135	156	130
S17-27	66	185	170	90	75	113	99	101	130	140
S17-28	72	200	190	80	80	129	118	128	177	156
S17-29	69	180	170	80	80	101	88	111	169	145
S17-30	63	180	170	90	80	117	89	112	140	147
S17-31	62	160	150	70	65	103	90	120	161	151
S17-32	68	210	195	00	85	116	98	127	151	147
S17-33	70	230	220	90	75	113	99	107	153	160
S17-34	70	195	190	95	80	131	113	115	147	154
S17-35	66	185	175	90	75	96	91	116	139	147
S17-36	51	165	155	65	65	82	74	89	105	147

APPENDIX III

TABLE 41 (continued)

ID	MEASUREMENTS									
	1	2	3	4	5	6	7	8	9	10
054-07	63	175	160	90	80	93	86	104	117	120
054-08	42	175	160	70	64	57	99	126	149	0
054-09	53	170	150	70	65	79	72	108	135	139
054-10	57	200	180	70	65	69	64	109	151	137
054-11	52	175	160	70	65	66	58	118	136	141
059B01	55	140	130	70	65	74	62	108	118	148
059B02	45	195	180	80	75	90	79	131	147	140
059B03	52	175	160	70	60	75	63	118	137	141
059C07	57	160	140	80	70	71	61	125	114	118
059C08	63	125	120	70	65	86	72	106	130	138
059D09	55	140	120	60	55	74	65	110	109	142
059D10	48	170	160	80	65	65	55	99	89	142
059D11	54	140	120	80	70	70	62	109	129	122
059D12	60	160	140	70	70	82	73	80	116	152
059D13	61	165	150	70	55	82	74	93	122	137
059D14	58	170	160	70	65	84	75	115	136	146
059D15	60	150	140	70	60	77	66	87	104	155
059D16	60	180	170	80	70	82	72	88	129	149
059D17	43	150	140	80	75	71	55	127	146	160
059D18	52	170	160	70	45	81	72	112	118	159
059F19	56	170	160	70	60	91	80	116	126	144
059F20	65	170	160	70	65	93	75	129	136	137
059F21	53	170	160	80	70	71	64	133	118	134
059F22	56	150	140	70	60	72	65	91	112	160
059F23	57	180	160	80	70	70	59	102	130	126
059F24	58	170	160	70	60	76	64	120	140	133
059F25	52	170	160	70	60	70	58	118	115	165
059F26	61	180	170	70	60	90	82	128	122	135
059F27	54	160	140	70	65	65	55	112	90	146
059F28	44	165	160	60	55	75	62	130	128	162
059F29	56	190	170	75	60	80	70	119	127	135
059F30	54	170	160	80	70	85	69	116	129	163
059G31	61	190	180	65	60	86	75	119	121	155
059G32	63	180	160	80	70	81	72	126	133	125
059G33	60	170	160	70	55	75	59	104	127	154
059G34	54	160	150	70	70	75	65	118	104	133
059G35	61	180	170	70	65	90	75	117	121	142
059G36	50	160	140	70	65	69	57	104	110	119
059G37	54	150	140	70	65	59	49	95	125	119
059G38	63	160	140	80	70	91	79	95	118	134
059G39	55	155	140	80	70	60	49	114	125	151
059G40	55	140	135	80	70	74	64	109	124	140
059G41	50	160	140	65	60	74	64	135	138	124
059G42	56	160	140	70	60	71	64	116	123	130
059G43	61	130	120	60	55	74	54	74	100	115
059G44	63	140	120	75	60	76	69	114	120	135
059G45	58	140	120	70	65	65	63	110	130	137

TABLE 41 (continued)

	MEASUREMENTS									
ID	1	2	3	4	5	6	7	8	9	10
059G46	50	160	140	80	70	74	61	96	132	136
059G47	45	170	160	80	70	70	56	112	115	163
059G48	62	170	160	70	65	76	65	98	135	113
059G49	52	170	160	80	70	68	59	99	136	138
059G50	54	160	140	80	70	64	51	109	133	136
059G51	60	150	140	75	70	85	76	122	117	148
059G52	49	170	160	60	55	68	63	91	111	136
059G53	54	145	140	70	60	69	62	106	125	156
059G54	52	170	160	70	65	70	64	109	125	141
059G55	52	150	140	70	60	56	51	99	117	160
059G56	63	160	140	80	70	73	68	109	143	140
059I57	61	135	120	70	65	72	64	103	121	131
059I58	57	155	140	65	65	70	63	106	118	122
059I59	50	170	160	70	65	81	71	100	151	158
059I60	55	170	160	80	65	71	63	116	105	135
061-01	53	155	140	70	60	71	58	102	102	143
061-02	49	170	160	65	60	79	67	78	155	154
061-03	60	170	160	70	65	86	76	126	107	133
061-04	45	150	140	65	60	57	52	95	107	165
061-05	60	170	160	60	60	82	68	117	134	140
076-01	57	200	190	65	55	83	70	142	121	156
076-02	60	165	160	70	55	92	71	111	98	159
076-03	62	165	160	60	50	76	60	113	92	177
093-01	51	145	130	70	60	65	56	136	128	142
093-02	61	165	160	70	70	87	76	89	67	150
096B01	58	160	160	75	65	84	77	107	108	168
096B02	60	160	160	80	60	85	77	112	98	185
096H03	53	135	130	70	60	65	57	115	115	158
096H04	56	190	180	75	65	85	70	142	127	153
096H05	53	150	140	80	75	60	53	110	129	146
096H06	55	180	170	80	70	73	65	118	122	150
096H07	57	150	140	70	65	85	78	108	139	141
108B01	65	160	160	80	70	99	89	102	62	165
108C02	62	190	170	70	65	82	74	130	146	144
108C03	52	175	160	75	70	90	74	166	144	160
108C04	52	175	160	80	70	73	55	132	128	145
108C05	65	185	170	80	60	94	84	127	116	136
108C06	50	170	150	65	65	70	60	119	132	140
108C07	60	165	150	70	70	82	70	138	156	140
108C08	49	145	130	70	65	74	58	119	147	142
108C09	48	150	140	65	65	72	61	98	111	162
108C10	50	175	170	70	65	75	62	133	147	172
108C11	53	180	170	75	70	65	56	141	121	163
108C12	48	140	120	75	75	59	50	107	125	125
108C13	52	205	190	70	65	90	80	130	147	159
108D14	53	130	120	70	60	65	55	116	95	146
108D15	60	160	140	90	80	82	65	140	167	140

APPENDIX III

TABLE 41 (continued)

				MEASUREMENTS						
ID	1	2	3	4	5	6	7	8	9	10
108D16	61	200	180	70	65	85	72	101	130	121
108F17	53	160	150	65	50	75	67	107	119	143
108F18	55	140	130	70	65	65	55	118	108	135
108F19	60	155	140	80	70	80	75	100	120	138
108F20	60	180	170	80	70	76	68	103	113	145
108F21	53	155	140	60	55	65	54	113	118	135
108F22	56	135	120	70	60	63	52	93	132	137
108F23	60	155	140	75	65	75	65	91	122	151
108F24	60	160	140	70	60	75	57	104	129	130
108F25	62	155	140	70	70	70	59	111	137	135
108F26	55	140	130	70	60	64	51	127	147	142
108F27	48	160	150	70	65	72	66	96	107	171
108F28	53	160	150	70	55	76	70	119	108	140
108F29	55	165	150	70	65	174	59	121	120	145
108F30	56	150	140	70	65	70	57	96	111	139
108F31	40	150	140	70	60	56	40	109	124	167
108F32	50	160	150	70	60	71	63	106	94	142
108F33	59	170	160	70	65	80	70	112	132	160
108F34	61	180	170	70	60	77	68	117	138	143
108F35	53	160	140	75	60	68	63	103	137	143
108F36	57	170	160	80	65	74	65	132	134	140
108F37	58	150	130	70	65	76	62	119	143	131
108F38	56	155	140	75	70	75	68	103	144	146
108F39	54	160	150	70	65	75	67	132	149	132
108F40	49	160	150	70	70	70	56	98	129	155
108F41	46	150	140	70	65	59	49	113	130	155
108F42	54	145	130	70	65	80	70	125	136	123
108F43	54	140	130	65	60	72	60	126	138	148
113A01	52	160	150	70	60	71	61	128	112	154
113A02	55	145	140	75	60	80	70	99	130	140
113A03	52	155	140	70	65	82	70	109	137	140
113A04	52	200	190	80	70	91	80	120	142	161
113C05	58	155	150	60	55	77	60	113	132	170
165B01	45	130	120	60	50	56	46	117	96	162
171A01	50	165	152	70	65	66	56	114	137	165
171A02	57	190	170	70	65	73	62	111	120	140
171A03	59	160	150	80	75	73	62	114	131	154
171A04	55	165	150	75	65	73	66	116	137	140
171A06	63	160	145	80	70	66	52	102	116	135
171A07	45	155	140	70	60	66	59	119	124	136
171B09	58	160	150	70	65	73	65	115	119	150
173-01	68	170	160	80	75	78	73	101	126	127
173-02	53	170	150	90	65	61	50	128	118	136
173-03	57	170	150	80	70	83	69	123	127	148
173-04	52	160	140	90	70	75	64	105	129	147
173-05	56	170	150	70	65	79	69	107	124	146
173-06	47	165	150	80	70	75	69	115	127	145

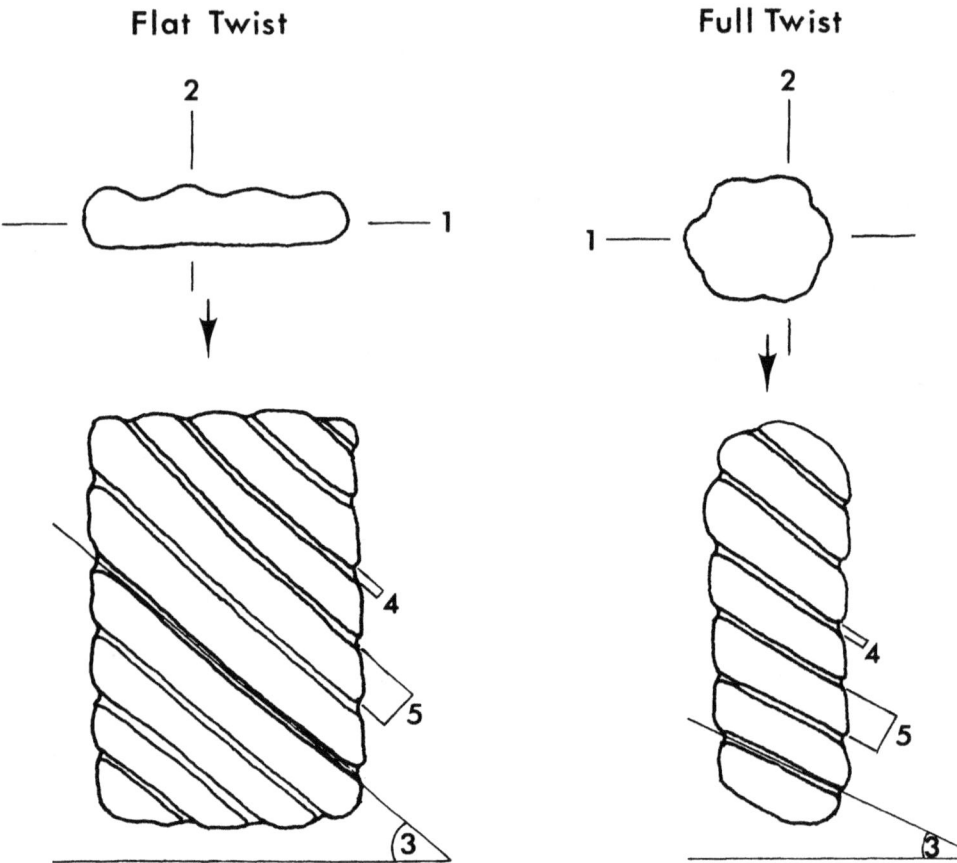

MEASUREMENT KEY

1 Handle Width
2 Handle Thickness
3 Ridge Angle
4 Groove Width
5 Ridge Width

Fig. 41. Uruk Twisted Handle Measurements

APPENDIX III

TABLE 42
URUK TWISTED HANDLE MEASUREMENTS

ID	\multicolumn{5}{c}{MEASUREMENTS}
	1	2	3	4	5
32-01	336	185	55	25	48
32-02	343	132	52	29	77
34A01	403	206	52	20	120
34A02	213	127	60	22	47
39E01	227	200	72	46	70
54-01	174	161	52	39	57
54-02	379	140	48	25	80
54-04	225	237	65	35	55
54-05	185	175	57	25	53
54-06	335	125	53	56	84
59G01	377	143	65	24	53
59F02	255	148	60	18	64
59I03	341	136	64	25	94
61B01	278	126	69	26	66
79A01	327	140	54	-1	94
79A02	212	196	56	16	35
79D03	269	274	62	43	135
79A04	255	226	70	39	129
79A05	392	178	51	26	87
79B06	317	111	58	11	87
96H01	198	209	55	26	40
96H02	319	162	63	34	63
96H03	297	234	75	24	81
96H04	243	123	64	16	57
96H05	216	147	62	18	52
96H06	283	163	52	19	50
96H07	208	179	61	25	76
96H08	533	175	60	28	100
113B01	152	119	52	25	32
171A01	193	183	61	27	116
171B02	209	177	65	21	135

BIBLIOGRAPHY

Adams, Robert McC.
    1962 Agriculture and Urban Life in Early Southwestern Iran. Science, Vol. 136, No. 3511, pp. 109-22. Washington.
    1966 The Evolution of Urban Society: Early Mesopotamia and Prehispanic Mexico. Aldine Publishing Company. Chicago.
    1970 The Study of Ancient Mesopotamian Settlement Patterns and the Problem of Urban Origins. Sumer, Vol. 25, pp. 111-24.

Adams, Robert McC. and Nissen, Hans J.
    1972 The Uruk Countryside. The University of Chicago Press. Chicago.

Amiet, Pierre
    1961 La Glyptique Mesopotamienne Archaique. Editions Du Centre National De La Recherche Scientifique. Paris.

Bascom, William
    1969 The Yoruba of Southwestern Nigeria. Holt, Rinehart and Winston. New York

Caldwell, Joseph
    1968 Tall-i-Ghazir. *In* Reallexikon der Assyriologie und vorderasiatischen Archäologie. Band III. pp. 349-55.

Carneiro, Robert L.
    1970 A Theory of the Origin of the State. Science, Vol. 169, pp. 733-738.

Childe, V. Gordon
    1951 Social Evolution. World Publishing Co. Cleveland.

Christaller, Walter
    1966 Die Zentralen Orte in Südeutschland. translation by Carlisle W. Baskin, Central Places in Southern Germany. Prentice-Hall Inc. Englewood Cliffs. 1966.

Delougaz, Pinhas
    1952 Pottery from the Diyala Region. Oriental Institute Publications, Vol. LXIII. University of Chicago. Chicago.
    1967 Excavations at Chogha Mish in Iran. (Annual Report of The Oriental Institute), pp. 29-38. The Oriental Institute. Chicago.

Delougaz, Pinhas and Kantor, Helene J.
    1969 New Light on the Emergence of Civilization in the Near East. The UNESCO Courier, Nov., pp. 22-25, 28. Paris.

Diakonov, Igor M.
    1969 The Rise of the Despotic State in Ancient Mesopotamia. *In* Ancient Mesopotamia, Socio-Economic History. Igor Diakonov (Ed.), pp. 173-203. Nauka Publishing House. Moscow.

Dollfus, Geneviève
    1971 Les fouilles à Djaffarabad de 1969 à 1971. *In* Cahiers de la Délégation Archéologique Francaise en Iran. No. 1, pp. 17-86. Librairie orientaliste Paul Geuthner. Paris.

Dyson, Robert H.
    1966 Excavations on the Acropole at Susa and Problems of Susa A, B and C. Unpublished PhD Dissertation, Harvard University.

Eliot, Henry Ware Jr.
    1950 Excavations in Mesopotamia and Western Iran: Sites of 4000-5000 B.C. Special Publication of the Peabody Museum of American Archaeology and Ethnology. Cambridge.

Falkenstein, Adam
    1936 Archaische Texte aus Uruk. Ausgrabungen der Deutschen Forschungsgemeinschaft in Uruk-Warka. Vol. 2. Deutsche Forschungsgemeinschaft. Berlin pp. 76-215.

Fallers, Lloyd A.
    1965 Bantu Bureaucracy: A Century of Political Evolution among the Basoga of Uganda. The University of Chicago Press. Chicago.

Flannery, Kent V.
    1972 The Cultural Evolution of Civilizations. Annual Review of Ecology and Systematics, vol. 3, pp. 399-426.

Frankfort, H.
    1924 Mesopotamia, Syria and Egypt and their Earliest Relations. Studies in Early Pottery of the Near East. I. Royal Anthropological Institute of Great Britain and Ireland. Occasional Papers No. 6. London.

Fried, Morton H.
    1967 The Evolution of Political Society: An Essay in Political Anthropology. Random House. New York.

Garner, B. J.
    1967 Models of Urban Geography and Settlement Location. *In* Models in Geography. Richard J. Chorley and Peter Haggett (Eds.). Methuen & Co. Ltd. London.

Gelb, I. J.
    1965 The Ancient Mesopotamian Ration System. Journal of Near Eastern Studies. Vol. 24 pp. 230-43.

Ghirshman, Roman
    1954 Village perse-achéménide. Mémoires de la Mission archéologique en Iran, Mission de Susiane Vol. XXXVI. Presses Universitaires de France. Paris.

Goff, Clare L.
    1971 Luristan before the Iron Age. Iran. Vol. IX, pp. 131-51. London.

Gremliza, F. G. L.
    1962 Ecology of Endemic Diseases in the Dez Irrigation Pilot Area. Development and Resources Corporation. New York.

Haggett, Peter
    1966 Locational Analysis in Human Geography. St. Martin's Press. New York.

Handy, E. S. Craighill (Ed.)
    1965 Ancient Hawaiian Civilization. Charles E. Tuttle Co. Rutland.

Hanson, Donald P.
    1965 The Relative Chronology of Nippur from the Middle Uruk to the End of the Old Babylonian Period (3400–1600 B.C.) *In* Chronologies in Old World Archaeology. Robert W. Ehrich (Ed.) The University of Chicago Press. pp. 201-213. Chicago.

Helbaek, Hans
    1969 Plant Collecting, Dry-Farming, and Irrigation Agriculture in Prehistoric Deh Luran. Appendix I of Frank Hole, Kent V. Flannery and James A. Neely. Prehistory and Human Ecology of the Deh Luran Plain: An Early Village Sequence from Khuzistan, Iran. Memoirs of the Museum of Anthropology University of Michigan. No. 1. Ann Arbor.

Hole, Frank, Kent V. Flannery, and James A. Neely
    1969 Prehistory and Human Ecology of the Deh Luran Plain: An Early Village Sequence from Khuzistan, Iran. Memoirs of the Museum of Anthropology University of Michigan, No. 1. Ann Arbor.

Hole, Frank and Mary Shaw
    1967 Computer Analysis of Chronological Seriation. Rice University Studies, Monograph in Archaeology. Vol. 53, No. 3. Houston.

Jacobsen, Thorkild and Robert McC. Adams
    1958 Salt and Silt in Ancient Mesopotamian Agriculture. Science, Vol. 128, No. 3334, pp. 1251-58. Washington.

Jéquier, Gustave
    1900 Travaux de l'hiver 1897-1898: Travaux de l'Apadana. Mémoires de la délégation en Perse. Vol. I, pp. 69-80. Ernest Leroux, Editeur. Paris.

Johnson, Gregory A.
    1972 A Test of the Utility of Central Place Theory in Archaeology. *In* Man, Settlement and Urbanism. Peter Ucko, Ruth Tringham and G. W. Dimbeleby (Eds.) pp. 769-785. Gerald Duckworth & Co. Ltd. London.

Kirkby, Michael and Kirkby, Anne V. T.
    1969 Provisional Report on Geomorphology and Land Use in Deh Luran and Upper Khuzistan. Preliminary Reports of the Rice University Project in Iran 1968-1969. pp. 1-8 (mimeo).

Krader, Lawrence
    1968 Formation of the State. Prentice-Hall Inc. Englewood Cliffs.

Kroeber, A. L. and Kluckhohn, Clyde
    1952 Culture: a Critical Review of Concepts and Definitions. Vintage Books. New York.

KWPA
    1964 Summary Report on Crop Evaluation: Fall-Winter 1963-64 (1342). DPIP

Crop Surveys & Evaluation Studies. Khuzistan Water and Power Authority: Dez Pilot Irrigation Project.

Labat, René
1963 Manual D'Epigraphie Akkadienne. Impremerie Nationale. Paris.

Le Breton, L.
1957 The Early Periods at Susa: Mesopotamian Relations. Iraq. Vol. XIX. pp. 79-124.

Le Brun, Alain
1971 Recherches stratigraphiques à l'Acropole de Suse (1969-1971). Cahiers de la Délégation Archéologique Française en Iran. No. 1, pp. 163-233. Librairie orientaliste Paul Geuthner. Paris.

Lees, G. M. and Falcon, N. L.
1952 The Geographical History of the Mesopotamian Plains. Geological Journal, Vol. CXVIII Part 1, pp. 24-39. The Royal Geographical Society. London.

Legrain, L.
1921 Empreintes de Cachets Elamites. Mémoires de la Délégation en Perse. Vol. XVI. Editions Ernest Leroux. Paris.

Lenzen, H.
1968 Vorläufiger Bericht über die von der Notgemeinschaft Der Deutschen Wissenschaft In Uruk Unternommenen Ausgrabungen, Nu. 24. Gebr. Mann. Berlin.

Lloyd, Seton F.S.A.
1948 Uruk Pottery: A Comparative Study of the Finds at Eridu. Sumer, Vol. IV Nu. 1., pp. 39-51.

Mallowan, M. E. L.
1965 Early Mesopotamia and Iran. McGraw-Hill Book Co. New York.

de Mecquenem, Roland
1928 Notes sur la céramique peinte archaïque en Perse. (Mémoires de la Mission archéologique de Perse, Mission de Susiane.) Vol. XX pp. 99-132. Librairie Ernest Leroux, Paris.
1934 Fouilles de Suse 1929 à 1933 (sur l'acropole et la ville royal). Mémories de la Mission archéologique de Perse, Mission de Susiane. Vol. XXV. p. 177-237.
1938 The Early Cultures of Susa. *In* A Survey of Persian Art A. U. Pope (Ed.) Vol. 1, pp. 134-50. Oxford Univ. Press. London.
1943 Fouilles de Suse, 1933-1939. Archaéologique Susienne. (Mémoires de la Mission Archéologique en Iran, Mission de Susiane.) Vol. XXIX. p. 3-161. Presses Universitaires de France. Paris.

de Morgan, J.
1900 Recherches Archéologiques: Fouilles a Suse en 1897-1898 et 1898-1899. Mémoires de la délégation en Perse. Vol. I. Ernest Leroux, Editeur. Paris.
1912 Observations sue les couches profondes de l'Acropole de Suse. Mémoirs de la Délégation en Perse. Vol. XIII, pp. 1-25. Ernest Leroux, Editeur. Paris.

Nagel, Wolfram
1963 Zum neuen Bild des vordynastischen Keramikums in Vorderasien–III. Berliner Jahrbuch für Vor- und Früh geschichte. Vol. 3, pp. 1-61.

Naroll, Raoul
   1956 A Preliminary Index of Social Development. American Anthropologist. Vol. 58 No. 4 pp. 687-715.

Nissen, Hans Jörg
   1970 Grabung in den Quadraten K/L XII in Uruk-Warka. Baghdader Mitteilungen, Vol. 5 pp. 102-191. Deutsches Archäologisches Institute. Baghdad.
   1972 The City Wall of Uruk. *In* Man, Settlement and Urbanism. Peter J. Ucko, Ruth Tringham and G. W. Kimbleby (Eds.) Gerald Duckworth & Co. Ltd. London.

Nöldeke, A., E. Heinrich, H. Lenzen, A. v. Haller
   1932 "Vierter Vorläufiger Bericht Über Die Von Der Notgemeinschaft Der Deutschen Wissenschaft In Uruk Unternommenen Ausgrabungen," Abhandlungen Der Preussischen Akademie Der Wissenschaften: Philosophisch-Historische Klasse, Nr. 6, Walter De Gruyter U. Co., Berlin.

Olsson, Gunnar
   1965 Distance and Human Interaction: A Review and Bibliography. Regional Science Research Institute Bibliography Series, No. 2. Philadelphia.

Pabot, H.
   1960 The Native Vegetation and its Ecology in the Khuzistan River Basins. FAO (mimeo)

Perkins, Ann Louise
   1949 The Comparative Archaeology of Early Mesopotamia. The Oriental Institute of the University of Chicago. Studies in Ancient Oriental Civilization, No. 25. The University of Chicago Press. Chicago.

Pirrie, L.
   1917 Map of the Dizful-Shushtar-Shush Area: prepared by the Basrah Survey Party, Indian Expeditionary Force "D" (copy available in the map collections of the University of Michigan General Library)

Porada, Edith
   1965 The Relative Chronology of Mesopotamia. Part I. Seals and Trade (6000-1600 B.C.) *In* Chronologies in Old World Archaeology. Robert W. Ehrich (Ed.) pp. 133-200. The University of Chicago Press. Chicago.

Redman, Charles and Watson, Patty Jo
   1970 Systematic, Intensive Surface Collection. American Antiquity, Vol. 25, No. 3, pp. 279-91.

Rowlands, J. J.
   1972 Defense: a factor in the organization of settlements. *In* Man, Settlement and Urbanism. Peter Ucko, Ruth Tringham and G. W. Dimbleby (Eds). pp. 447-62. Gerald Duckworth & Co. Ltd. London.

Sanders, William T.
   1968 Hydraulic Agriculture, Economic Symbiosis and the Evolution of States in Central Mexico. *In* Anthropological Archeology in the Americas. Betty J. Meggers (Ed.) pp. 88-107. The Anthropological Society of Washington. Washington.

Sahlins, Marshall D.
   1958 Social Stratification in Polynesia. University of Washington Press. Seattle.

1968a Tribesmen. Prentice-Hall, Inc. Englewood Cliffs.
1968b Poor Man, Rich Man, Big Man, Chief: Political Types in Melanesia and Polynesia. *In* Peoples and Culture of the Pacific. Andrew P. Vayda (Ed.) pp. 157-76. The Natural History Press, Garden City.

Schulze, Erich
    1959 Interim Report on Soil Fertility Investigations in the Khuzistan Region Headwaters. FAO. Rome.

Service, Elman R.
    1962 Primitive Social Organization: An Evolutionary Perspective. Random House. New York.

Simon, Herbert A.
    1944 Decision-Making and Administrative Organization. Public Administration Review, Vol. IV, pp. 16-30.

Smith, Philip E.L. and Young, T. Cuyler
    1969 The Evolution of Early Agriculture and Culture in Greater Mesopotamia. Unpublished Manuscript circulated for the Colloquium on Population, Technology and Social Organization. Philadelphia.

Steve, M. J. and Gasche, H.
    1971 L'Acropole De Suse: Nouvelles Fouilles (Rapport Préliminaire). Mémoires de la Délégation Archéologique in Iran. Vol. XLVI. P. Geuthner. Paris.

Taylor, Clara Mae and Orrea, Florence Pye
    1966 Foundations of Nutrition. The Macmillan Co. New York.

Veenenbos, J. S.
    1958 Unified Report of the Soil and Land Classification of Dezful Project, Khuzistan Iran. Reprint by the Ministry of Agriculture, Soil Institute of Iran.

Watt, K. Bernice and Merrill, Annabel L.
    1963 Composition of Foods. Agriculture Handbook No. 8. Consumer and Food Economics Research Division Agricultural Research Service, United States Department of Agriculture.

Whallon, Robert Jr.
    1969 Early Bronze Age Development in the Keban Reservoir, East-Central Turkey. Current Anthropology, Vol. 10, No. 1, pp. 128-33.

Wirsing, Wolf
    1973 Political Power and Information: A Cross-Cultural Study. American Anthropologist. Vol. 75 No. 1, pp. 153-170.

Wise, John H.
    1965 The History of Land Ownership in Hawaii. *In* Ancient Hawaiian Civilization. E. S. Craighill Handy (Ed) pp. 81-93. Charles E. Tuttle Co. Rutland.

Wittfogel, Karl A.
    1957 Oriental Despotism: A comparative study of total power. Yale University Press. New Haven.

Wolf, Eric R.
    1966 Peasants. Prentice-Hall, Inc. Englewood Cliffs.

Wright, Henry T.
   1969*a* The Administration of Rural Production in an Early Mesopotamian Town. Museum of Anthropology University of Michigan. Anthropological Papers, No. 38. The University of Michigan. Ann Arbor.
   1969*b* Tepe Varukhabad. Iran, Vol. VII, pp. 172-3. London.
   1970 Toward an Explanation of the Origin of the State (mimeo)
   1972 A Consideration of Interregional Exchange in Greater Mesopotamia: 4000–3000 B.C. *In* Social Exchange and Interaction. Edwin N. Wilmsen (Ed) pp. 95-105. Museum of Anthropology University of Michigan. Anthropological Papers No. 46. The University of Michigan. Ann Arbor.

Plate I

Key to Ceramic Types Illustrated

Figure	Description	References
a	Bevel Rim Bowl—Rim to Base Profile, Chaff Temper	Steve and Gasche, 1971: Pl. 86:1,2
b	Proto Bevel Rim Bowl—Rim to Base Profile, Chaff Temper	Steve and Gasche, 1971: Pl. 86:3,7
c	Tray—Rim to Base Profile, Chaff Temper	Steve and Gasche, 1971: Pl. 86:11,12
d	Band Rim Bottle—Rim, Mineral Temper	Steve and Gasche, 1971: Pl. 84:10
e	Ledge Rim Bottle—Rim, Mineral Temper	Steve and Gasche, 1971: Pl. 86:6
f	Thumb Impressed Bowl Base, Chaff Temper	
g	Sinuous Sided Cup with Lip Spout—Rim, Mineral Temper	Le Brun 1971: Fig. 47:1

Plate I

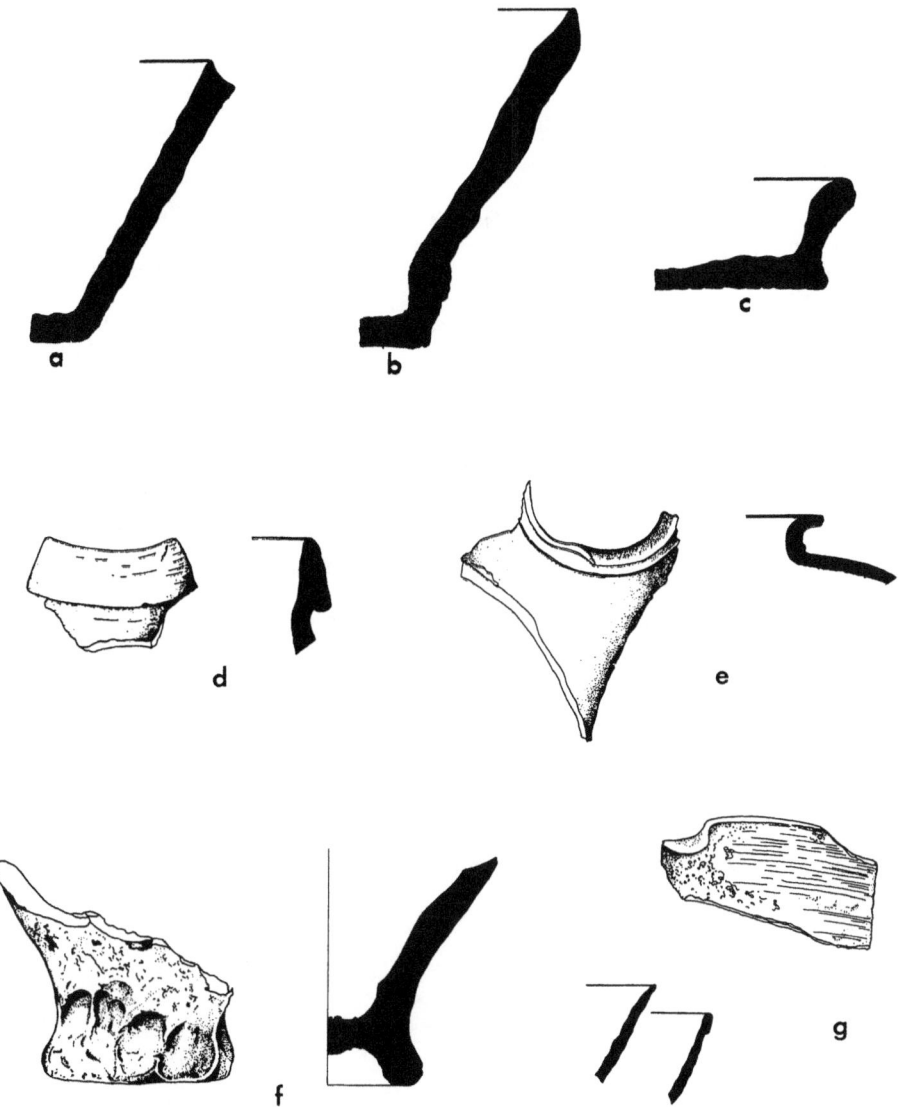

Plate II

Key to Ceramic Types Illustrated

Figure	Description	References
a	Round Rim Bowl–Rim, Mineral Temper	Steve and Gasche, 1971: Pl. 86:8
b	Flat Rim Bowl with Impressed Strip–Rim, Fine Mineral Temper	Steve and Gasche, 1971: Pl. 85:1
c	Flat Rim Bowl with Incised Rim–Rim, Mineral Temper	
d	Impressed Strip Bowl–Rim, Mineral Temper	
e	Beveled Rim Bowl–Rim, Mineral Temper	Le Brun, 1971: Fig. 45:11
f	Expanded Ledge Rim Bowl–Rim, Mineral Temper	
g	Ledge Rim Bowl–Rim, Mineral Temper	Steve and Gasche, 1971: Pl. 86:10
h	Beaded Rim Bowl–Rim, Mineral Temper	Steve and Gasche, 1971, Pl. 90:10,11

Plate II

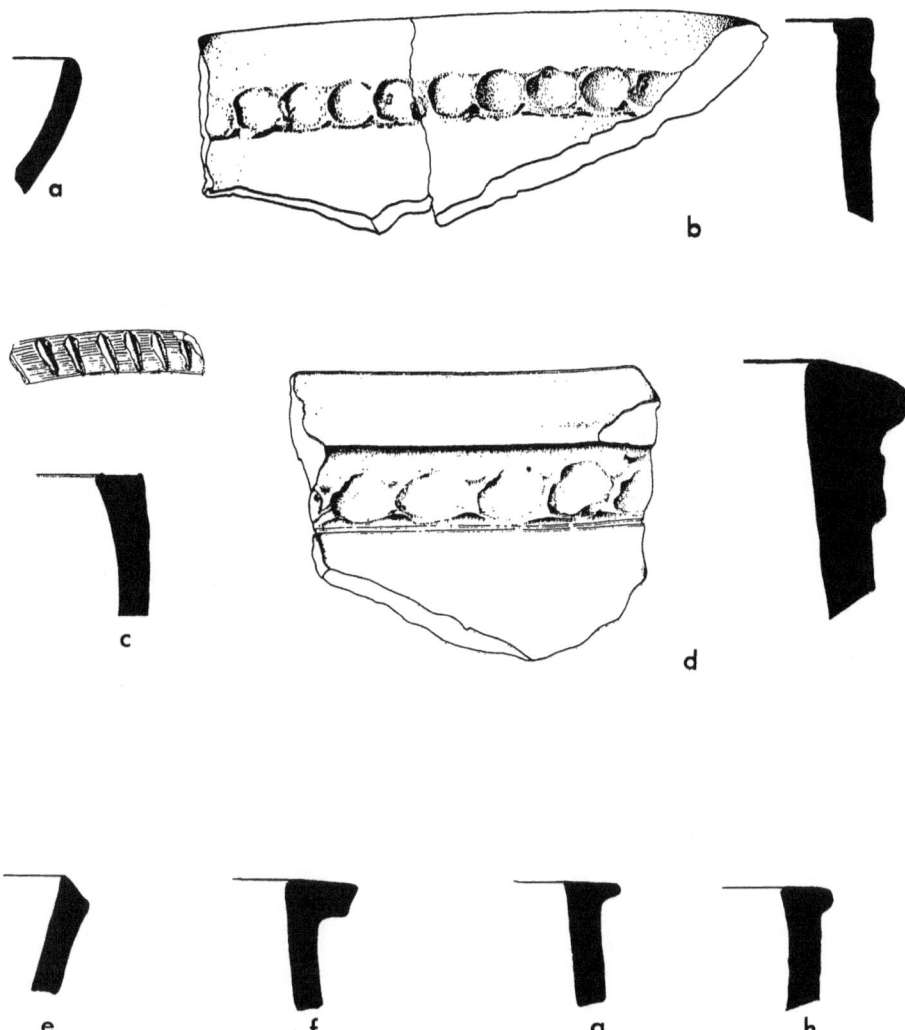

Plate III

Key to Ceramic Types Illustrated

Figure	Description	References
a	Straight Round Rim Jar—Rim, Mineral Temper	Le Brun, 1971: Fig. 49:3
b	Heavy Round Rim Jar—Rim, Mineral Temper	
c	Grooved Round Rim Jar—Rim, Mineral Temper	
d	Flared Round Rim Jar—Rim, Mineral Temper	Le Brun, 1971: Fig. 49:16
e	Straight Expanded Rim Jar—Rim, Mineral Temper	Le Brun, 1971: Fig. 49:4
f	Flared Expanded Rim Jar—Rim, Mineral Temper	Steve and Gasche, 1971: Pl. 84:5,8
g	Out-turned Expanded Rim Jar—Rim, Mineral Temper	
h	High Expanded Band Rim Jar—Rim, Mineral Temper	
i	Low Expanded Band Rim Jar—Rim, Mineral Temper	
j	Ledge Rim Jar—Rim, Mineral Temper	
k	Expanded Ledge Rim Jar—Rim, Mineral Temper	
l	Neckless Ledge Rim Jar—Rim, Mineral Temper	Steve and Gasche, 1971: Pl. 85:2
m	Hatched Strip Jar Shoulder, Mineral Temper	
n	Punctate Jar Shoulder, Mineral Temper	

Plate III

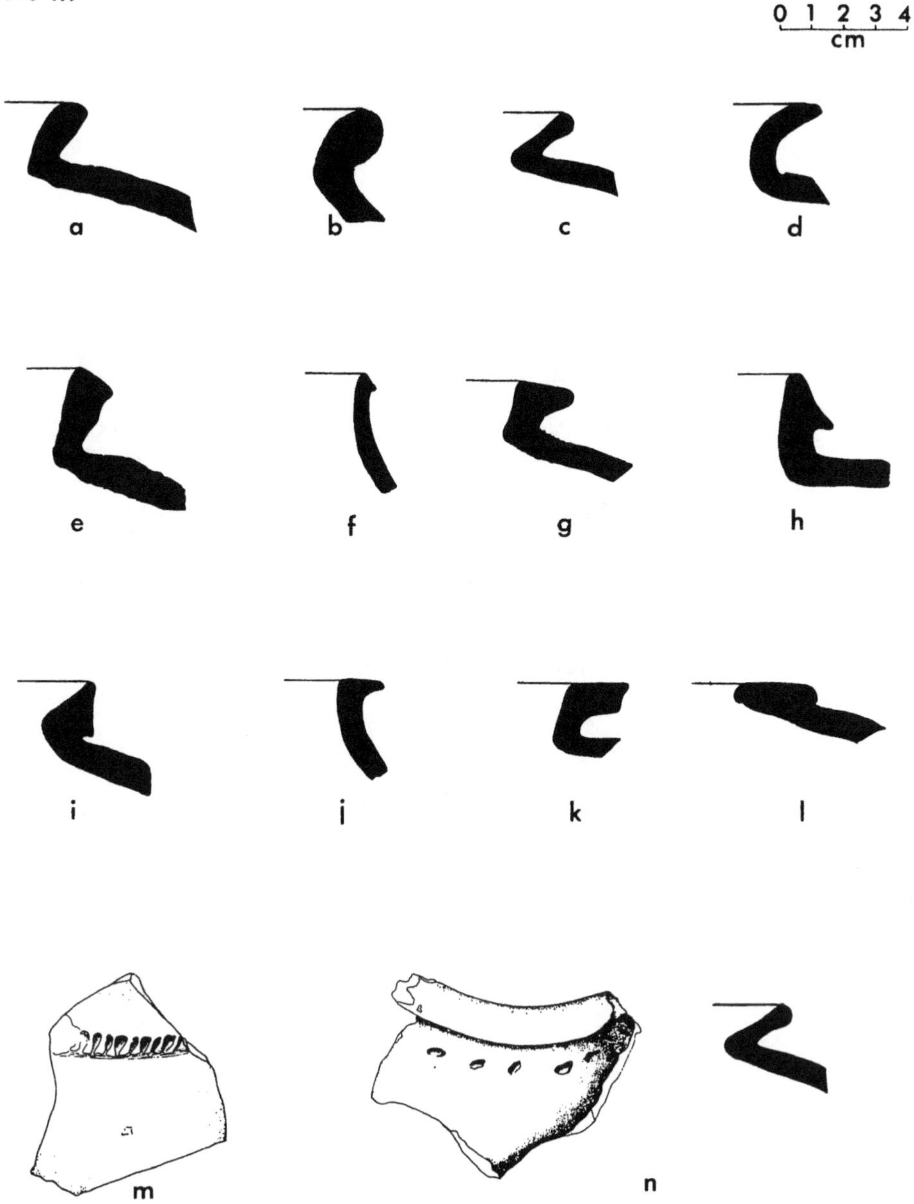

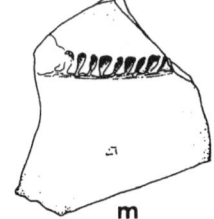
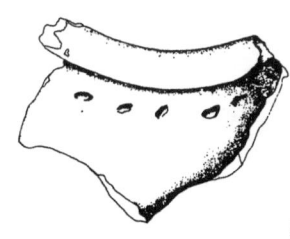

Plate IV

Key to Ceramic Types Illustrated

Figure	Description	References
a	Reserve Slip and Punctate Jar Shoulder, Mineral Temper	Steve and Gasche, 1971: Pl. 87.1
b	Incised Cross Hatch Band and Incised Cross Hatch Triangle Jar Shoulder, Mineral Temper	Steve and Gasche, 1971: Pl. 87:8
c	Incised Oblique Band Jar Shoulder, Mineral Temper	Le Brun, 1971: Fig. 51:4
d	Incised Groove and Oblique Jar Shoulder, Mineral Temper	
e	Rocker Stamp Jar Shoulder, Mineral Temper	
f	Combed Jar Shoulder, Mineral Temper	

Plate IV

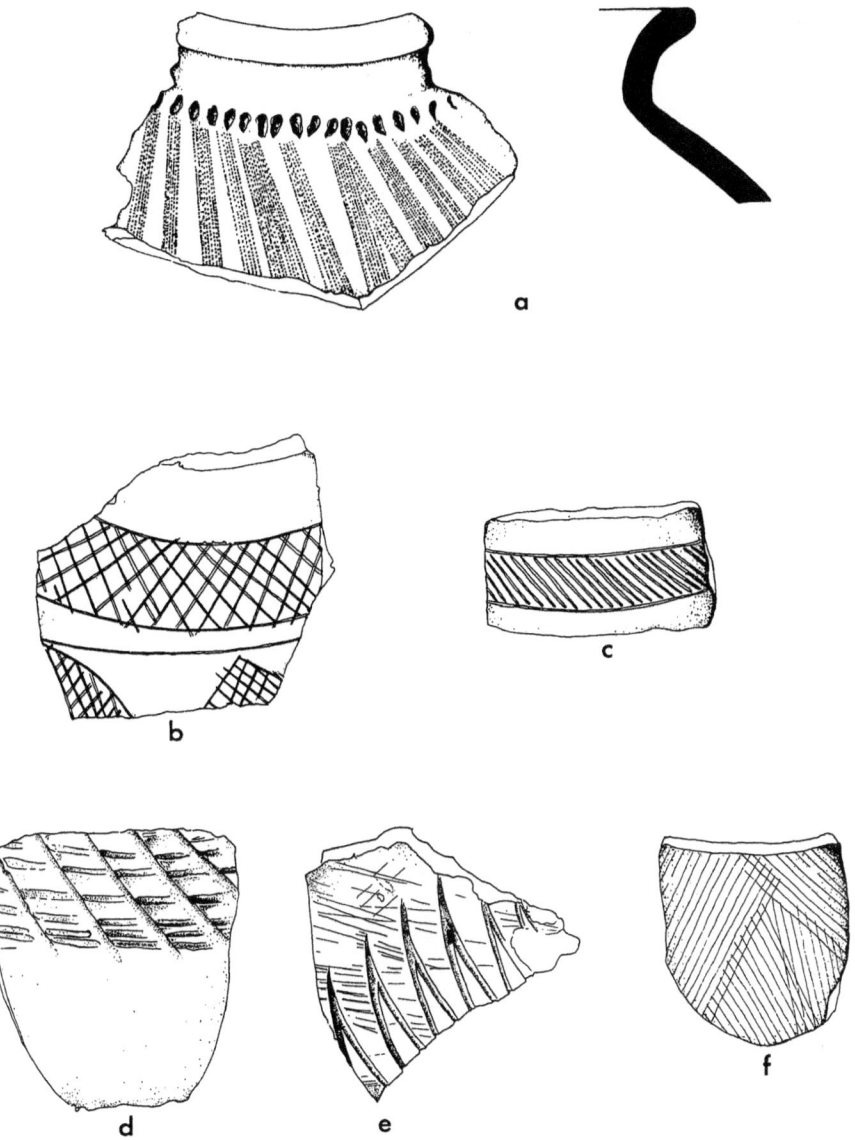

Plate V

Key to Ceramic Types Illustrated

Figure	Description	References
a	Nose Lug, Mineral Temper	Le Brun, 1971: Fig. 51:1-11
b	Nose Lug, Mineral Temper	
c	Heavy Lug, Mineral Temper	
d	Straight Spout, Mineral Temper	Steve and Gasche, 1971: Pl. 84:5

Plate V

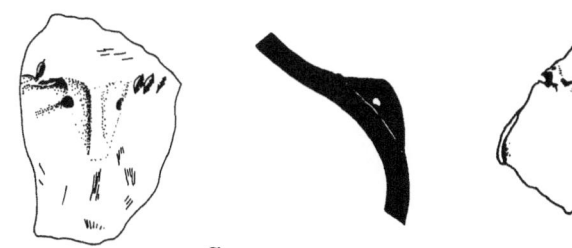
a

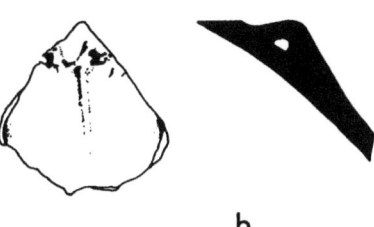
b

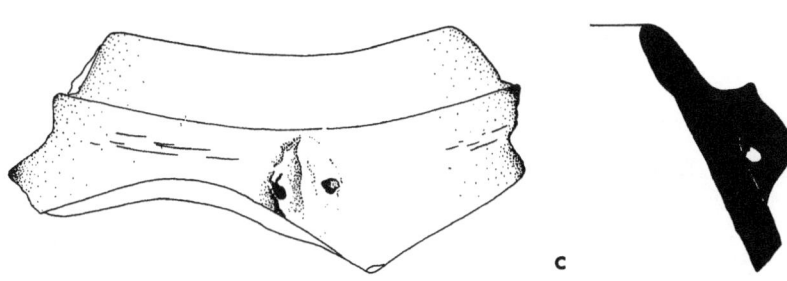
c

d

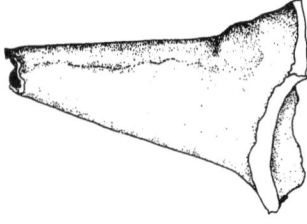

Plate VI

Key to Ceramic Types Illustrated

Figure	Description	References
a	Droop Spout, Mineral Temper	Steve and Gasche, 1971: Pl. 87:3
b	Conical Spout, Mineral Temper	
c	Truncated Straight Spout, Mineral Temper	
d	Cut Spout, Mineral Temper	Steve and Gasche, 1971: Pl. 84:9

Plate VI

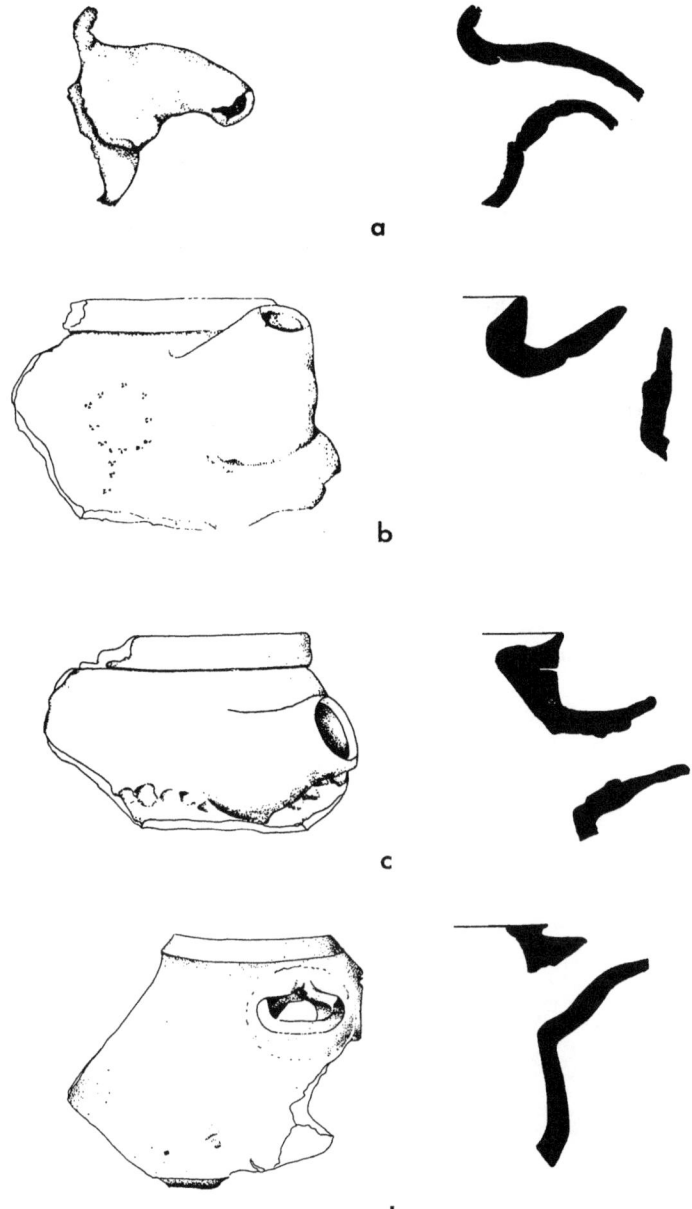

Plate VII

Key to Ceramic Types Illustrated

Figure	Description	References
a	Attached Spout, Mineral Temper	
b	Open Spout, Mineral Temper	
c	Strap Handle, Mineral Temper	Le Brun, 1971: Fig. 49:8, 9, 10
d	Incised Strap Handle, Mineral Temper	
e	Flat Twisted Handle, Mineral Temper	

Plate VII

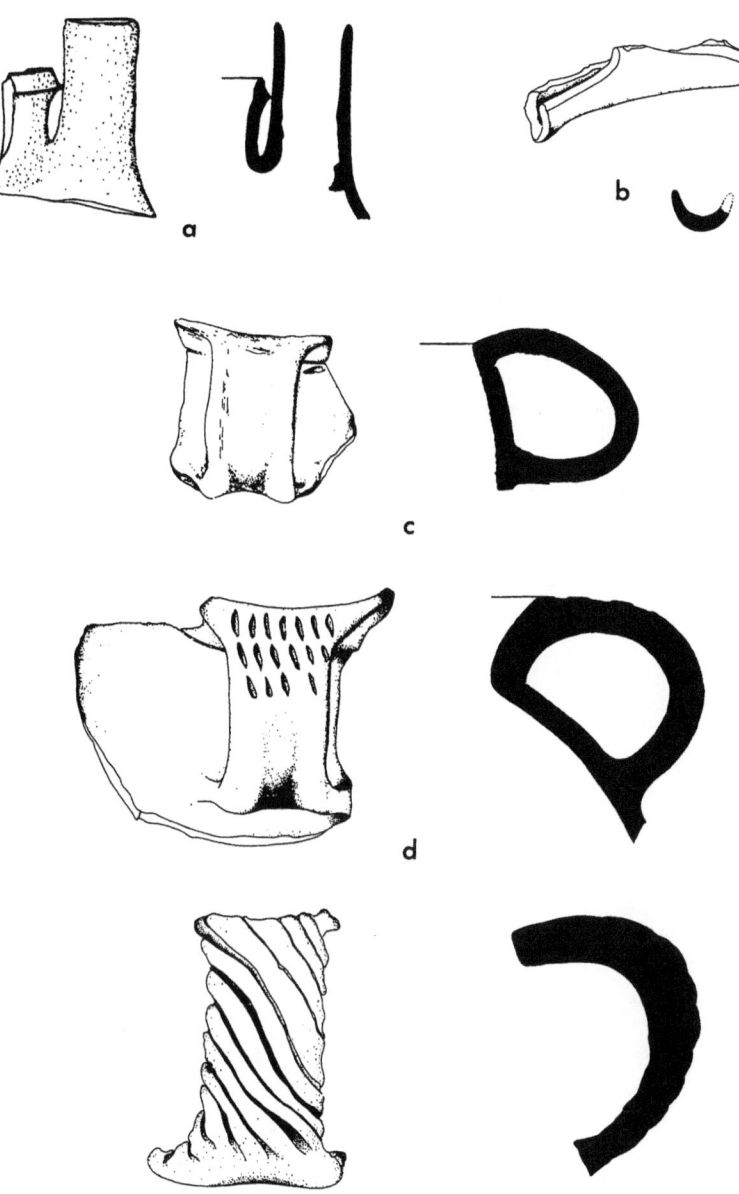

Plate VIII

Key to Ceramic Types Illustrated

Figure	Description	References
a	Full Twisted Handle and Grooved Shoulder, Mineral Temper	
b	Horizontal Full Twisted Handle, Mineral Temper	Le Brun, 1971: Fig. 49:12
c	Incised Rim Lug, Mineral Temper	Steve and Gasche, 1971: Pl. 87:5
d	Sickle, Mineral Temper	Steve and Gasche, 1971: Pl. 85:17

Plate VIII

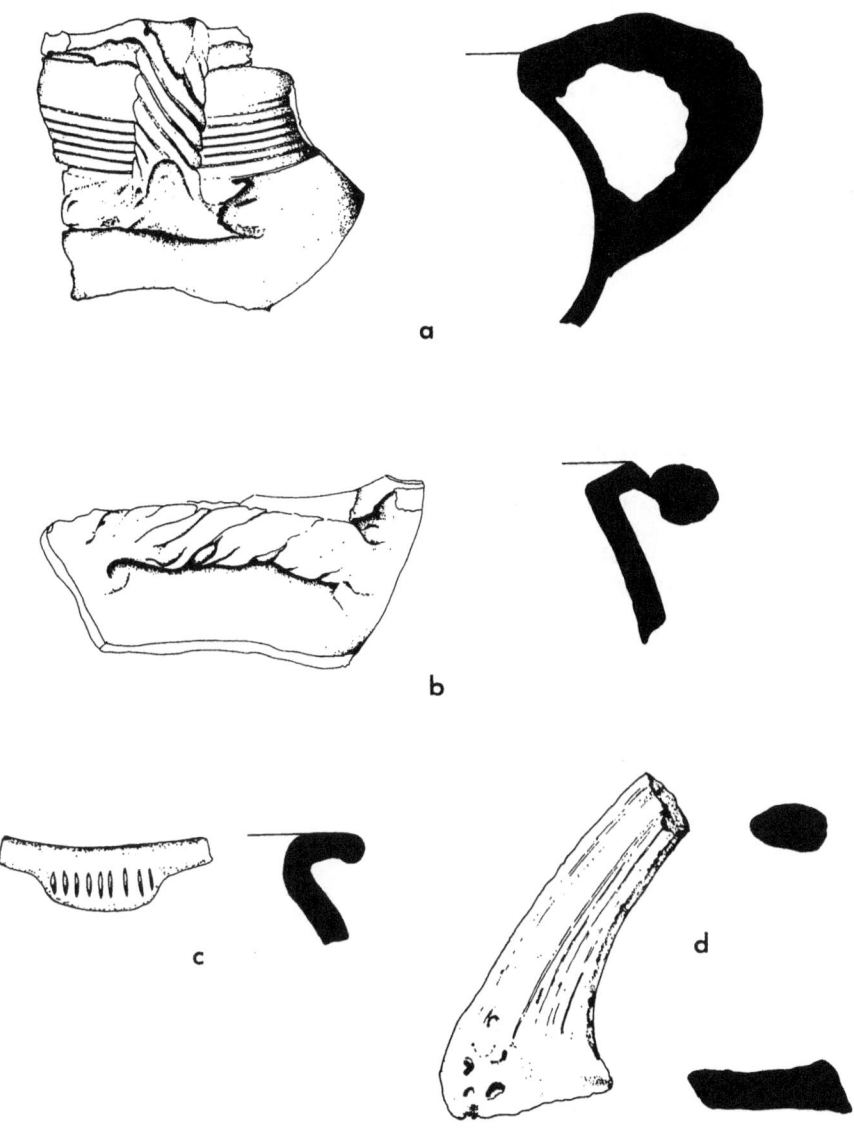

Plate IX

Key to Ceramic and Lithic Types Illustrated

Figure	Description	References
a	Ceramic Wall Cone, Mineral Temper	Steve and Gasche, 1971: Pl. 89:4,6,13
b	Fine Jar, Mineral Temper	
c	Black on Red Painted Jar, Fine Mineral Temper	
d	Terminal Susa A Painted Jar, Fine Mineral Temper	
e	Uruk Blade Core	

Plate IX

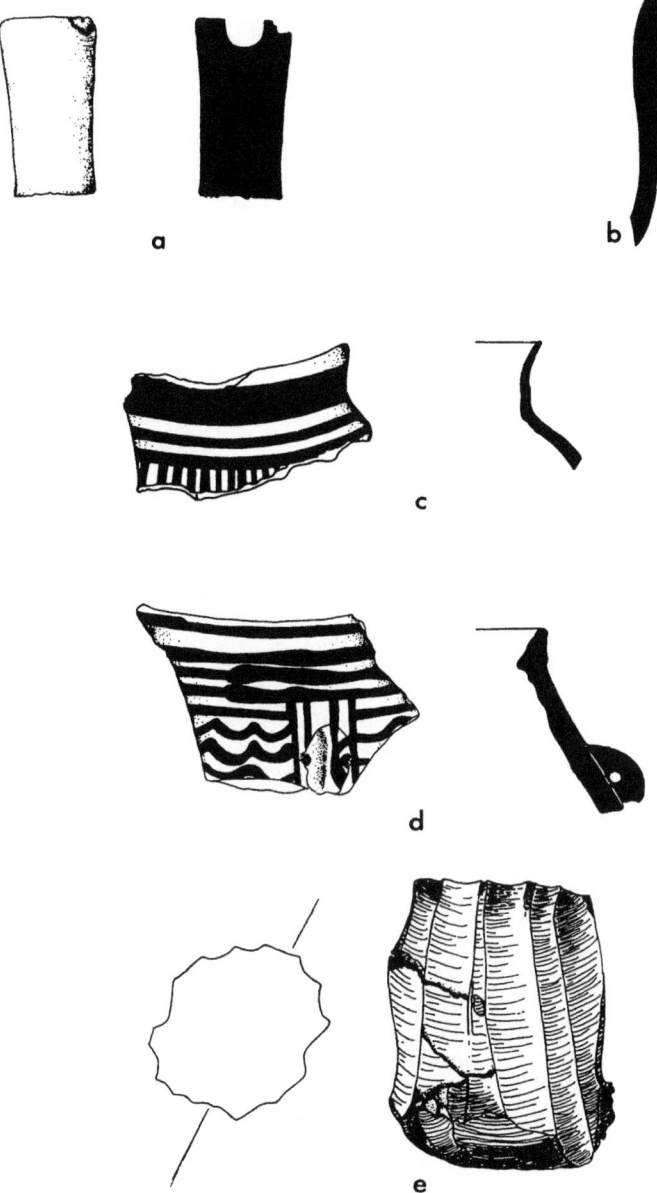

Plate X

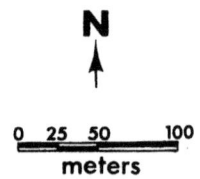

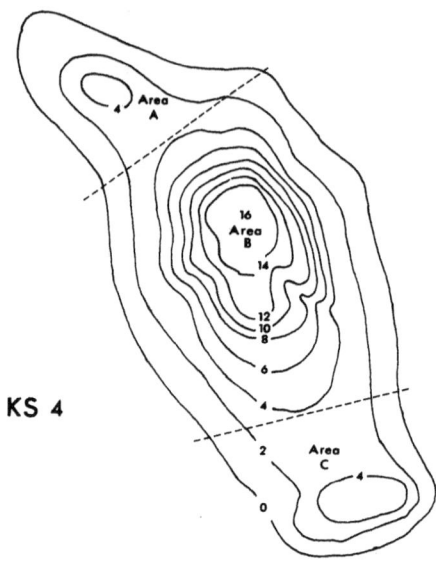

KS 4

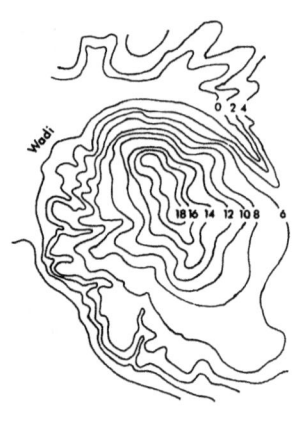

KS 5

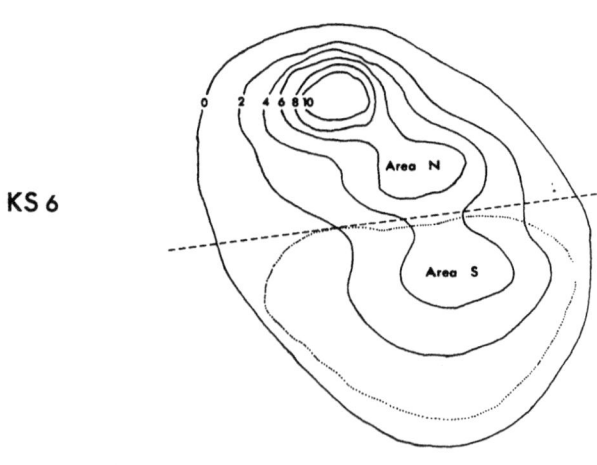

KS 6

Plate XI

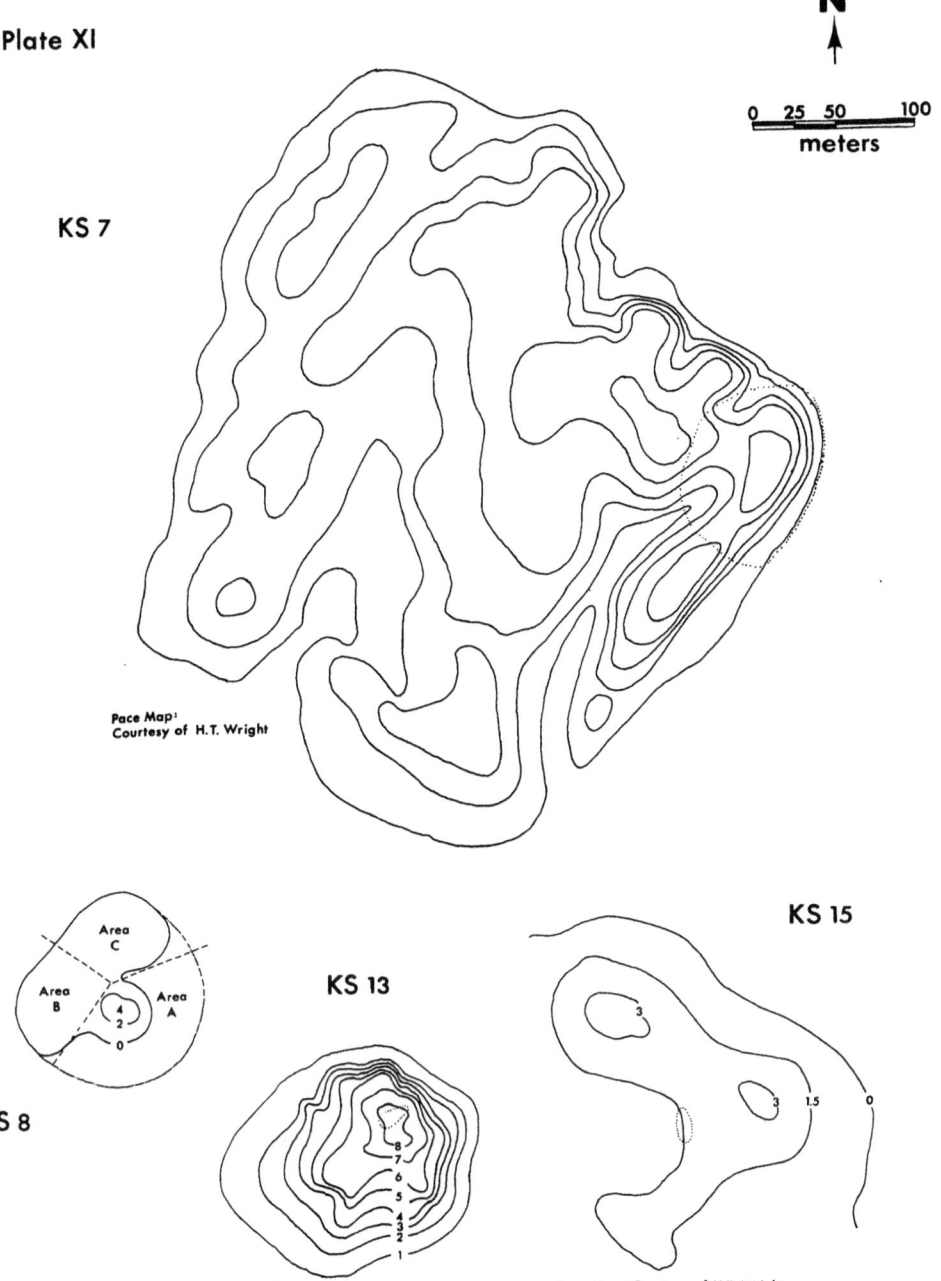

Plate XII

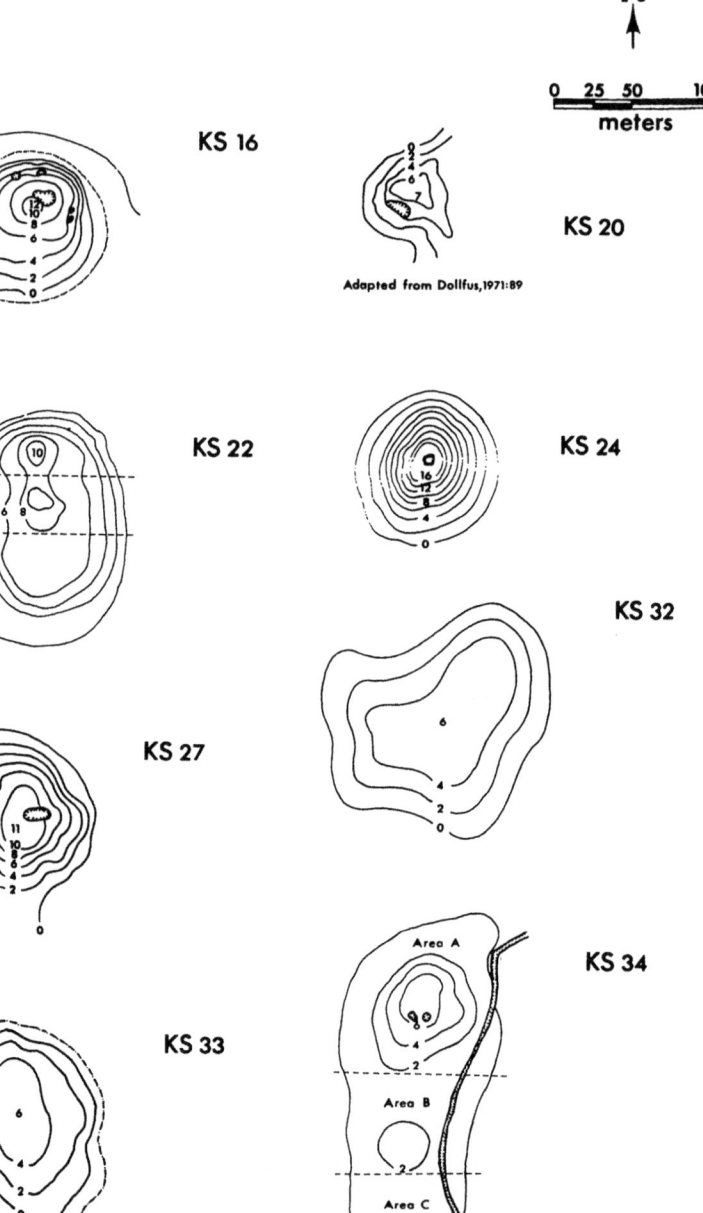

Plate XIII

KS 35

KS 36

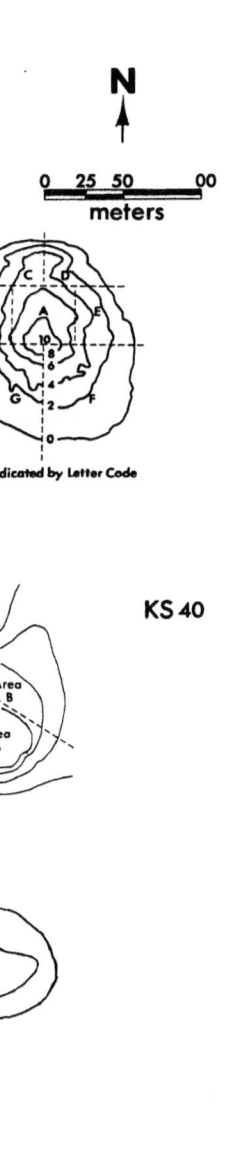

KS 39

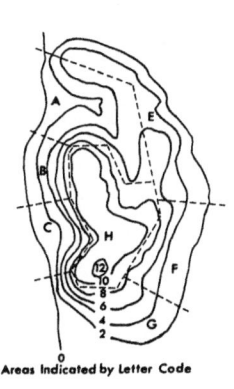

Areas Indicated by Letter Code

KS 40

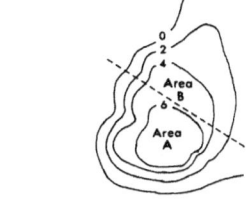

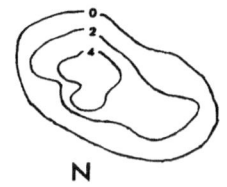

N

KS 44

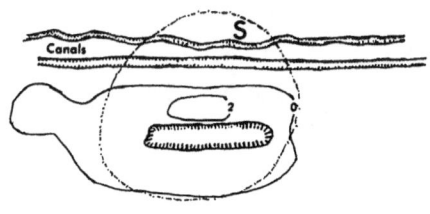

Plate XIV

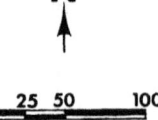

KS 45

KS 49

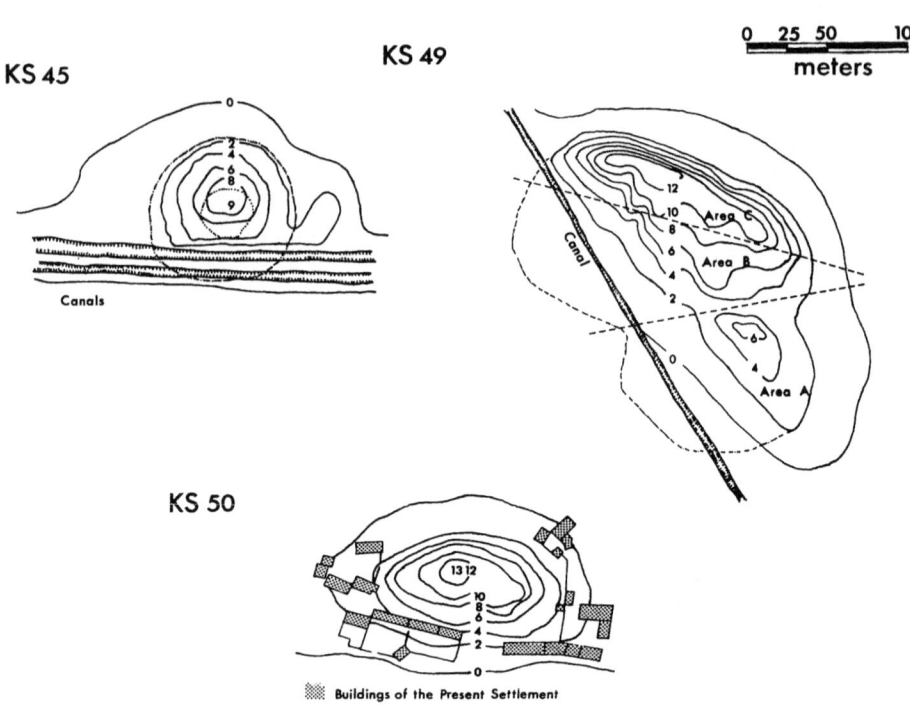

KS 50

KS 52

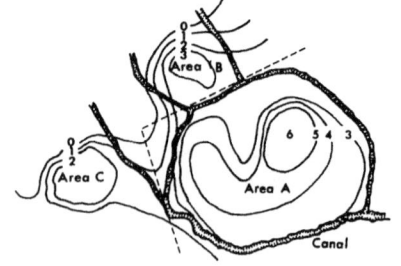

KS 54

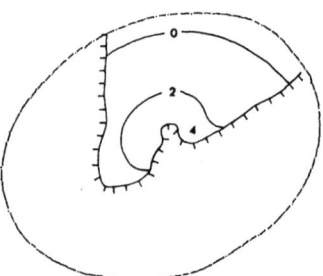

Plate XV

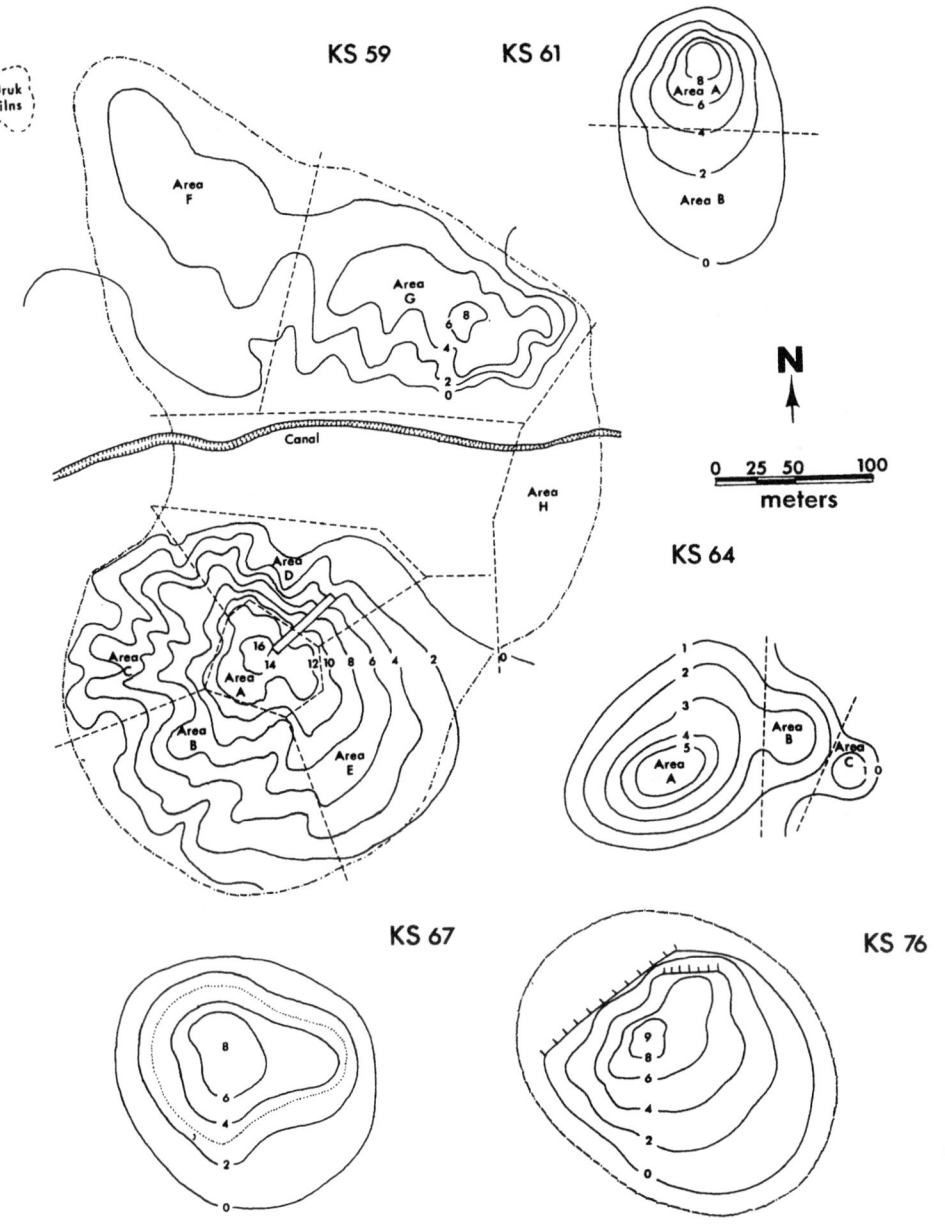

Plate XVI

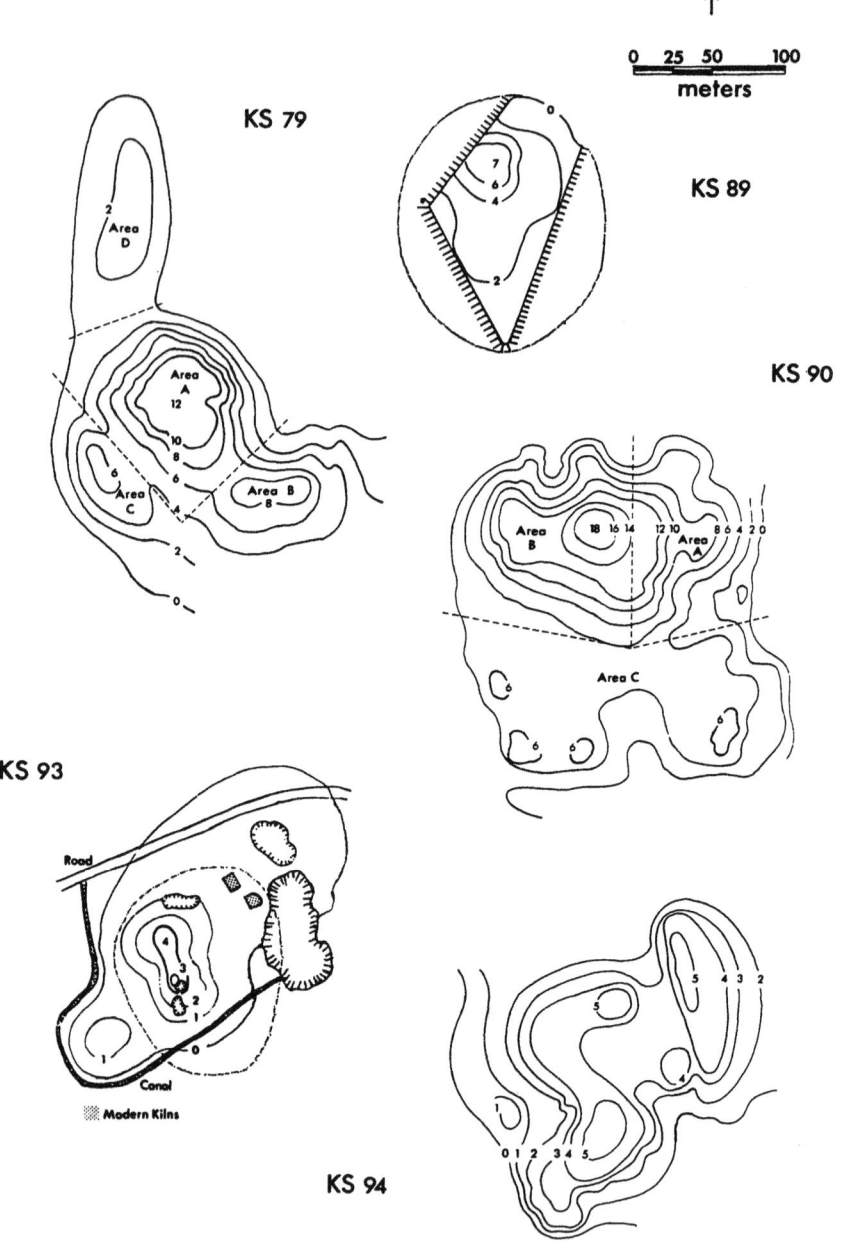

Plate XVII

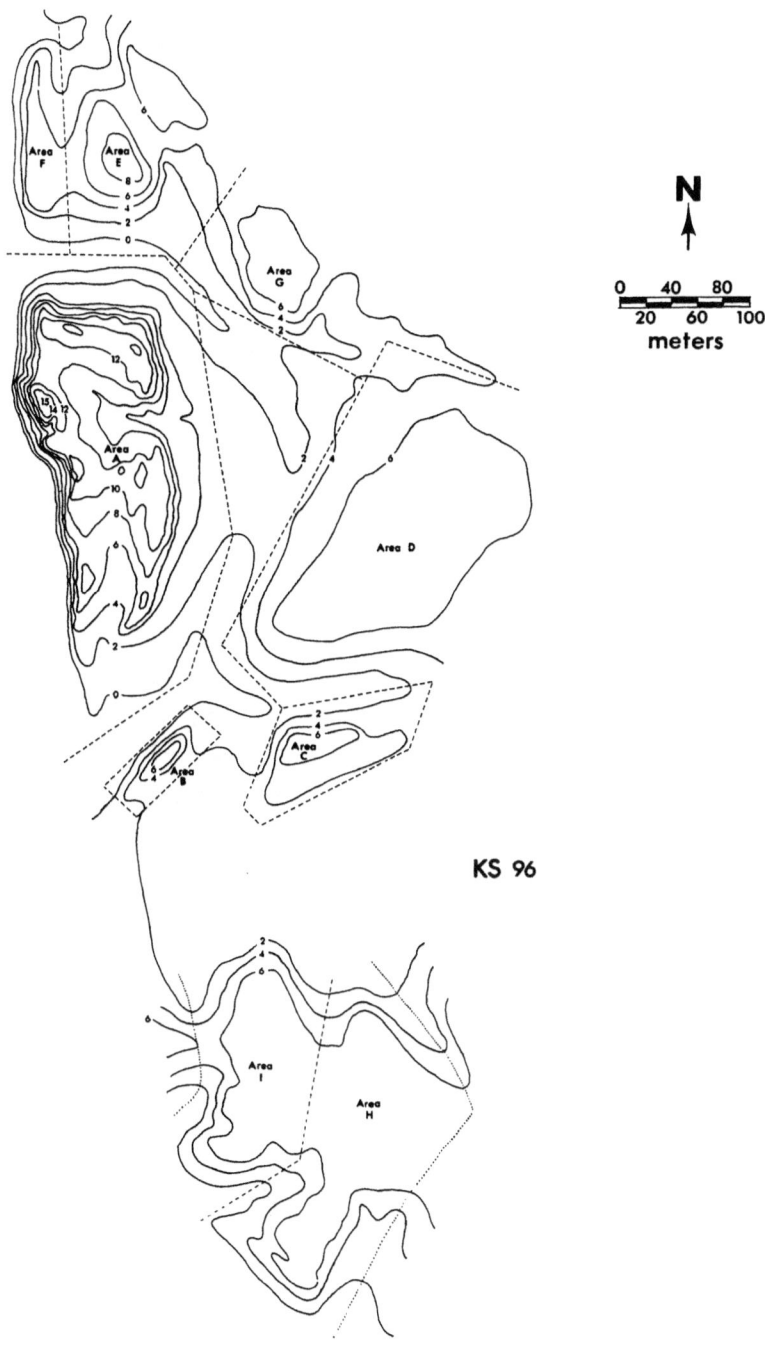

KS 96

Plate XVIII

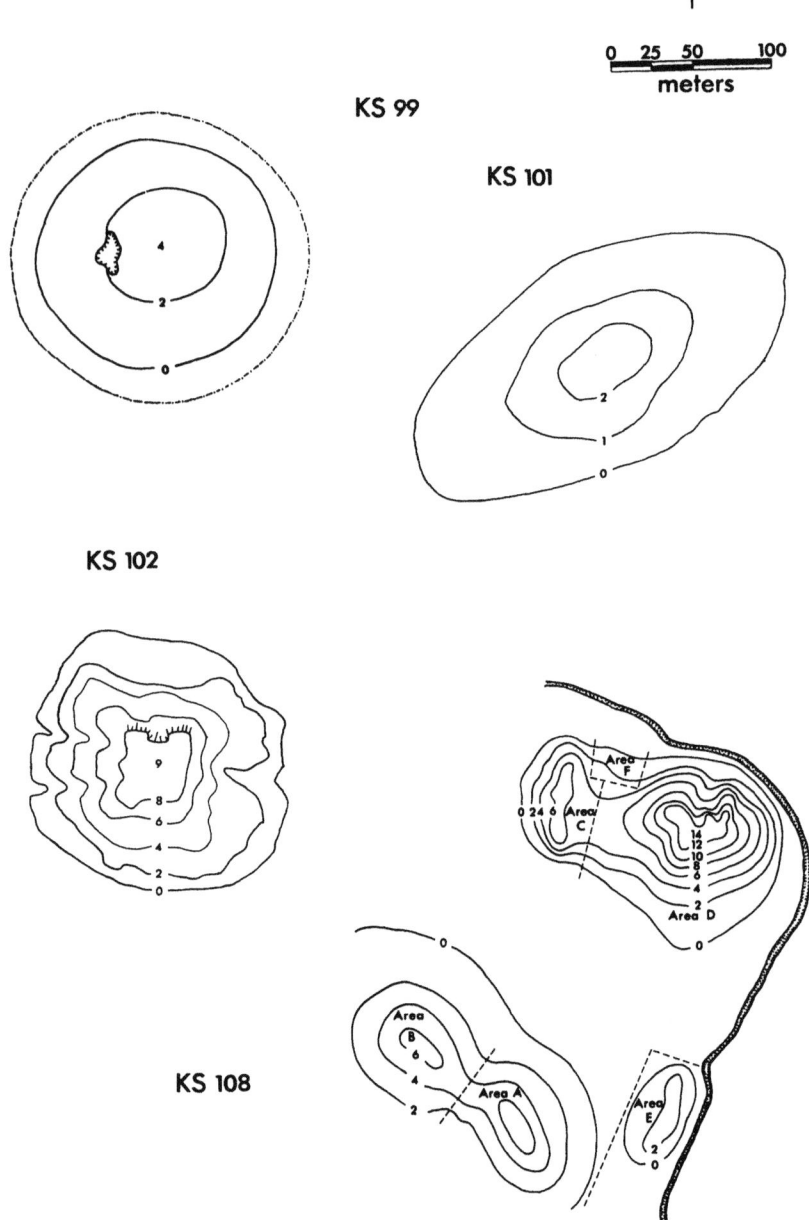

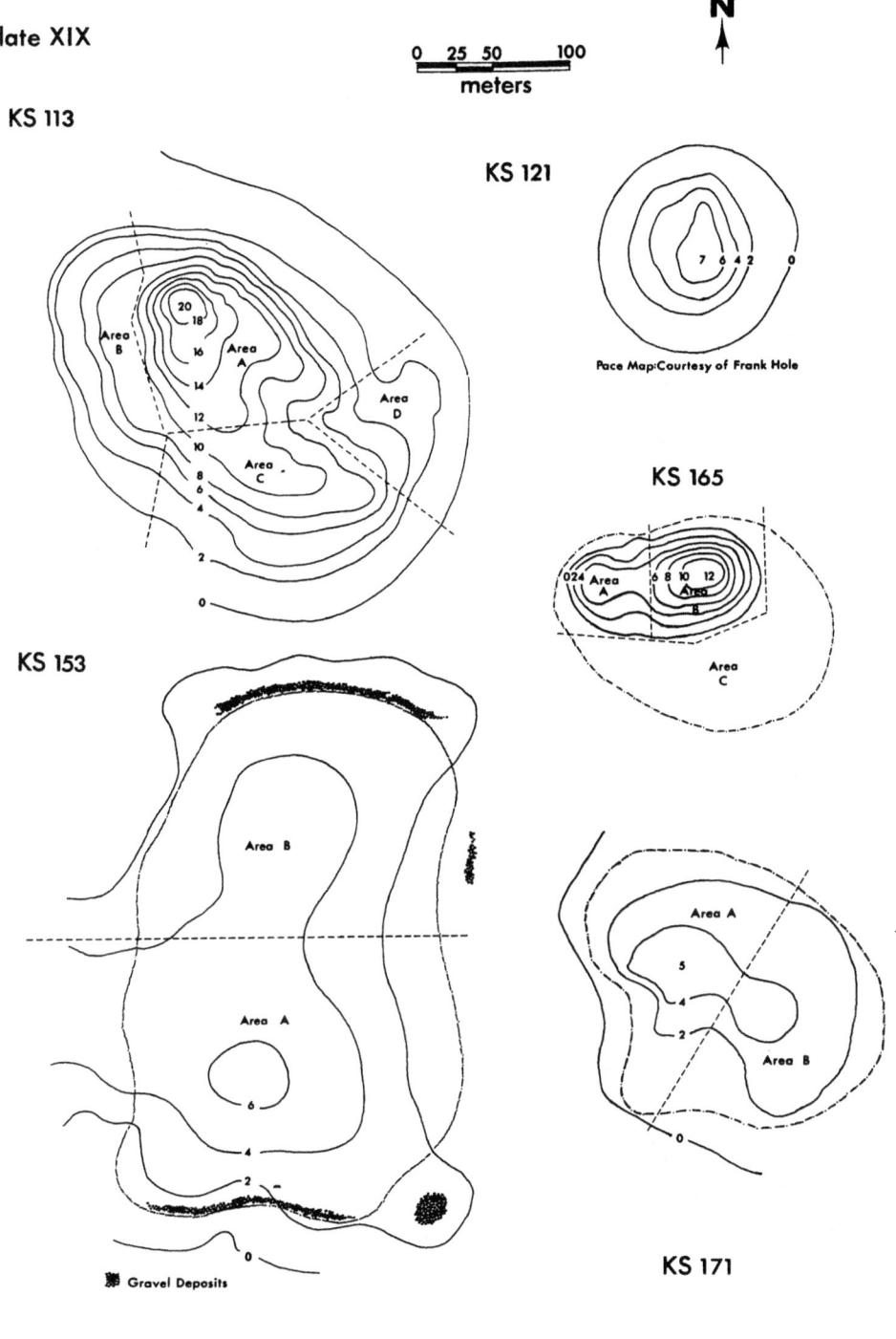

Plate XX

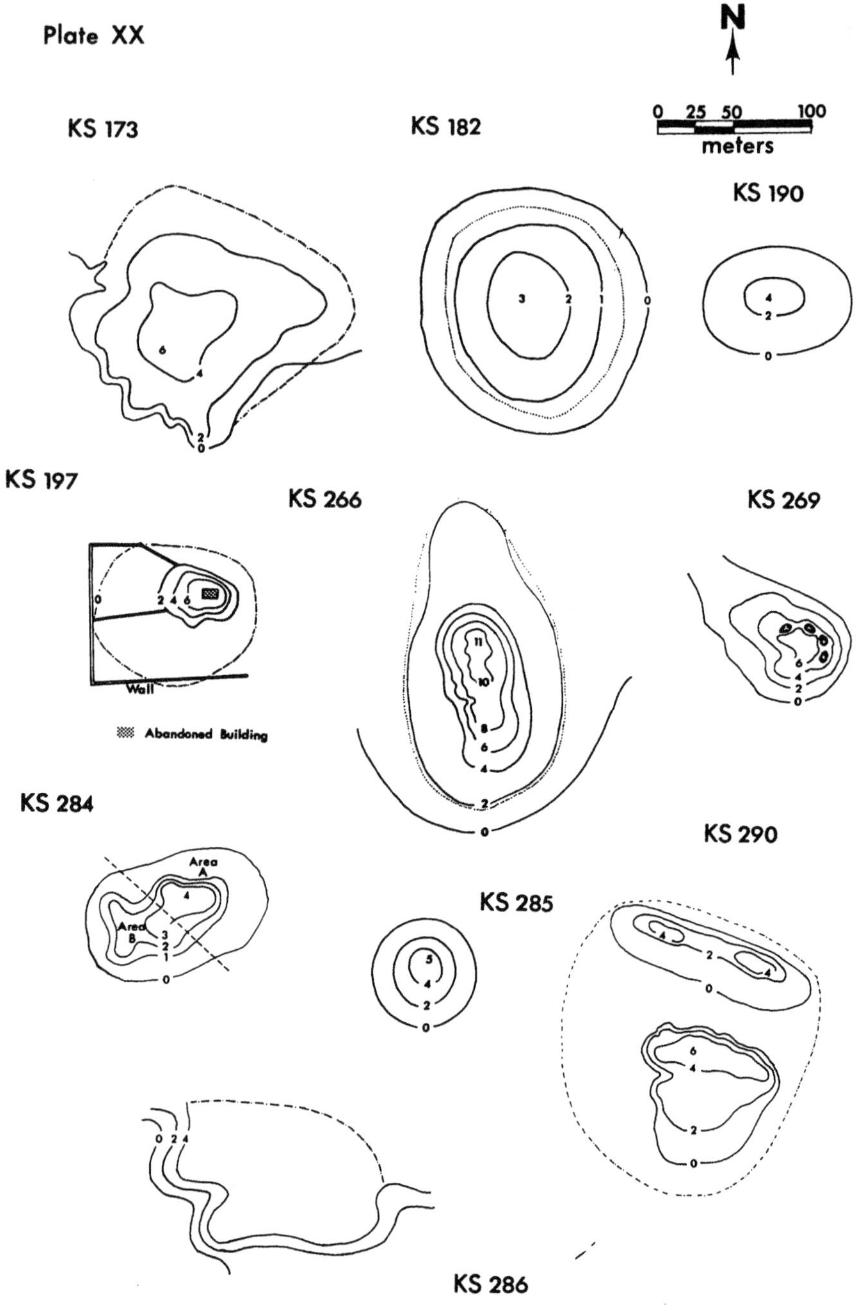
N
0 25 50 100
meters
KS 173
KS 182
KS 190
KS 197
Wall
Abandoned Building
KS 266
KS 269
KS 284
Area A
Area B
KS 285
KS 290
KS 286

www.ingramcontent.com/pod-product-compliance
Lightning Source LLC
Jackson TN
JSHW070313120426
100741JS00007B/39